Handbook of Group Decision and Negotiation

Handbook of Group Decision and Negotiation

Seyed Ali Fallahchay

SOCIETY Publishing

www.societypublishing.com

Handbook of Group Decision and Negotiation

Seyed Ali Fallahchay

Society Publishing
224 Shoreacres Road
Burlington, ON L7L 2H2
Canada
www.societypublishing.com
Email: orders@arclereducation.com

ISBN: 978-1-77469-096-3 (Hardcover)

ABOUT THE AUTHOR

Seyed Ali Fallahchay, Ph.D, has International experience in academia and industry. He received his Ph.D in Business Management from De La Salle Araneta University, Philippines. He earned his Bachelor in Engineering of Industrial Forestry from Islamic Azad University, Iran. He held professorial positions at Raffles Design Institute (Indonesia), University of Mansford (California, USA), and several universities and colleges in Philippines. He also managed his manufacturing business in Philippines during the period of post-graduate studies. Further, he had held university administrative position as Senior Program Head Administrator and Director of Research (Philippines).

TABLE OF CONTENTS

LIST OF FIGURES

LIST OF TABLES

LIST OF ABBREVIATIONS

BATNA	Best Alternative to a Negotiated Agreement
BM	Bonferroni mean
CNSS	combined negotiation support system
DSS	group-based support system
FI	fuzzy integrals
GDN	group decision and negotiation
GDSS	group decision support systems
GSS	group support systems
IFOWA	Intuitionistic Fuzzy Ordered Weighted Averaging
MCDM	multiple criteria decision making
MSRP	manufacturers suggested retail price
NSS	negotiation support systems
OGA	order weighted averaging
PA	power average
POC	protection of civilians
POWA	power ordered weighted average
RCEP	Regional Comprehensive Economic Partnership
RH	representative heuristic
SES	socioeconomic level
UNITAR	United Nations Institute for Training and Research

ABSTRACT

Organizational groups are continually settling on choices that impact on the adequacy of their performance and the organization at large. This volume makes reference to the nature of cooperative decision making, which despite being more beneficial than individual decision making, is still prone to risks including different personalities and incongruity of ideas. Some of the chapters in this book include: Chapter 1: Group Decision-Making, Chapter 2: The Essentials of Negotiation, among others, Chapter 3: Classes of Multi-Person Decisions, Chapter 4: Group Decision Making Problems, Chapter 5: Formal Models for Group Decision Making and Negotiation, Chapter 6: MCDM and Negotiation Support, Chapter 7: Emotion in Negotiation, Chapter 8: Role of Justice in Negotiation, Chapter 9: Advantages and Disadvantages of Group Decision Making, and Chapter 10: Factors that Affect Negotiations and Group Discussions.

Strategies for improving collective decision making have been developed to such an extent that they can be utilized to guarantee top notch decisions in company settings. Cooperative decision-making measures are usually embraced to strengthen social bonds within the company. In this volume, the author examines the impacts of collective decision making on organizational goals, recognizing the strengths and result impacts of the strategy. In particular, it builds on the likelihood of attaining better results in comparison to individual decision-making strategies. Different ideas are presented, and the most ideal ones are chosen.

PREFACE

Group decision making is a process of settling on a decision from the variety of choices presented by people. As per this volume, the group is perhaps the main tool of administrative authority and center of action. The significance of responsibility, support for the group's objectives and goals lead to expanded adequacy of the choices. The point of this volume is to characterize, which factors have the best effect and how they contribute to a decision being made. The group can boost dynamism through social interaction, looking at and assessing a variety of options and among which pick the best arrangement. Notwithstanding, employees settle on choice based on the most popular arrangement, which is agreeable to most of them. The technique, which they use, it's called democracy.

This volume further mentions the risks and vulnerability of democracy within a group. After group voting, the members are hundred percent sure that all results will be positive for the organization and they need to pick the most advantageous one. In any case, most of the choices have a type of risk; subsequently, it's fundamental to expect the probability of its outcome based on experience and information on the individual roles. Choices made in a group can be difficult for everyone to agree with, but they must for the sake of progress.

Group thinking requires everyone to make progress toward unanimity and abrogate their inspiration simultaneously. The individuals don't defy the group's reasoning, since they are hesitant to disturb the agreement. The group loses freedom to settle on the best choices, in light of the fact that the risks and choices are mulled over. The cohesiveness, for the most part connected with constructive outcomes can lead additionally to the ideal results. In like manner, before any conversation begins, the people ought to record their perspectives on a subject and rate them on one to ten scales for review.

The topics covered in this volume include: Chapter 1: Group Decision-Making, Chapter 2: The Essentials of Negotiation, Chapter 3: Classes of Multi-Person Decisions, Chapter 4: Group Decision Making Problems, Chapter 5: Formal Models for Group Decision Making and Negotiation, Chapter 6: MCDM and Negotiation Support, Chapter 7: Emotion in Negotiation, Chapter 8: Role of Justice in Negotiation, Chapter 9: Advantages and Disadvantages of Group Decision Making, and Chapter 10: Factors that Affect Negotiations and Group Discussions.

Brainstorming is a procedure, which seeks to improve the collective decision making. The supposition will be that individuals who are cooperating can discover more viable and inventive solutions than the people, who work independently. The motivation behind this idea is to discover, however, many imaginative concepts as could be allowed and recognize the best one. There are a few standards, which must be trailed by the group to make the interaction more efficient. Above all else, the group must scrutinize everyone's thoughts, remarks and give input. The people should share all choices, even the most bizarre ones with the group. While a group represents the common good of everyone, each member should not lose focus of their individuality.

Chapter 1

Group Decision-Making

CONTENTS

1.1. INTRODUCTION

Group decision-making (also known as collaborative decision-making or collective decision-making) is a scenario in which a group of people must make a unilateral decision from a set of options. The conclusion is then no more attributed to any solitary group member. It is because the result is influenced by all people and social group dynamics such as social influence. Personal choices are frequently distinct from those made by organizations. Consensus-based decision is among the most effective ways to gain buy-in from other stakeholders, develop harmony, and stimulate positive work environments. Decisions made collaboratively, and per the concept of synergy, are likewise more productive than those owned by a single individual (Wu et al., 2012). Several collaborative arrangements, in this spirit, have the potential to produce greater net organizational performance than people acting alone. When there is time for full consideration, discussion, and interaction, collaborative or group decision-making is often favored and generates more rewards than solo decision-making in regular everyday situations. This can be accomplished through the employment of committees, teams, groups, partnerships, and other forms of social collaboration.

Nonetheless, there may be disadvantages to this strategy in some circumstances. Other types of decision-making may be preferred in dire situations or crisis circumstances; as urgent measures may need to be undertaken more swiftly with much less time for debate. When evaluating the suitability of a decision-making structure, however, additional variables must be factored into the equation. Group polarization, for example, can happen at times contributing to certain groups making more radical decisions than their individual members, in the line of their particular preferences. There are other instances in which a group's decisions are faulty, like in the case of the Bay of Pigs invasion, the scenario that the groupthink model of group decision-making is based off of.

Group decisions are influenced by factors that influence other social group activities. For instance, groups with strong cohesiveness have been shown to have a negative influence on group decision-making and thus on group performance when combined with other antecedent variables. Furthermore, when individuals make decisions as part of a group, they are more likely to debate shared knowledge rather than unshared knowledge.

For various reasons, group decisions can differ significantly from those made by individuals. This potential for variance in outcomes is one of the reasons why collective decision making is appealing (Ambrus et al., 2009).

Moreover, when individuals are making critical decisions as part of a group, they have a propensity to favor discussing shared information over unshared information (i.e., shared information bias).

1.2. UNDERSTANDING SOCIAL GROUPS

Although it may appear that we can quickly recognize a social group when we encounter one, defining what constitutes a group of people a social group is not so simple. Consider the situation of a half-dozen persons in a grocery checkout queue. You had probably agreed that this collection of people should not be classified as a social group because they are not affiliated in any significant way. Individuals taking a huge lecture class or viewing a movie in a theater may also be seen simply as individuals who are in the same location at the same time but are not interconnected as a social group.

In fact, a group of people who chance to be in the same place at the same time might easily become a social group if anything happens to draw them altogether. For example, if a man in the grocery checkout line unexpectedly slumped on the ground, it is likely that those surrounding him would band together to assist him. Somebody would call for an ambulance, anyone else would perform CPR, and another would try to reach his relatives (Weller et al., 2007). Likewise, if a movie theater were to burst into flames, a crowd would grow as people tried to flee the building. Even the class of students can start to feel like a group if the lecturer kept praising it as the finest (or worse) class he or she had ever had. It is difficult to define what it is about a group that makes it a unit, but one term that has been used is *entitativity*.

Entitativity is a concept that describes to the notion that a group of people is a grouping, whether that impression is held by the group members themselves or by others. It is a critical characteristic, both in regards of how we perceive and act around our in groups or how we perceive and act towards out-groups. Strong views of in-group entitativity, for instance, can help people maintain their sense of common self-esteem in the face of adversity. Considering our ingroups as more entitative might also assist us in meeting our own psychological demands. Our attitudes about our out-groups, as well as our pro – social and antisocial acts toward them, are influenced by our views of their entitativity. People might feel more xenophobic to out groups that they regard as more entitative in certain circumstances, but they may opt to contribute more funds to support more entitative out groups in several other scenarios.

Figure 1.1. Two businessmen shaking hands at international business meeting.

Source: https://opentextbc.ca/socialpsychology/part/chapter-11-working-groups-performance-and-decision-making/.

1.2.1. Similarity

A cognitive is one of the determinants of entitativity, the perception of similarity. Similarity is essential across many dimensions, including beliefs, values, and qualities, as we saw in our studies of liking and loving. A group can be called a group only if its members possess something in commonality; at the very least, they are similar since they are all part of the same group. If a group of people are engaged in the same topics, have similar thoughts and values, or work together on the same common goal, they should be regarded as a group by themselves and others. However, if there are many differences among individuals, especially in their goals, values, beliefs, and behaviors, they are less likely to be seen as a group.

Given the numerous disparities between members of collectivist and individualist cultures in respect of how individuals perceive their social environment, it should stand to reason that various types of similarity are more strongly associated with views of entitativity in each culture. For example, similarity in terms of personal attributes was shown to be more strongly connected with entitativity in American versus Japanese individuals, whereas similarity in terms of personality traits was shown to be the inverse pattern in regards to shared goals and results (Bazerman & Moore, 2012). As a result, people tend to establish groups exactly because they are alike. Maybe they all enjoy playing poker, or they all support the same soccer team, or they all enjoy kung fu. Then when group members grow diverse and hence no longer have that much in commonality to hold them together, groups are more prone to fall apart.

1.2.1.1. Communication, Interdependence, and Group Structure Are All Important Factors to Consider

Additionally, similarity is important but, it is not the sole factor that leads to the formation of a group. When there is regular interaction and communication among the members of the group, then groups have more entitativity. Whilst communication might happen when groups gather in one location, it can also take place amongst individuals who are separated by enormous distances. For instance, the members of a Marketing team works remotely, but regularly communicate via Video chat, might have frequent interactions feel like they belong to a group though they never or seldom meeting in person.

When interaction is coupled by *interdependence*—the degree to which group members are jointly reliant on one another to achieve a goal—it becomes even more significant. *Interdependence* refers to the requirement to collaborate in order to complete a task successfully in various situations, especially in working groups. Individuals who play baseball rely on one another to be able to play the game and do it well. In order for the group to work, each member must do his or her part. When we collaborate to write a report or develop a class project, we are also interdependent. When members of a group are interdependent, they report like each other more, are more likely to collaborate and communicate with one another, and maybe more productive (Van Ginkel & Van Knippenberg, 2009).

Another feature of working groups whose participants spend a bit of time together and appear "group-ish" is that they create group structure—the stable norms and roles that govern the group's as well as an individual's appropriate actions. Customs, traditions, rules and regulations, and the group's basic ideals include the important social regulations for groups. Injunctive standards specifying how members of the group should comply are especially notable. Some of these are regulatory standards that tell the group members what to do, while others are prohibitive standards that tell them what not to make. Generally speaking, the more precisely defined and universally established standards in a group, the more entities they are.

Effective groups also establish and allocate to group members social roles (expected behaviors). For example, a number of organizations can be configured to have a chairman, a secretary, and multiple working committees. Often there are multiple jobs and these hierarchies with various levels of prestige or perceived authority. Generally, groups are more productive if each member's function is clearly defined and suitable for the abilities and goals of those persons. In addition, for example, when members perform and coach more than one role, it is crucial that these responsibilities are not contradictory but rather compatible. This allows high-performance groups to avoid stressing their duties. This happens when people experience incompatible demands and expectations within or among roles that they hold, often negatively affecting their capability to succeed.

1.2.2. Social Identification

Although cognitive variables such as perceived similarity, communication, interdependence, and structure typically plays a significant role in what we mean as a group, they may not always appear to be needed. In some cases, even though they have little independence, communication, or structure groups can still be called as groups. Perhaps because of such a problem, an alternate method to group thinking, and an approach which in social psychology was highly important, uses the affective responses we have towards the groups we adhere to. As we learned, social identity pertains to the element of the self-concept that comes from our social membership. In principle, because we choose to stay in groups that we feel comfortable with, the result of the group membership is a positive sociological identity – we feel comfortable with our members.

And per the concept of the social identity group, the members feel a social identity whenever part of them are defined by the group to which they belong and feel comfortable about membership in their cohort. This identification can be seen as an individual's predisposition to talk to others favorable about the group, the overall pleasure of belonging to the group, and a feeling of pride from being part of the group. Since identity is quite an important element of our group, we might try to create it to make both our group and ourselves feel good (Tang & Liao, 2021). Probably you know some people, maybe yourself even, who wear their sports team outfits to underline their identity with the unit since they wish to belong to the other group members and to be welcomed by them. In fact, even if we have enticing options, the more we view our social identities as part of our group membership, the more inclined we are to stay in that group.

1.2.3. The Development Stages

It is important to talk about the stages of group development because we must be aware that decisions are made all through the lifespan of said group. While many groups are essentially static and execute the same kinds of duties every day, other groups are more dynamic. Actually, at least some changes occur in nearly all groups; members come and leave, and the group's purpose can alter. Even groups that are reasonably stable over lengthy periods can, suddenly, change dramatically when facing crises, for example, a change in work objectives or the death of a leader. Groups can sometimes lose their meaning and their identity as they achieve their objectives.

The probable steps groups usually undergo are one way to understand group growth. The model established by researchers Bruce Tuckman and Mary Jensen is a regularly utilized strategy here. In Figure 1.2, the individual stages entail forming, storming, norming and performing, and adjourning.

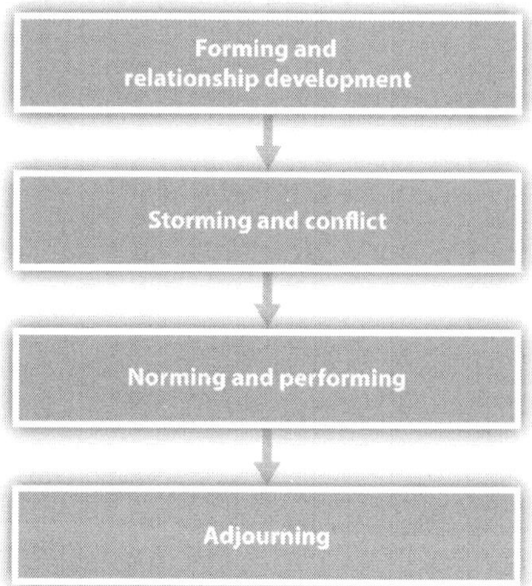

Figure 1.2. Stages of group development.

Source: https://opentextbc.ca/socialpsychology/chapter/understanding-social-groups/.

Forming stage occurs when the group members decide to get together and start to exist as a group. In some circumstances, if a new group, such as a jury in the courtroom, is able to achieve an objective, the training phase takes place quite rapidly and is called the first stage of the group appropriately. However, in some circumstances, the process of group training takes place continuously over a lengthy period of time, for example, when industrial workers are left and replaced by new staff.

In this stage, it is vital for the group and for the new members as well. The group and the individual shall at this period exchange knowledge of relevant standards, including existing group structures, processes, and routines (Sorkin et al., 2001). Each member must learn about the group and identify how they fit into it. And the group can inspect the qualities and suitability of the individual as a group member. This initial study may result in the rejection by the individual or in the refusal of the group.

Figure 1.3. The forming stage ("team orientation" stage).

Source:https://clockify.me/blog/business/stages-of-group-development/.

Storming stage can be equated to puberty if you can contrast the formation with your childhood. As members of the group become acquainted, they may not always agree on everything. In the storm, the members might try to make their own opinions, exhibit their individuality and convince the group to embrace their ideas. Storming may take place from the beginning of the group and at any moment during the development of the group, especially if a group has stress produced by a bad occurrence such as a reversal towards the group objective. In other circumstances, the dispute could be so great that the members of the organization determine that they do not work and dissolve. In fact, field investigations of real working groups have demonstrated that a considerable proportion of new organizations never pass through the stages of formation and storm before they collapse (Schulz-Hardt et al., 2002).

Furthermore, storming can be destructive to organizations, and therefore, groups have to endeavor to prevent its escalation, some conflicts between group members may really help. Oftentimes, the most effective groups are those which have passed a stormy stage successfully since conflicts can boost the group's output if the disagreement is not as extreme as it disintegrates prematurely. Groups that do not clash at all may be ineffective, since the members are bored, unaffected and uninspired, and do not engage about the issues that are relevant to them creatively or honestly. In order for growth to be made, the group needs to generate new ideas and approaches, and this compels members to discuss the decisions they have to make.

Figure 1.4. The storming stage ("power struggle" stage).

Source: https://clockify.me/blog/business/stages-of-group-development/.

If the storms do not grow too far, the group will continue onto the standardization step, when appropriate standards and roles are defined for the group.

After these standards are set, the group enters the *stage of performance*, which is to build a routine and to work together efficiently. At this point, each group member can be highly satisfied with, identified with and strongly identified with the group. Groups who have entered this stage successfully are able to achieve objectives and survive adversities and finely tuned to its mission and can successfully carry out the task. The teams were chosen such that they would all work within a set time frame, although that time frame varied greatly—from 8 to 25 meetings spread out across durations ranging from 11 days to 6 months.

Norming and performing stage, in this stage, the group created clear guidelines for how it would approach the work in its very first discussion. During the first half of the time given, each team continued with this method with very little variance (Song, 2009). However, the group abruptly had a meeting midway through the period it had been assigned to execute the task (whether it was after four sessions or after a dozen), in which it decided to rethink its approach. Then, for the remainder of the time allocated, each group employed this new way to complete the work. At the halfway point, it was as if a buzzer ringed, causing each squad to reconsider its strategy.

Most groups will finally get at the *stage of adjournment*, where the group will prepare to end. This transpires in some circumstances because the work which the group was founded upon has been done, and in others because group members have discovered new interests outside of the group. In any event, since individuals who have operated in a group have likely built a deep bond with the group and its members, the adjournment period can be unpleasant, and individuals may oppose the split. In the face of these circumstances, people are often planning to re-join and exchange addresses and telephone numbers even though they know that they are probably not going to. Sometimes it is helpful for the organization to prepare members for the division in advance.

Figure 1.5. The adjourning stage ("sense of closure" stage).

Source: https://clockify.me/blog/business/stages-of-group-development/.

Bear in mind that this model merely gives an overview of the group phases, starting with formation, and ending with postponement, and is not equally relevant to all groups. For example, the steps are not strictly sequential some groups can cycle back and forward in response to their circumstances through earlier and later stages. Not all groups are necessary going through all stages, too. The model was nevertheless effective to describe the development of a wide range of groups

1.3. WORKING GROUPS: PERFORMANCE AND MAKING OF DECISIONS

Though individuals and their worldviews have significantly over the course of our history, one fundamental aspect of human existence remains the same. Just as our prehistoric predecessors lived in small social groups, families, tribes and clans, even until this era of modernization people spend most of their time in social groups (i.e., eating in the restaurants, group study, working together in a particular project as a team, or in any businesses). We are forming governments, playing sports teams together, and communicating with others using social media. It looks like people will always be social creatures no matter how much our world is changing. It is likely incorrect to claim that human group is the foundation of human existence; we would simply not be humans without our relationships with one another and there is no human culture.

A *social group* can be defined as a set of people with a common purpose who usually share a good social identity. Whereas social groups provide the foundation of human culture and productivity, some of our deepest failures also arise. Groups sometimes create a very opposite of what we could expect, for example when a group of highly intelligent and prominent advisors lead their president with poor decision, when peaceful protest becomes violent upheaval or when a clique teases other pupils in a secondary school until they go violent (Schulze & Newell, 2016).

When one psychologist put all the evidence together, he reportedly went so far as to say that "humans without groups would do better." Probably, that scholar meant recognizing the tremendous strength of social organizations and stressing the significance of realizing that these forces may have both positive and harmful implications. Take account of this essential idea should be kept in mind as we continue.

In addition to obtaining high levels of performance, a crucial group task is to make decisions. In fact, we often commit the crucial decisions in our societies, for instance via juries and political parties, to the groups rather than individuals. A crucial point here is, if we are right to make sound decisions by groups of trust rather than by individuals. From the old saying that, "two heads are better than one."

This question can prove to be difficult to reply to. Firstly, it is difficult to examine the making of decisions, since the quality of decisions on the basis of the knowledge at the time, regardless of their results, is difficult to measure. This is especially problematic because typically, when we assess decision making, we tend to look too closely at the results. In addition, the study of decision making in laboratory conditions usually entailed supplying more information to group members than would normally be available in the actual world, and so it is not always possible to generalize conclusions.

However, taking into account these reservations, some speculative conclusions may be drawn concerning when and why groups makemake better decisions than individuals, and also when and why they end up making superior choices.

1.4. PROCESS GAINS IN GROUP VERSUS INDIVIDUAL DECISION MAKING

The type of dependency they have is a crucial feature helping groups overcome individuals in decision-making activities. In general, positive interdependent (cooperative) groups tend to make better choices, particularly in complicated activities, compared to negatively interdependent (competitive) organizations and individuals. These process benefits are based on a number of things. The first is that group members typically provide fresh ideas and solutions that they would not have reached separately when they engage (Sari, 2008). Group members are also more likely to recognize and remedy errors that can damage sound decision-making than individual people. They have a greater collective memory, such that many minds have more knowledge than one, and greater transactive memory, which happens when interactions among groups make key materials easy to retrieve. Furthermore, the total number of data that the group can draw upon in order to make good decisions increases if individual group members contribute information unique to them.

Individual Decision Making		*Group Decision Making*	
Pros	Cons	Pros	Cons
Typically faster than group decision making	Fewer ideas	Diversity of ideas and can piggyback on others' ideas	Takes longer
Best individual in a group usually outperforms the group	Identifying the best individual can be challenging	Greater commitment to ideas	Group dynamics such as groupthink can occur
Accountability is easier to determine	Possible to put off making decisions if left alone to do it	Interaction can be fun and serves as a team building task	Social loafing-harder to identify responsibility for decisions

Figure 1.6. Advantages and disadvantages of different levels of decision making.

Source: https://saylordotorg.github.io/text_principles-of-management-v1.1/s15–04-decision-making-in-groups.html.

1.5. PROCESS LOSSES DUE TO GROUP CONFORMITY PRESSURES

The above-mentioned advantages with group membership are the basis where a group can make effective decisions. However, these conditions are not usually gain in real groups. One example of a group process which might lead to very bad group decisions was groupthink, as we have already mentioned. Failed group process and conformity pressures results a poor decision making even though the group is consist of highly competent individuals with exceptional decision making capability.

Groupthink is more likely to happen in groups in which the members are feeling strong social identity, for example, at moments of stress and crisis when the group needs to take the chance to make an important decision when a powerful and director develops positive group feelings. The difficulty is that groups who think of a group do not wish to search, discuss or discuss discrepancies or disturbances on the subject, and the groups do not voice contradictory ideas (Saaty & Peniwati, 2013). Since the group member's fear expressing thoughts that contradict the leaders or bringing in foreigners with more information, a fully informed decision is avoided. Figure 1.7 outlines the fundamental causes and effects of groupthink.

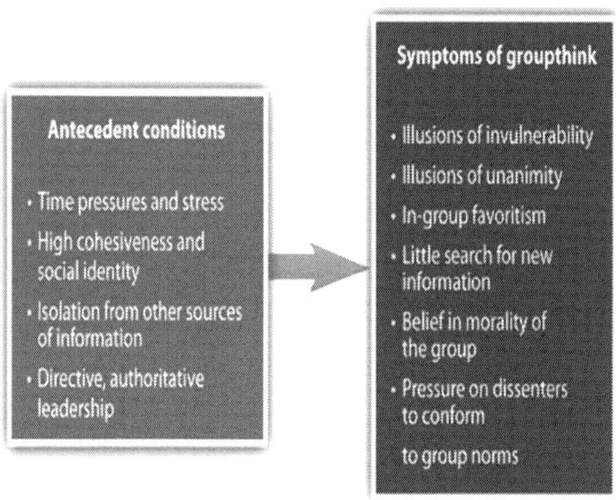

Figure 1.7. Antecedents and outcomes of groupthink.

Source: https://opentextbc.ca/socialpsychology/chapter/understanding-social-groups/.

Although some researchers at least are skeptical of the usefulness of groupthink in genuine group decisions (Kramer, 1998), many others have indicated that groupthink has been engaged in a number of major, but very poor, government- and business-level decisions. Key historical decisions analyzed in terms of groupthink include President George Bush's and his advisors' choice to attack Iraq with prominent support of other foreign governments such as UK, Spain, Italy, South Korea, Japan, Singapore, and

Australia; President John F. Kennedy and his adviser's decision in 1962 to commit US forces to aid in an invasion of Cuba with the purpose of deposing Fidel Castro; and many European leaders' strategy of appeasement of Nazi Germany in the 1930s, leading up to World War II. In several lesser-known but also essential sectors, such as pack journalism, Groupthink has also been employed. Groupthink was fascinatingly even utilized to try to explain social psychologists' alleged anti-right political inclinations.

The function of conformity pressure was recorded through careful analyses of the decision-making process in the historical situations listed above. In fact, the group process frequently appears to be set up to promote compliance rather than to encourage free and open dialogue. President Kennedy, for example, requested that group members offer a voice vote on their individual thoughts before the group considered the benefits and drawbacks of a new plan during sessions of the Bay of Pigs advisory committee. These conformity constraints lead to a general aversion to expressing thoughts that differ from the social norm (Saka et al., 2008).

Conformity demands also reach a point in which just a few of the group members are actively engaged in discourse, while the others remain silent. Whenever there is little or no opposition in the organization, the members begin to believe that they are all in agreement. In rare situations, the leader may even appoint mind guards, who are tasked with suppressing opposition and increasing obedience to the leader's views.

Because these groups have such high levels of conformity, they grow to perceive themselves as incredibly valuable and significant, highly adept at making high-quality decisions, and invulnerable. In other words, the members of the group generate exceptionally high levels of social identification and conformity. While this social identity can produce certain positive results in contexts of a dedication to working towards group objectives (and certainly makes the group members feel good), it also leads to misconceptions of invulnerability, which make them feel superior and not need to discover data from outside the group. In such a setting, bad decision-making is common, which can have tragic effects.

Surprisingly, the structure of the group can have an impact on the likelihood of groupthink. For example, more varied groups can assist ensure that the group has a broader range of viewpoints when making its choices that can minimize the risk of group thinking. The more homogenous the group is in internal qualities such as beliefs and external traits such as gender, considering our case study, the more at danger of group thinking.

Mixed-gender business boards are then, perhaps, somewhat more efficient because they can actually avoid a dangerous group thinking phenomena.

1.6. LAKE OF INFORMATION SHARING IN THE COGNITIVE PROCESS

While group discussions generally enhance the quality of decisions of a group, this will only happen if the group discusses the most useful facts for decisions to be taken. One problem is that groups are more inclined than others to discuss certain kinds of knowledge. Besides the pressure to concentrate on information from leaders, which complies with group norms, discussions are impacted by the method that the information is initially disseminated between the members of the group (Risco & Duffy, 2011). The difficulty is that group members are inclined to talk about information that they all have access to, while ignored information that is equally significant, which is made available only to a few members.

1.6.1. Poor Group Sharing of Information

Figure 1.8. Poor communication or poor coordination.

Source: https://www.alert-software.com/blog/the-causes-of-poor-communication-in-the-workplace.

Social psychologists employed an experimental design, as indicated in a demonstration of the shared information distortion, based on the work of the hidden profile. Students read descriptions of two candidates for presidential elections for the imaginary student body and then gathered in groups to discuss and select the best nominee. Candidate's information was so prepared that in contrast with the other candidates Candidate A had overall more good traits than Candidate B. In view of this superiority, the members elected Candidate A 83% of the time following their debate in groups in which all members received information about the two candidates.

Table 1.1: An Example of the Type of "Hidden Profile "That Was Used by Stasser and Titus (1985) to Study Information Sharing in Group Discussion

Group member	Information favoring Candidate A	Information favoring Candidate B
X	a1, a2	b1, b2, b3
Y	a1, a3	b1, b2, b3
Z	a1, a4	b1, b2, b3

Source: https://opentextbc.ca/socialpsychology/chapter/understanding-social-groups/.

Nevertheless, in certain situations, it was made harder by the experimenters to create a disguised profile in which only part of the information was received by each member of the group. In these circumstances, even if the group had the opportunity to have all the knowledge available, the right choice had to be shared. In particular, where Candidate B information was supplied but Candidate information was not supported, just 18% of the groups chose A whereas other groups preferred the lower candidate. This happened because even if the members of the group had cumulatively access to all of the good information, the information originally not shared among the members of the group was not debated. In addition, this prejudice also happened in participants who received specific directions to ensure that their initial views were not expressed and all the relevant evidence was examined.

Although the tendency of sharing information appears to be poorly happens more frequently, it does not emerge equally under all settings, at least in groups generated artificially. For example, groups have been observed to exchange information more effectively when group members think if there is enough debate, a proper solution can be achieved, and they are expected to undergo their conversation even after they believe they have covered all pertinent material. These results demonstrate that one of the group leader's most essential responsibilities is to keep the group talking until he or she is satisfied that all pertinent information has been addressed (Reynolds et al., 2009).

The group's design will also have an impact on information sharing. Groups with members who are physically isolated from one another and consequently have trouble communicating with one another may need to restructure themselves to better communication. The group member's status can also be significant. Lower-status individuals of a group may lack confidence and hence be less likely to offer their ideas. Another study discovered that members of groups with higher rank were more inclined to share new information. Those with higher social status, on the other hand, may occasionally control the discussion, even if the information they possess is not more accurate or significant. When group members are unaware of the alternatives that must be determined or the preferences of the other group members, they are more likely to provide unique information.

Findings indicating that groups do not disclose or discuss previously unshared information have alarming implications for group decision-making since they imply that group debate is likely to result in very poor conclusions. Unshared information is not only not discussed, but just because shared information is discussed frequently, it is more likely to be perceived as more genuine and have a stronger effect on decisions as a consequence of high cognitive availability (Reinalda & Verbeek, 2004). People in a working group frequently bring diverse sorts of information to the debate, and this unrecognized information must be communicated. In a development team meeting for a new building, for example, the architects, engineers, and customer representatives will all have separate and perhaps incompatible information. As a result, working group leaders must be aware of the issue and work hard to create open environments that stimulate information sharing and debate.

Given its obvious drawbacks, it's worth considering why shared information bias appears to be so widespread. Remembering the confirmation bias, it's possible that this propensity is reflected at the group level, where members work to give confirming arguments for each other's opinions. Following on from this, it may also represent people's desire to use groups to reaffirm their own beliefs. Perhaps some organizations devolve into places where members strive to mutually confirm one other's shared opinions at the expense of exploring alternatives.

If these ideas are correct, given that we often choose to associate with similar others, then it may be important to seek out the views of group members that are likely to be most different from our own, in seeking to weaken the damaging effects of the shared information bias (Morrow & Deidan, 1992).

1.7. COGNITIVE PROCESS LOSSES: INEFFECTIVE BRAINSTORMING

If these theories are right, and we tend to associate with people who share our interests, it may be necessary to seek out the perspectives of group members who are most likely to vary from our own in order to mitigate the negative consequences of shared information bias. Brainstorming is a strategy that is widely utilized in working groups to generate creative decisions. Osborn (1953) created the concept in an attempt to improve the efficacy of group sessions at his advertising agency. People would be able to efficiently use their brains to "storm" a challenge by discussing ideas in groups, according to Osborn. As a result, brainstorming was guided by the following guidelines:

- Each group member was required to generate as many ideas as possible, regardless of how foolish, insignificant, or impracticable they were deemed to be.
- The group was to create as many ideas as possible.
- No one was permitted to express an opinion on the merit of an idea (including one's own).
- Members of the group were pushed and expected to improve and expand on each other's ideas.

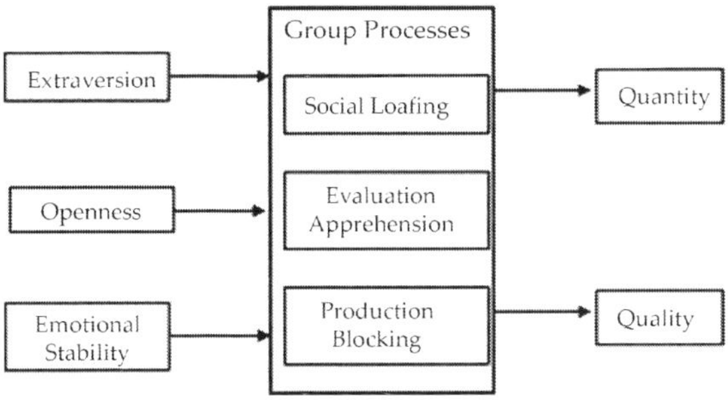

Figure 1.9. Personality, process, and performance in interactive brainstorming groups.

Source: https://link.springer.com/article/10.1007/s10869–005–9000–7.

Experts have put a lot to test the efficiency of Brainstorming, but there is very little evidence of efficacy given the creativity of this idea itself. Indeed, almost everyone in these research findings as well as in meta-analyses finds that, irrespective of the precise commands that a group receives, brainstorming groups do not produce as many concepts as one would anticipate, and the suggestions they yield are normally of less value than the ideas generated by an equal number of people who work alone and then share their findings. Thus brainstorming is another case of a circumstance in which a process loss is instead observed despite the anticipation of a group process gain (Rassin et al., 2008).

There have been a lot of explanations that brainstorming failure is effective, many of which have been found relevant. Social loafing of the group members is an obvious problem, and at least some research shows that this leads to part of the problem. Experts, for example, observed that social loafing in brainstorming groups happened in part because people felt that the other team members didn't work too hard and complied with the perceived norm. Researchers contrasted face to face brainstorming groups with the same numbers of persons who operated alone to further directly assess the function of social labor; they discovered that face to face brainstorming groups created less and less innovative solutions comparing to equal equivalents working on their own. But, for a few of the face-to-face groups, the researchers have created a TV camera to capture the members' participation in order to identify the individual contributions to the debate. To be able to identify reduced social loafing and boost individual productivity in face-to-face gatherings.

Even if people in brainstorming groups are assured that there is no review of the value of concepts and that therefore all ideas are acceptable, they could still not be willing to say some of their suggestions in brainstorming groups, since they fear that the other group members would assess them adversely. If you are taught that people in other groups are known more than they are, you minimize their own efforts, and if you are sure that you are experts, you boost your efforts.

Despite social loafing or assessment fears tend to cause some of the trouble, it seems that being with others in a group is preventing possibilities for idea development and expression that is the main difficulties that diminish the efficacy of brainstorming in face-to-face groups. In a group only one person can talk at a time and this can make people forget their ideas because they attend to others or because other people don't know what they say as they concentrate on their own ideas – an issue that is known as *blocking production*. In other cases, blocking production is because although individuals working by themselves can spend the whole time producing ideas, they must also execute other activities in face-to-face groups, which lowers their creativity (Pérez et al., 2010).

In another experiment compared to individuals with groups, Researchers proved how important production blocking is. In this experiment, they created production blocking in individual conditions via a turnaround process instead of changing things in the real group, which required that individuals, who were working in individual cubicles, verbally express their ideas into the microphone, but only could speak if no other person spoke. The performance of individuals declined so that they were no longer better than face-to-face groups had to be coordinated. The biggest cause of productivity loss in face-to-face brainstorming groups, according to a follow-up study, is that group members are unable to make effective use of the time they are compelled to spend waiting for others. They tend to forget their thoughts while they are waiting because they have to focus on bargaining when it is their turn to speak. Indeed, even if the researchers gave the individual groups more time to accomplish the assignment (to make up for waiting for others); they still didn't achieve the individual production level. This reduces the ability to think in creativity by the need to monitor the behavior of others and the delay in waiting to speak one's views.

Although conceptualizing is a typical case of a group process loss, it can be more efficient. The nominal group methodology is called a variation on the brainstorming idea. A nominal group methodology builds on the usage of individual sessions to develop the initial ideas and then to discuss and develop on face-to-face group meetings. With these approaches, the initial jobs of the participants to produce their ideas and write them down before the group discussions begin. A round tap approach is also employed to ensure that everyone has an opportunity to share their opinions (Patalano & LeClair, 2011). Current technological improvements have enabled users to collaborate on creative endeavors through their computers. In many companies and other organizations, these computer systems, often referred to as group support systems, are used. Brainstorming in creative endeavors includes one use. Every person in the group works on the problem on his or her own computer. When he or she writes proposals or thoughts, they are transferred via the computer network to other members, so that all of the group members can see their own proposals.

Groups working together more than face-to-face were also shown to share unique information more commonly. Each person can read the remarks of all the other members of the group and, as appropriate, read them. The person may alternate between reading other people's comments and making his/her own remarks and not waiting to voice his/her thoughts. Electronic brainstorming may also be useful since it eliminates the assessment fear, especially in anonymous circumstances.

To sum up, the most significant conclusion from brainstorming literature is that the methodology is not as effective as expected, given that groups are not just creative but also obliged to accomplish other things. This does not always mean, however, that brainstorming is not generally productive, as changes to original brainstorming methods were proven to be beneficial in creating group ideas. The finest tactics for brainstorming and group creativity are techniques used by the first individual thought, and then followed by group discussions. You can apply this knowledge when you are in a group that has to make a choice. Ask the members of the group to consider and write down their ideas before their conversation begins.

1.8. GROUP POLARIZATION

One of the group's regular decision-making tasks is to agree to an award such as where a party should hold, whether an accused is innocent or guilty, or how much funds a business should invest in a new product. If a majority of the group supports a specific opinion, even if it is relatively small, it is likely that the group finally adopts that position. This outcome would, of course, be expected because the ultimate judgment of the group should reflect an average of the first opinions of group members due to conformity demands. Although groups usually demonstrate pressure for conformity, there is nevertheless a larger inclination to be on the side of the majority following group discussions. It is frequently discovered that, given the starting opinions of the group members, the groups make even more extreme decisions in the direction of the current standard than we would expect.

Figure 1.10. Difference between groupthink and group polarization.

Source: https://www.youtube.com/watch?v=VbdpxcgLuEc.

Group polarization is said to develop when the sentiments of the individual group members are more extreme after discussion than before the group started to debate the subject. The popular idea that groups tend to encourage people to reach consensus and the middle ground in decision-making may sound strange. Indeed, they can often lead to more radical actions than individuals alone would have done. Group polarization was seen at first by means of challenges in which the group members were to recommend how a person should pick a risky yet extremely favorable result with a certain but unwanted result. Take the question as follows:

Frederica's got a safe position at a big bank. Her wages are sufficient, but will not increase. Frederica was nevertheless offered a job with a relatively unknown start-up company with a high probability of failure and a wage contingent on the firm's performance. What is the minimal likelihood of the success of the start-up business that you think would make Frederica worth taking on the job? (Select one).

- 1 in 10,
- 3 in 10,
- 5 in 10,
- 7 in 10,
- 9 in 10.

Research has found a group polarization of such decisions that the suggestion from the Group is riskier than the average of the initial opinions of each group member (in this case, needing a lower chance of new company success). In these instances, the diffusion of culpability can partly explain polarization. Since the group as a whole is responsible for the decision, a person may be prepared to take a more extreme posture because the person can share responsibility with other group members if the dangerous decision fails. But polarization of groups is not restricted to risk-related choices. For example, during a study conducted by a group of researchers in 1976, the accuser's guilt or innocence in trafficking instances was examined by student groups.

In some groups, the evidence was strong, and in other groups, the evidence was weak. The researchers have adjusted the strength of the evidence against the defendant (Beynon, 2005). This resulted in two groups, some with a majority of students (based on substantial evidence) originally backed guilt and others with a majority initially favoring acquittal (on the basis of only weak evidence). The researchers asked people to comment both before and after the jury had deliberated on the defendant's guilt. As in Figure 10.10, Polarization group views were shown to be more extreme after discussion that the persons had on the culpability or innocence of the accused before discussions began on average. Thus, jurors where most of the people who initially backed conviction believed that the defendant was guilty, and jurors in whom most of the people who were original advocates of acquittement believed that the respondent was innocent after the discussions, it became more likely to believe. In 1970, similarly, researchers observed that college-level groups with attitudes initially racist got more racist following group discussion, but university-level groups with attitudes initially anti-racist became less racist after group discussion. For groups who talk about a variety of topics and many different cultures, similar findings have been reported.

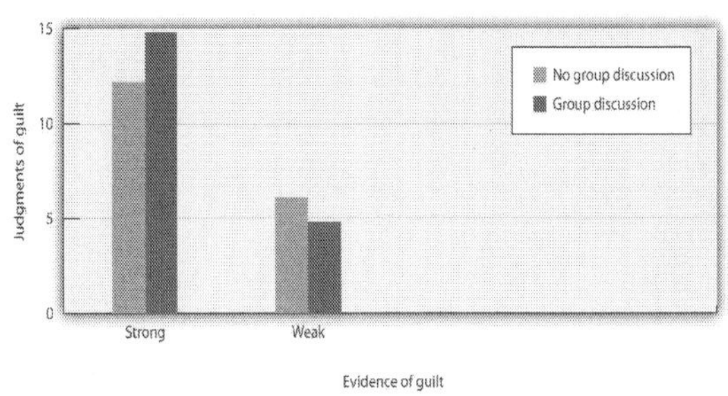

Figure 1.11. Group polarization.

Source: https://opentextbc.ca/socialpsychology/chapter/understanding-social-groups/.

The juries get strong or weak proof of a defendant's guilt in this research and can then discuss the evidence before making a judgment. The juries that discussed the matter took far more radical decisions as shown by group polarization than those juries which did not examine the issue; evidence from research and studies given in 1970.

Groupthink in all groups and circumstances doesn't really occur but most frequently occurs when two conditions occur: Firstly, the members of the group must first rely on a particular viewpoint or judgment. If the group members support liberal policies generally, after discussions, their views will probably grow even more liberal. But if both liberals and conservatives make up the group, there would not be group polarization. Secondly, the debate of the topic enhances group polarization. For example, in the 1976 research, the group members had merely given their views, but did not discuss the subject in certain experimental settings, and the groups were less polarized than the groups that discussed the problem. Polarization of the Group has also occurred in key real-world circumstances, such in corporate finance decisions (data presented from studies in 2008 and 2010) (Nutt, 2006).

As the group members, all of whom initially have some radical beliefs, meet and discuss their concerns and desires, their opinions polarize, allowing them to become progressively more extreme. Because they are also away from any other influences that might moderate their opinions, they may eventually become mass killers. It was also alleged that the recent political polarization among "blue" Democratic States in many countries versus "red" Republican States for example, in the United States is largely due to each group spending time communicating with other members of this same-minded group leading to more extreme views on both sides. And some suggested that the group polarization that happens in the interaction of terrorist groups develop their extreme ideas and participate in acts of violence.

Cognitive as well as affective elements occur from group polarization. The general idea of the persuasive discussion technique is cognitive in orientation. This strategy presupposes that there are a number of potential reasons supporting each view and a series of potential arguments refuting this view. In addition, the present view of an individual about the subject is projected to be based on his or her current knowledge of the arguments. Each member will put forward arguments to support their individual perspectives in the group debate. Initially, because the members of the group lean in a single way, many arguments will be produced that support the group members' initial leaning (LeClair, 2010). As a consequence, additional arguments are exposed for each member supporting the Group's initial lean, which polarizes the viewpoints of the group members by the dominance of arguments in one direction. The study has demonstrated that the number of new arguments mentioned in the discussion corresponds to the level of polarization and that there can be little polarization in a group without debate in support of the predictions of persuasive arguments.

Please note here the links between the persuasive group polarization technique and the concept of information compliance. The polarization of groups, however, is founded in certain respects on the emotive responses of people and especially their social identity. The theory is that members of groups try to distinguish their group from others by embracing extreme beliefs in order to establish a positive social identity. Thus, not only the standards of the internal group but also a distance from the norms of others of significant external groups are likely to determine the apparent level of group polarization. In summary, it suggests that groups with well-defined (strong) values can establish social identity better for members than groups with moderate (and potentially less clear) ideas. Once again, note that this polarization explanation is comparable to the concept of regulatory conformance. The consequences of group polarization are larger if the group members are socially identical. A 1986 researcher had three participants listening to a topic so that he could familiarize himself with the subject in order to enable them to decide on their own.

The people they heard were, though, members of a group they would join in the next experimental session, members of a group they would not anticipate to join, or some people who were not a group.

A scientist discovered that the perceived (future) standards in the Group were more extreme than those of the other group and more inclined than the individuals to accept the arguments of the group. This finding supports the assumption that group standards for groups with which people associate are viewed more harsh (in this case, because they were expecting to join it in the future). Another experiment carried out by a scientist in 1986 also supported the prediction of social identity that the existence of a competing out-group enhances polarization as members try and separate from the other group by taking more radical opinions (Beekun & Westerman, 2012). Together, the research then indicates that it is possible to polarize another potential challenge for group decision making. These swings towards more extreme opinions have different origins and occur more under certain settings than under other conditions, but they should be remembered whenever major choices are made by groups together.

1.9. SOCIAL PSYCHOLOGY IN THE PUBLIC INTEREST

1.9.1. Decision Making By a Jury

Although many countries depend on judge's decisions in civil and criminal proceedings, in many other countries, the jury provides the cornerstone for the legal system. The idea of a trial by one's colleagues is founded on the concept that, if people work together in groups, regular people may make informed and fair judgments. However, given the issues faced by groups, social psychologists and others often ask if the jury is the best solution to these critical decisions and if the composition of a jury affects the possible outcome of its discussions. Juries can make good or poor decisions as tiny working parties, according to several of the criteria that we explored in this chapter. And once again it is based on both individual's features and group processes that the jury has the potential to make a sound choice. There is at least some evidence, in terms of person variables, that the characteristics of the jury members matter. For one thing, people who have previously serving on jurors are more likely to be considered experts, to be picked as a precursor to the jury and to provide more information during discussions (Leclercq, 2018).

The status issues were also found to be more likely for jurors with higher professions and education as opposed to women, and those who speak first were chosen to be the foreperson. As in other minority group members, the jury discussion was usually dominated by minorities, and often a tendency exists. Consequently, crucial information or viewpoints may not be communicated since certain persons are never or rarely involved in the conversation.

The most powerful proof of the importance of the members' traits in decision-making is perhaps the selection of death-qualified juries in proceedings involving a death sentence. The prospectors must state that, in principle, they are ready to suggest the death penalty as a penalty to be selected for such a jury. Potential jurors who are against the death sentence in certain nations are not eligible for these jurors. This selection process does, however, create potential partiality because people who say they won't vote for the death penalty under any conditions are more likely to be rigid, punitive and therefore to find the defendants guilty more often, a situation which increases the chances for the defendant to convict himself. Although there are at least certain member features affecting jury decision-making, group processes, as in other working groups, have a greater effect than membership features in the outcome of jury decisions.

Like any organization, juries adopt their own standards, and their judgments can have a tremendous impact. Analyzing the group process injuries demonstrates that various jurors adopt very varied tactics in order to achieve a judgment. Some spend a lot of time planning initially, while others start talking immediately (Bolaños et al., 2005). And some juries base their discussions upon an examination and reorganization and wait until they have all taken a vote, other judges decide first, by taking a poll, which decision will be preferred by the team and then organize their discussion around the opinions (in the event that the first vote does not lead to a final verdict).

These two approaches are employed equally commonly, but can lead to differing decisions in some instances (presented in a research in 2008). Most importantly, conformity demands have a significant impact on the decision making of the jury. As you can see in Figure 10.11, as the majority of the judges are more and more members of the jury, their perspective is increasingly clear during debate. This does not mean that minorities can't ever be convincing, but for them, it is incredibly tough. The majority impact is likely attributable both to informational conformity (this is supported by more reasons) and to normative conformity (Many are less inclined to disagree with the opinion of the majority).

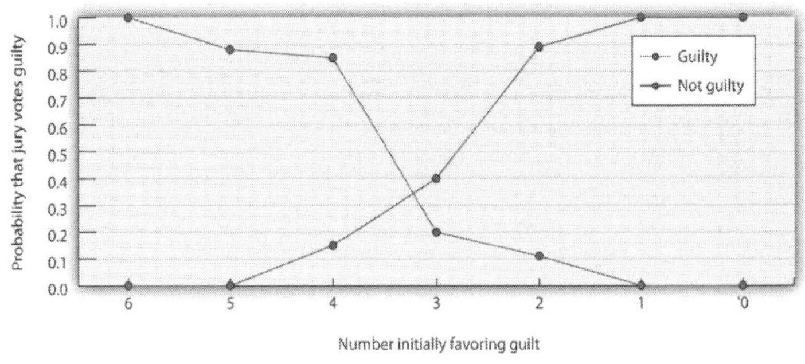

Figure 1.12. Conformity injuries.

Source: https://opentextbc.ca/socialpsychology/chapter/understanding-social-groups/.

This figure depicted the six-member mock jury rulings making "majority rules." When most of the six initially favored votes, the jury almost always voted guilty, and the jury almost always voted innocent when the majority of the six initially favored voting. When the original division was three to three, the jury was often hanging (cannot make a decision) (data are from the work of three researchers in 1982).

Research has also indicated that juries which are evenly divided (three or six to six) tend to be lenient by voting for acquittal more often than by deciding to culpability.

This is in part because jurors are normally told to take innocence unless adequate evidence to affirm guilt is available—they have to apply "beyond any reasonable doubt" to the burden of proof of guilt. The leniency factor does not always exist injuries, although when the possible sentence is more serious, it is more likely (Brodbeck et al., 2002).

Given your knowledge of the many problems facing groups in sound decision making, you could be concerned that the judgments of juries may not be very effective, accurate, or fair. Despite these worries, however, there is evidence that jurors may not do as well as we would hope. The deliberation process appears to have reversed a large number of juror privileges and the relevance of the judgment motivates jurors to examine the facts thoroughly.

We began this chapter by looking at the definition and perception of groups. A cognitive factor of a group's perspective is the impression of similarity. A group can be only a group insofar as it has something in agreement with its members. A group will also have more entity if the group members frequently engage and communicate. The amount to which the group members are mutually dependent upon one another in order to attain a goal is especially crucial when supplemented by Interdependence. Also more likely to be seen as a group is a group developing a group structure. The effect we have on the group to which we belong – social identity—also contribute to produce a collective experience. During your time together, the majority of groups pass a series of stages—the formation, storming, standardization and performance.

As groups comprise numerous members, group performance is often better than any individual operating alone and Group choices are often more precise. On the other side, work in groups also cost – we call them losses in the process.

Various investigations have demonstrated that the presence of others can provide social support for a wider range of jobs. However, the presence of others sometimes creates poorer individual performance—social inhibition. As per Robert Zajonc's theory, we feel more excited than when we are alone, if we are with others, and this excitement raises the probability that we're going to respond dominantly, the response that we most likely issue in any circumstances. Although Zajonc's arousal model is likely the most attractive one, alternative reasons for social facilitation and social inhibition have also been presented (Caemmerer et al., 2021).

By using the following formula, we may compare the group's productivity level, that is, with its membership, with the group's actual productivity:

Actual productivity = potential productivity − process loss + process gain.

A group's actual production relies in part on the qualities of the group – its respective qualities, skills or competencies. However, group performance is also dependent on environmental circumstances such as work type. The work is reliant, whether or not it can be broken down into smaller subprojects, on the ability of the best or worse member of the group to do the task, on the particular product created by the group and on the empirically correct conclusion for the task.

Operational losses are produced by occurrences within the group which make it harder to achieve the full capacity of the group. They are partly because of synchronization losses that occur when individuals collaborate and partly because people are not as hard in a group as they are alone—social loafing.

As regards decision-making, we examined numerous reasons why individual groupings can and often make better decisions, e.g., because of broader base of knowledge, greater collective and active memory as well as their greater capacity to detect and correct errors. However, we have also seen several events which illustrate when groups are able to make inferior choices than people.

Group thinking is one such mechanism that can lead to very poor group decisions. This group thinks when, as a result of faults in the group process and severe compliance demands, a body that comprises individuals who can indeed be very competent and thus able to make outstanding decisions ends up making a bad conclusion (Colombo et al., 2003). And process losses also arise as group members tend to share the information, that is to say, they all have access to information while ignoring equally vital information that only some members have access to.

Brainstorming is one strategy widely employed in working groups to develop creative decisions. Brainstorming, though, often commonly causes process loss in groups as a consequence of social loafing, concern for evaluation and production obstruction. Brainstorming methods, such as group support networks, can be successful which lessen the blockade of production. Group polarization happens when the attitudes of each group member are more extreme than before the group began to debate the subject. Cognitive as well as affective elements occur from group polarization.

Group members often overestimate their group's output—the illusion of group effectiveness. It is due to the high level of work of the whole group and the high social identity of the group. Groups therefore need to be more motivated to work and aware that they can overestimate their values by their pleasant sensations.

Perhaps the most straightforward approach to getting people to work harder in groups is to provide rewards for performance. This approach is frequently, but not always, successful. People also work harder in groups when they feel that they are contributing to the group and that their work is visible to and valued by the other group members.

Groups are also more productive when they adopt adequate social standards, such as information sharing standards. Information is more likely to be shared if the group has time to decide. In order to promote standards of free debate, the group leader is vitally crucial.

The definition of the objectives that the group uses to direct its work is one part of planning, which has been closely linked with effective group performance. Groups that set defined, challenging and yet achievable objectives do better. There are advantages and disadvantages in terms of group variety. Although diverse groups may have some advantages, the groups—particularly the group leaders—must try to ensure that the group members have a happy impression.

You can help in your daily life by fresh understanding about working groups. If you are in a working group, make sure you use this knowledge to make your group more functional and your working groups more efficient

Chapter 2

The Essentials of Negotiation

CONTENTS

2.1. INTRODUCTION

A negotiation is a planned dialogue that aims to resolve a problem in a way that is agreeable to both parties. Each party in a negotiation seeks to persuade the other to agree with their point of view. By bargaining, the parties concerned aim to avoid disputing and instead agree to find a solution.

Negotiations entail a certain amount of give and take, which implies that one party will always come out on top. The other, on the other hand, must concede—even if it is only a token concession. The parties to a negotiation can be diverse. They can involve discussions between buyers and sellers, an employer, and a potential employee, or two or more governments.

Two or more parties participate in negotiations which are joined together for a final goal by means of a compromise or resolution which is acceptable to all concerned. One party puts forward its position, whereas the other accepts the conditions or opposes their position (Charness & Sutter, 2012). The process continues until a resolution is approved by both parties. Before negotiations begin, participants learn to their fullest extent the strengths and weaknesses that the other party must take on, how to prepare themselves to defend their positions, and whatever counterarguments that the other party is likely to make.

Figure 2.1. Illustration of negotiation technique for resolving disagreements.

Source: https://www.inc.com/david-finkel/which-of-these-5-negotiation-rules-are-you-breaking-every-day-hint-its-costing-your-thousands-of-dollars.html.

The duration of negotiations depends on the situation. The negotiations take time. Negotiations can take just a couple of minutes or much longer, in more complex cases. For instance, for minutes or hours a purchaser and seller may negotiate for selling a car. However, it may take months or years for governments of two or more countries to negotiate terms of a trade agreement. Many people believe that pricing and offerings are set in stone and cannot be changed. But this isn't always the case. Many people are, in fact, adaptable. Negotiating can be used to settle a range of issues, including debt reduction, lowering the sale price of a home, improving contract terms, and getting a better bargain on a car.

Let's say you would like to buy a new SUV. The manufacturer's suggested retail price (MSRP) is usually the starting point for negotiations between you and the salesperson. This is the suggested selling price by the manufacturer for the SUV. Many individuals are unaware that, unless the make and model is extremely popular, most dealerships sell below MSRP. You can approach the dealer with a lower-than-MSRP offer, which the dealer may accept or reject. You might be able to negotiate a better deal than the vehicle's invoice price if you have good negotiation skills. This is the exact price that the manufacturer charges the dealer) (Cheek & Goebel, 2020).

Negotiations are also an important ability to accept a new job. The first compensation offer by the employer is often not the best offer of the company and employees can negotiate different terms, such as higher salaries, more holidays, better pension benefits, etc. Negotiation of an employment offer is especially important because the initial offer will be based on all future compensation increases.

Figure 2.2. Illustration of the important role of negotiator in negotiation.

Source: https://corporatefinanceinstitute.com/resources/careers/soft-skills/negotiation/.

There are certain key factors in negotiations. There are some essential components or factors in the negotiations that come into play if you succeed:

- *Involved parties*: What are the interests of the parties involved in the negotiation? What is everyone's background, and how does that affect their viewpoint in the debate?
- *Relations*: What is the nature of the connection between the parties and their negotiators? What is the nature of the parties' relations, and what function does this play in the negotiation process?
- *Communicating:* What are the best ways of communicating the needs of the parties involved to secure their pacts through negotiations? How can the desired results and needs be transmitted most effectively? How can the parties rest assure that they are heard?
- *Alternative options:* Does any party at first want any alternative? If no direct agreement is possible, will it be necessary for the parties to seek alternative results?
- *Options that are realistic:* Which options can an outcome are reached? Where can flexibility in their demands are expressed by the parties? (Dalal & Brooks, 2013).
- *Legitimate claims*: Does each party have legitimate requests and promises? What proof do the parties present to support their claims and demonstrate the validity of their requests? How will they ensure that the results of the negotiations are followed up?
- *Commitment level*: What level of commitment is needed to complete the negotiation's result? What is at risk for each party, and do the discussions consider the effort required to attain the agreed-upon outcomes?

2.2. THE VARIOUS NEGOTIATION TYPES

A multilateral conference with all UN members to establish a new international standard (e.g., the United Nations Convention on the Law of the Sea), to a gathering of the parties to a conflict to halt violence or treat the underlying problem are all examples of negotiation (e.g., constitutional talks in South Africa between 1990 and 1994 or in Colombia with the FARC in 2012 and 2015). Mediation is a method of bargaining with the assistance of a third-party catalyst that assists the parties in reaching an agreement when they are unable to do on their own.

Arbitration, on the other hand, is a process in which a third party decides that the disputing parties are bound to accept. There are two types of negotiations, according to negotiation theorists. The difference in how the two types are used depends on the negotiator's mindset as well as the situation: one-time encounters with no long-term relationships are more likely to result in distributive negotiations, whereas long-term relationships are more likely to necessitate integrative negotiating. Various theorists give the two general categories different names and identify them in different ways.

Figure 2.3. The steps in negotiation.

Source: https://www.negotiationacademy.com/negotiation-tactics-techniques/master-negotiation-skills/.

2.2.1. Positional Negotiations

Positional or hard-bargaining negotiation, also known as distributive negotiation or compromise, aims to share a "set pie" of rewards. Distributive negotiation works on a zero-sum basis, which means that any benefit made by one party comes at the loss of the other. As a result of the premise that one person's gain is another person's loss, distributive bargaining is frequently referred to as win-lose. Haggling prices on the open market, such as the price of a car or a home, are examples of distributive negotiation (Mustakallio et al., 2002). One side often takes an extreme or fixed view in a distributive negotiation, knowing that it may not be accepted, and then tries to abandon the agreement as little as possible. Distributive negotiators see negotiation to disperse a fixed value. While there is a distributive element in all negotiations, there is often distributive discussion with those who have never had an interactive interaction before and are unlikely to do so soon.

Since each negotiator is contending in the division approach to the greatest possible part of the pie, it is more likely that the parties will consider one another as an enemy than a colleague and take a harder position. Since people are more aware of the value of losses than profit and more risk-averse of losses, concession-convergence negotiations are harsher and less productive, according to Prospect Theory.

2.2.2. Interest-Based Negotiation

Interest-based, principled, or merit-based negotiating are all terms used to describe integrative negotiation. It's a set of tactics aimed at improving the value and possibility of a negotiated agreement by leveraging the fact that different party's value different outcomes differently. While the negotiation process assumes that the parties have a fixed value (the "fixed pie") in which to spread the negotiation, the integrative negotiation tries to create value through either "compensating" a lost item with gains from another item ("trade-offs" or registration) or constructing or restructuring conflict issues in a way that boosts them ("win-win" negotiation).

Even integrative negotiation, on the other hand, is likely to include some distributive components, particularly when the party's value different items equally or when specifics are left to be allocated at the end of the discussion. While capitulation is a necessary part of any negotiation, research suggests that people who capitulate fast are less likely to consider all integrative and mutually beneficial options. As a result, early concessions lower the likelihood of a successful integrative negotiation (Davenport, 2009).

Interest-based negotiation frequently necessitates a higher level of trust as well as the building of a bond. It can also entail creative problem-solving with the goal of mutual benefit. It defines a good agreement as one that maximizes individual advantage while also benefiting all participants. Gains are made with the other rather than against it in this scenario. Each wants to provide enough value to the other that it will stick to an arrangement that gives the first party a satisfactory result, and vice versa. The focus of productive negotiations is not on their starting spots, but on the aspirations of the parties as fundamental interests; they approach negotiating process as a shared solution of problems instead of an individualized fight and stress that objective, principles of agreement must be respected.

Figure 2.4. Illustration of possible conflict in negotiation.

Source: https://www.openside.group/managing-difficult-negotiations-how-to-develop-a-negotiation-framework/.

2.2.3. Text-Based Negotiations

Wording-based negotiation is the process of developing an agreement's text that both parties are prepared to accept and sign. Parties to a negotiation may start with a draft text, evaluate additional textual suggestions, and try to find a middle ground between various perspectives. The United Nations' text-based negotiation on UN Security Council reform and the creation of the international agreement underlying the Regional Comprehensive Economic Partnership (RCEP) in the Asia-Pacific Region, where the involved parties refused to concur on a text that would suit India in 2019, are two examples of text-based negotiation.

2.3. NEGOTIATION PROCESS STAGES

Negotiators, on the other hand, do not have to forsake good negotiating to maintain a healthy relationship between the parties. Instead of conceding, each side can recognize that the other has their own feelings and reasons and utilize this to their advantage when debating the matter. Perspective-taking, in fact, can assist parties in moving toward a more integrative solution. In their book getting to Yes, Fisher et al., outline a few tactics for improving perspective-taking, and negotiators might use the following to distance people from the problem:

- Seek out ways to act contrary to his or her beliefs – It's probable that the other side has preconceived notions and expectations about you. The other side can conduct in a way that clearly contradicts those preconceptions, successfully sending the message that the other party is interested in a collaborative discussion.
- Putting yourself in their shoes – People are more likely to seek out information that confirms their own opinions, while ignoring facts that contradict them. It is critical to sympathize with the opposing party's point of view to negotiate effectively. One should be open to other points of view and try to see things from their point of view.
- Discussion of each other's views – Explicitly discussing each other's views is a more direct method to understanding the other party. Without attributing blame or judgment to the other, everyone should openly and honestly convey his or her perceptions (Mukherjee et al., 2016).
- Face-saving – In a negotiation, these strategies refer to defending a position based on previously proclaimed ideals and ideals. This solution to a problem is less subjective, and thus more comprehensible from the standpoint of the opposing party.
- Furthermore, certain communication skills can be used by negotiators to strengthen relationships and generate more effective negotiation solutions:
- Listening actively – It is more than just listening to what is said from the other side. Active attention should be paid to what is spoken nonverbally and verbally. It requires that the person regularly seeks further clarification. When asked exactly what they mean, they may realize that you don't just walk through a routine but take it seriously.
- Purposefully speaking – Too much data can be just as dangerous as not enough. Determine exactly what you want to say to the other person before delivering an essential issue. Determine the precise purpose for which this information will be provided.

2.4. INTEGRATED NEGOTIATION

Integrated negotiation is a strategic strategy to impact that maximizes value in each one negotiation by astutely combining and scheduling other negotiations and choices linked to one's operations. In complicated circumstances, the best way to implement this strategy is to map out all possibly important negotiations, conflicts, and operational decisions to integrate positive linkages while minimizing potentially negative ones. Another concept (as outlined above) related to the non-zero-sum approach to value-building in negotiations is integrated negotiations.

Figure 2.5. Illustration of professional negotiator.

Source: https://blog.procureport.com/negotiation-skills-procurement-director/amp/.

In his book Negotiating with Giants, international negotiator and author Peter Johnston recognized and classified interconnected negotiations for the first time. J.D. Rockefeller's decision to build his first major oil refinery is one of the examples mentioned in Johnston's book. Rockefeller chose to build his refinery in Cleveland instead of the simpler, cheaper route from oil fields in Pittsburgh to refine his petroleum. Why does this happen? Di Fabio et al., (2015) states that it is because railways would carry its refined oil to the market. Pittsburgh had only one major railroad, which allowed it to impose rates during talks, whereas Cleveland had three railways, all which Rockefeller knew would compete for his business, potentially lowering his expenses dramatically. The additional operating costs of sending his oil to Cleveland for refining were more than offset by the leverage gained in these rail negotiations, helping to establish Rockefeller's empire while undermining his competitors who failed to integrate their core operating decisions with their negotiation strategies. The following are some further examples of integrated negotiation:

- Athletes in their final year of contracts should aim for full capacity so that they may negotiate solid, long-term contracts to their advantage.
- Before approaching management to negotiate a new contract, a union must first negotiate and resolve any serious internal disagreements to maximize its collective bargaining power.
- Identifying and merging orders into one high volume purchase can assist establish buying power and potential savings in talks with suppliers if comparable goods or services are purchased independently by multiple government agencies?
- A tech start-up that hopes to be acquired by a larger industry player in the future might increase its chances of success by ensuring that its systems, technology, skills, and culture are as compatible as feasible with those of its most probable acquirer.
- A politician who is negotiating presidential backing may want to keep any prominent supporters out of business, who risk alienating other prospective allies while preventing any unforeseen policy that may also reduce the amount of their increasing coalition.

If a party purports to be negotiating, but secretly does not intend to compromise, it is deemed to be negotiating in bad religion. Bad faith is a concept in the theory of negotiations, which parties claim, but do not intend, to find a settlement (Martinsons & Davison, 2007). For example, a certain political party can pretend to negotiations for political purposes with no intention of compromise. In political science and political psychology, the term "bad faith negotiations" refers to negotiating methods or a model of information processing in which there is no genuine effort to seek a settlement. Ole Holsti first proposed the "inherent bad faith model" of processing information to describe the relationship between John Foster Dulles' ideas and his model of information processing. It is the most researched opponent model. Contra-indicators of this are overlooked when a state is assumed to be unwaveringly hostile. They're brushed aside as ruses or evidence of weakness.

2.5. THE NEGOTIATION PIE

Negotiations can be straightforward or difficult, combative, or collaborative, depending on the situation. In today's corporate world, conducting a collaborative, non-adversarial negotiation with a "win-win" outcome is frequently desirable to create and maintain cordial relationships between corporate partners. When bargaining with a used car salesperson, though, you don't want to go for a "win-win" situation. It's vital to understand the type of negotiation you're about to enter and tailor your tactics accordingly.

Figure 2.6. Elements of negotiation.

Source: https://www.stratechi.com/negotiation-strategy/.

When both parties benefit with the scope, price, and contract terms, they reach an agreement. It can take a lot of patience, teamwork, and ingenuity to reach an agreement that is satisfactory to both sides. Distributive bargaining assumes that the pie is fixed, and that the winner and loser are selected by taking extreme positions, haggling, bluffing, and brinkmanship. Integrative negotiation, on the other hand, assumes that value may be cooperatively produced, and the pie may be enlarged in a negotiation by exploring interests, collaborating on problems, and stretching one's thinking to find "win-win" solutions.

The term "negotiation pie" depicts the entire number of benefits and drawbacks to be allocated in a negotiation. The outcome of the negotiations could result in an increase, decrease, or stagnation in these values. A win-win situation is feasible if the negotiating parties can enlarge the entire pie if both sides benefit from the extension of the pie. In practice, however, the so-called little pie prejudice, or the psychological underestimating of the negotiation pie's size, frequently thwarts this maximization method. Similarly, due to the so-called incompatibility bias, the prospect of increasing the pie may be underestimated. During discussions, the pie may shrink rather than grow, for example, due to (excessive) negotiation expenses (Dyer et al., 2008).

The desired outcome is the main distinction between talks. There are essentially two ways to deal with negotiations: to ensure that you win and lose, or to work towards a satisfactory and mutually beneficial solution. We will investigate the difference between these two negotiation types and the best way to distinguish between them.

Competitive, distributive, or positional, negotiation; fixed-pie negotiation; and zero-sum game are all terms used to describe a negotiation with one winner and one loser. Both parties begin as adversaries in this sort of negotiation and tend to stay that way throughout the process. Manipulation is a typical approach. The parties are rigidly positional, neglecting the fundamental challenges and requirements that lie beneath their views.

Because the conclusion is commonly imagined as a pie, each party wants the largest piece, this form of negotiation is known as a "fixed-pie" negotiation. Because the amount of the pie does not change, the party with the largest slice wins and the other loses; there is no way for a win-win situation to emerge. It's also known as a "distributive" negotiation since the pie is divided evenly between the parties, or a "zero-sum game" since any gain on one side equals a corresponding loss on the other: total gains minus total losses equals zero. Buying a used car is a typical example of a fixed-price negotiation, and it provides some insight into what makes this sort of negotiation unique. The sole issue in a used-car deal is price, and there are two sides to the argument: the buyer wants to pay as little as possible, and the dealer wants to collect as much as possible. As a result, we can observe that in a fixed-pie negotiation, there is only one core topic, no complex underlying interests, and no compromises. Each side is just interested in maximizing their profit at the expense of the other.

No long-term relationship: it is unlikely that the buyer and the seller will have a long-term relationship. It's an adversarial and competitive negotiation. No one of the parties is concerned with the level of satisfaction of the other or if the result is satisfactory in a fixed-pie negotiation. This can result in many rough and manipulative methods of negotiation and bargaining (Kugler et al., 2012).

Figure 2.7. Illustration of planning for effective negotiation.

Source: https://www.intheblack.com/articles/2019/11/12/key-to-a-successful-negotiation.

Terms used to describe a potential win-win situation are inclusive, collaborative, or principal negotiations. Both parties work to establish or maintain a long-term, cooperative relationship in which, in this form of negotiations, both parties can obtain mutual satisfaction. The aim of this kind of negotiation is "to broaden the gap" and to find a mutually beneficial solution. As the needs of the parties vary, both can be achieved and a win-win situation. Because they have different needs. The fixed-pie scenario is different from collaborative negotiations or win-win negotiations.

There are several issues to work through, with its set of reasons and interests.

It is feasible to make compromises, concessions, and tradeoffs, concessions. Finding out what each side genuinely wants and collaborating to raise the size of the pie requires a multi-issue discussion. The other party is someone with whom you would like to keep a positive working connection. A mutually satisfactory solution is advantageous if the parties or their companies will be dealing with each other again in the future. If you don't want to lose a business partner, don't make them over the coals! (Kulcsár et al., 2020).

If you don't have a relationship with the other party, it's a one-time deal with only one issue on the line. In most commercial talks, though, you'll be dealing with a long-term connection, a more complicated scenario, and the desire to find a win-win solution. Before you begin, be sure you understand the type of negotiation you're about to engage in.

2.6. STRATEGIES USED IN NEGOTIATIONS

The main elements of negotiation can be classified in a variety of ways. Negotiation has three key parts, according to one perspective: method, behavior, and substance. The process relates to how the parties negotiate, including the background of the discussions, the parties involved, the tactics employed by the parties, and the order and stages in which all of this occurs. The term "behavior" refers to the interactions between these individuals, as well as their communication and communication styles. The agenda, the issues (positions and – more helpfully – interests), the possibilities, and the agreement(s) made at the end are referred to as the substance.

A different perspective on negotiation includes four components: tools, process, strategy, and tactics. The top-level goals, which usually include the relationship and the result, are referred to as strategy. The procedures to take and roles to play in preparing for and negotiating with the other parties are outlined in processes and tools. More comprehensive words and acts, as well as responses to others' statements and acts, are included in tactics. Some add persuasion and influence on this list, claiming that these are now essential to modern-day negotiation success and should not be overlooked. Considering the best time to make concessions, making concessions in installments, and ensuring that the opponent is aware that a concession has been made rather than expressing an existing position and that he is aware of the costs incurred in making the concession, especially if the other party is unaware of the cost, are all strategic approaches to concessions.

2.7. EMPLOYMENT OF ADVOCATES

A competent negotiator can serve one of the negotiating parties as an advocate. The lawyer works to ensure the best outcome for the party. In this course, the negotiator seeks to determine what a small conclusion the other side (or parties) are prepared to accept and then amend their requests properly. A "successful" negotiation takes place in the advocate strategy when the negotiator can achieve all or most of his party's desired results without forcing the opponent to permanently conclude negotiations.

Negotiation hypnosis, a direct presentation of requests or creation of prerequisites, and more misleading ways such as cherry picking are all methods used by skilled negotiators. Salami and intimidation tactics may also be used to influence a negotiation's outcome. Another bargaining strategy is the "bad guy/good guy" strategy (Hwang & Lin, 2012). When one negotiator acts as a bad guy by utilizing threats and fury, this is known as bad guy/good guy. Through being kind and sympathetic, the other negotiators act like a wonderful man. While attempting to elicit concessions and cooperation from the opponent, the good person blames the bad guy for all the troubles.

Figure 2.8. Both parties must be involved in negotiation agreement.

Source: https://www.tradeready.ca/2016/topics/supply-chain-management/negotiating-with-suppliers-walk-away/.

The most favorable course of action, if a dealer fails to reach agreement in the current discussion, is the best alternative to the negotiated agreement, or BATNA. The quality of a BATNA may enhance the negotiating results of a party. A person can become more empowered and set higher targets when it comes to understanding BATNA. Alternatives must be real and workable to be useful. Negotiators can also analyze during negotiations the BATNA of the opposing party, and how it compares to what they propose.

2.8. STYLES IN CONFLICT

Five styles or negotiations responses were identified in Kenneth W. Thomas. The five strategies are often outlined and based on the two-fold model in the literature. A perspective that presupposes the preferred method of handling conflict is based on two themes or dimensions, the dual concern conflict resolution model:

- assertiveness (concern for one's self);
- Empathy (concern for others).

Individuals balance their personal wants and interests with the needs and interests of others using this paradigm. The five styles listed below can be adopted based on an individual's preferences and pro-self or pro-social goals. Individuals can have strong preferences for a variety of styles, and these preferences can vary over time.

2.8.1. Accommodation

Individuals who like resolving problems for others and maintaining personal relationships. Accommodators are aware of the other party's emotional states, body language, and vocal messages. They may, however, feel exploited in instances when the other party does not place a high value on the relationship. Accommodation is a conflict resolution strategy that is both passive and pro-social. Giving in to the demands of others is how people resolve both huge and little conflicts (Herrera et al., 2005). They may yield because they recognize that their perspective is incorrect, and they concur with others' viewpoints. In other circumstances, they may retract their requests without honestly believing the opposing side is correct, but for the sake of team cohesion or expediency, they do so. As a result, yielding can indicate either true conversion or feigned cooperation.

2.8.2. Avoidance

Individuals who dislike negotiating and only do so when necessary. When it comes to bargaining, avoiders tend to postpone and avoid the more aggressive portions of the process; nonetheless, they may be viewed as diplomatic and courteous. Inaction is a passive strategy for resolving conflicts. Those who avoid confrontations take a "wait and see" approach, thinking that issues will resolve themselves. Conflicts are commonly tolerated by avoiders, who allow things to stew without doing anything to resolve them. People that rely on avoidance alter the subject, miss meetings, or even leave the group altogether rather than directly discussing disagreements. They may just agree to disagree (a modus vivendi).

2.8.3. Collaboration

Persons enjoying negotiations that involve creatively solving difficult problems. The employees are good enough to use the negotiations to understand other parties' concerns and interests. Collaborating in resolving conflict is an effective, pro-social, and self-employed approach (Haghani et al., 2019). Working with people, they identify the problems behind the dispute and then work together to find a solution that is mutually acceptable. This approach, which is also described as cooperation, solving problems or a win-win approach, invites both sides to take account of the results and the results of their opponents.

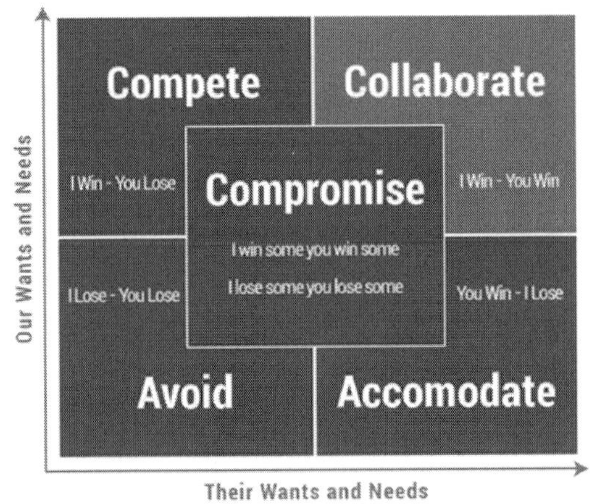

Figure 2.9. Negotiation styles adopted from Thomas Khimann's conflict styles.

Source: https://www.negotiations.com/definition/negotiation-styles/.

2.8.4. Competition

People who enjoy negotiating because it gives them a chance to win anything. Competitive negotiators are strategic and have great instincts for all parts of negotiation. Competitive negotiators frequently overlook the importance of connections since their style can dominate the bargaining process. Competing is an aggressive, pro-self-method of resolving dispute in which one forces others to accept one's point of view. This strategy's practitioners regard disagreement as a lose-lose situation, thus they employ competitive, forceful measures to scare others. Fighting (forcing, dominating, or contesting) can take a variety of forms, such as authoritative mandates, challenges, disputing, accusations, insults, grumbling, retribution, and even physical violence (Morrill, 1995). These methods of dispute resolution are all problematic since they entail imposing one's solution on the opposing side.

2.8.5. Compromise

Individuals willing to conclude the agreement by doing fairly and equal things for all negotiating parties. Compromise can be useful if there is little time to conclude the deal; but compromises often rush the negotiation process unnecessarily and make concessions too fast.

2.9. DIFFERENT TYPES OF BARGAINERS

Researchers working on The Harvard Negotiation Project have discovered three types of negotiators. Hard bargainers, soft bargainers, and principled bargainers are the three categories of negotiators.

2.9.1. Soft

Negotiation is too near to rivalry for these folks, so they opt for a mild approach. They make deals that are not in their best interests, they give in to other people's requests, they avoid conflict, and they keep good relationships with other negotiators. Their goal is accord, and their perception of others is one of friendship. They do not distinguish between persons and problems but are soft on both. They avoid battles of wills and prefer to reach agreements by proposing solutions, trusting others easily, and modifying their minds.

2.9.2. Hard

These people utilize inflammatory language to persuade others, such as "this is my final offer" and "take it or leave it." They threaten others, are suspicious of others, are adamant about their position, and use pressure to bargain. Others are adversaries, and victory is their goal. Furthermore, they look for a single answer and urge that you accept it. They don't isolate individuals from problems (as soft bargainers do), but they are harsh on both the people and the problem.

2.9.3. Principled

Individuals who deal in this manner seek holistic solutions while avoiding commitment to specific ideas. They are more concerned with the problem than with the people involver's intents, goals, and needs. They detach people from the problem, investigate interests, avoid bottom lines, and arrive at results based on criteria that aren't influenced by personal desires (Gillet, 2009). They make decisions based on objective criteria rather than power, pressure, self-interest, or a haphazard decision-making process. Moral norms, justice ideals, professional standards, and tradition can all be used to create these criteria. The Harvard Negotiation Project recommends that negotiators consider a variety of options to find the best solution to their difficulties, however, this isn't always the case (When you're dealing with a person who uses soft or hard negotiation tactics, for example).

2.10. TECHNIQUES

Negotiating tactics are always an important element of the process. They are frequently subtle, difficult to spot, and employed for a variety of objectives. When it comes to distributive talks and taking as much value off the table as possible, tactics are more commonly used. There are numerous negotiation strategies available. A few common strategies are listed below.

Figure 2.10. Negotiation techniques.

Source: https://www.negotiations.com/questions/effective-negotiator/.

- *Auction* – The purpose of the bidding procedure is to foster competition. When a group of people wants the same goal, put them against each other. People desire something even more when they are aware that they may lose it. They want not only the item being bid on, but they also want to win, just to win. Using all a competitor's competitive nature can lead to a price increase.
- *Chicken* – Extreme measures, typically bluffs, are proposed by negotiators to force the opposing party to cave in and give them what they want. When parties are unwilling to back down and

follow through with the drastic option, this technique can be deadly.

- ***Calling a higher authority*** – To avoid making too many concessions, de-escalate a situation, or break an impasse, one party makes the next step in the negotiating process reliant on the judgment of a decision maker who is not present at the table.
- ***Brinksmanship*** – One side pursues a set of demands vigorously until the other bargaining party has no choice but to acquiesce or walk away. Brinkmanship is a form of "hard nut" bargaining strategy in which one party drives the other to the "brink" or limit of what that party is willing to accept. Successful brinkmanship persuades the opposing party that they have no choice but to accept the offer and that the proposed deal is the only option (Eden & Ackermann, 2001).
- ***Bogey*** – The bogey approach is used by negotiators to make it appear as if a little problem is enormously important. The problem can then be swapped for a substantial concession of actual importance later in the negotiation.
- ***Deadlines*** – Offer the other party a deadline to meet to force them to make a choice. This strategy employs the utilization of time to exert pressure on the other side. Actual or fictitious deadlines can be set.
- ***Defense in depth*** – Every time the contract passes via a separate level of authority, several layers of decision-making authority are used to allow for more compromises. To put it another way, each time the offer is presented to a decision maker, the decision maker requests more concession to complete the sale.
- ***Generous Tit Tat or Forgiveness Math*** – According to computer simulation study, the best tactic is to extend an olive branch or give the opponent the option to participate and come up with a win-win solution. Of course, the worst negotiators are oblivious to their own self-interest; therefore negotiators must safeguard their own interests and anticipate a lack of collaboration.
- ***Flinch*** – A significant negative natural response to a proposal is flinching. Gasping for air or a visible show of surprise or shock are common examples of flinching. It's possible to flinch intentionally or unintentionally. The flinch communicates to the other party that you believe the offer or proposition is ridiculous,

in the hopes that they will reduce their ambitions. It's more credible to see someone's physical reaction than to hear someone remark, "I'm astonished."

- ***Bad guy / Good Guy*** – Positive and unpleasant tasks are frequently divided between two negotiators on the same negotiation side, or unpleasant activities or choices are assigned to a (real or hypothetical) outsider, in the good guy/bad guy method (synonyms are good policeman/bad cop or black hat/ white hat). The good guy is in favor of the contract being completed and emphasizes the positive parts of the negotiation (mutual interests). The antagonist criticizes the negative qualities of the situation (opposing interests). The separation of the two roles helps individual negotiators to be more consistent in their behavior and credibility. The good guy can establish trust with the opposite side by promoting the contract (Gati et al., 2011).
- ***Ambits claim or Lowball/Highball*** – Sellers or buyers utilize an absurdly high or stupidly cheap opening offer that is not achievable, based on whether they are selling or purchasing. According to the theory, the extreme offer causes the opposing party to reconsider their initial offer and move closer to the resistance point (as far as you are willing to go to reach an agreement). Another advantage is that when the party making the excessive demand makes concessions toward a more realistic goal, they appear more flexible. One disadvantage of this strategy is that the other party may believe that negotiating is a waste of time.

Figure 2.11. The four stages of negotiation.

Source: https://www.tutorialspoint.com/management_concepts/negotiation_skills.htm.

- ***Snow Job*** – Negotiators bombard the opposing party with so many facts that they have trouble identifying what is significant and what is a distraction. Negotiators may also employ jargon or technical terminology to hide a straightforward solution to a non-inquiry (Forbes & Milliken, 2008).
- ***Generous Tit for Tat*** – Numerous negotiators try to emulate the world's use and abuse of power by adopting a macho and deceptive attitude. They puff up their chests and appear as if they're smart when they've never studied or practiced effective negotiating. It exemplifies some of the world's worst and ugliest leadership. The advantages of a skilled and informed collaborative style have been proven through studies. For research-based and effective strategies, see Forgiveness Math above.
- ***Mirroring*** – The result of a negotiation is more likely to be positive when participants get along well. A negotiator may replicate or replicate the opponent's behavior and repeat what they say to build trust and rapport. Mirroring is when a person repeats the main points of what another person has just said, or when a person repeats a certain expression. It shows that you're paying attention to the issue of the discussion and that you've heard what the other party has to say. Mirroring can aid in the development of trust and the establishment of a connection.

2.11. NON-VERBAL COMMUNICATION

Negotiation relies heavily on communication. Participants must be able to effectively communicate and comprehend information to negotiate effectively. Body language and gestures are used by participants in a negotiation to transmit information not just vocally but also nonverbally. A negotiator who understands how non-verbal communication works, is better able to grasp the information that other participants are leaking non-verbally, while keeping hidden those items that might impair his or her capacity to negotiate.

Figure 2.12. Illustration presents the importance of communication in negotiation.

Source: https://zoetalentsolutions.com/course/advanced-negotiation-skills-course/.

Some examples are given in the following subsections.

2.11.1. Non-Verbal "Anchoring"

A person can obtain an advantage in a negotiation by verbally declaring a stance first. Anchoring one's position is the position from which the negotiation progress is established. Similarly, nonverbal (body language) clues can be used to "anchor" and gain an advantage:

- By leaning back and whispering, one can successfully create a dominant physical position that can give them the upper hand in negotiations.
- Beginning with pleasant gestures and excitement, make a good first impression. With sincerity, look at the person in the eyes. If you are unable to keep eye contact, the other person may believe you are concealing something or are being disingenuous. Make a firm handshake.
- Personal space: The individual at the head of the table appears to be the person in charge. Negotiators can counteract this strategic advantage by surrounding that person with sympathizers in the room.

2.11.2. Reading Non-Verbal Communication

Being able to understand another person's nonverbal communication can greatly assist in the process of communication. Negotiators can reach better outcomes by recognizing and reconciling differences between a person's verbal and nonverbal communication. Inconsistency in body language can be seen in the following examples:

- Nervous Laugh: A laugh that is inappropriate for the situation. This could be an indication of anxiety or discomfort. When this happens, it's a good idea to ask probing inquiries to find out what the person's genuine feelings are.
- Negative body language while speaking positive words: If somebody asks if their negotiation partner is upset, and they smash their fist and answer forcefully, "what makes you think anything is troubling me?" (Escobar & Moreno-Jimenéz, 2007).
- Arms raised in a clinched position: Even when smiling, the individual raising his or her hands in this stance shows irritation. This is a clue that the individual doing it is suppressing a bad emotion.
- If feasible, it may be beneficial for negotiating participants to spend more time together outside of the negotiating room in a comfortable atmosphere. Knowing how each party interacts nonverbally outside of the negotiation setting can aid negotiation partners in detecting inconsistencies in nonverbal and verbal communication.

2.11.3. Conveyance of Receptivity

The way negotiating partners position their bodies in relation to one another may have an impact on how open they are to the other's ideas and message.

- Eyes and face – Negotiators who are receptive smile and make a lot of eye contact. This provides the impression that the individual is more important than what is being stated. Non-receptive negotiators, on the other hand, rarely, if ever, initiate eye contact. It's possible that their eyes are squinted, their jaw muscles are tensed, and their heads are turned slightly away from the speaker.
- Hands and Arms – Negotiators should widen their arms and open their hands on the table or rest on their lap to show receptivity. When a negotiator's hands are clasped, crossed, in front of

their lips, or scratching the back of their neck, they exhibit low receptivity (Escobar & Moreno-Jimenéz, 2007).

- Feet and Legs – Negotiators that are receptive sit with their legs together or somewhat in front of the other. They stand with their weight equally distributed and their hands on their hips, their bodies angled toward the speaker. Negotiators who are not receptive stand with their legs crossed and their backs to the speaker.
- Torso – Negotiators who are receptive sit on the edge of their chairs, unbuttoning their suit coats and tilting their bodies toward the speaker. Non-receptive negotiators should recline back in their chairs and button their suit coats. With their hands open and palms visible, receptive negotiators tend to appear comfortable.

Figure 2.13. Sample of body language/gesture in negotiation.

Source: https://sirdargroup.com/negotiation-101-knowing-when-to-walk-away/.

Some barriers of good negotiations include:

- spoilers;
- structural impediments;
- negotiators dilemma and informational vacuums;
- lack of trust;
- die-hard bargainers;

- gender and cultural differences;
- communication issues; and
- the power of dialogue.

2.12. EMOTIONS

Emotions play a significant role in the bargaining process; however, their impact has just recently been explored. Emotions can play a beneficial or negative impact in the negotiation process. During negotiations, emotional elements play a role in deciding whether to settle. Negative emotions can lead to unreasonable and even irrational behavior, escalating disagreements and breaking down discussions, but they can also help you get concessions. Positive emotions, on the other hand, can assist you reach an agreement and maximize your joint gains, but they can also assist you get concessions. Negative and positive discrete emotions can be purposefully presented to influence task and higher performance, and they may manifest differently across cultures (Escobar & Moreno-Jimenéz, 2007).

Effect Affect: The manner the other party and their intents are seen, their readiness to reach an agreement, and the final negotiated outcomes are all influenced by dispositions for impacts. Positive affectivity (PA) and negative affectivity (NA) of one or more bargaining parties might result in drastically different outcomes.

Positive Affect: Individuals in a good mood have more assurance and are more likely to prepare to utilize a cooperation technique even before the negotiating process begins. Negotiators that are in a good mood enjoy the interaction more, are less irritable, employ less confrontational techniques, and use more cooperative strategies throughout the negotiation. As a result, the chances of parties achieving their instrumental aims increase, as does their ability to find integrative gains. Positive affectivity negotiators reached more deals and inclined to honor those commitments more than negotiators with negative or natural affectivity.

Better decision-making processes, such as willingness to take chances, creative problem-solving, flexible thinking, respect for others' perspectives, and increased confidence, are responsible for the positive outcomes. Positive effect after a discussion might also be advantageous. It influences one's desire for future encounters by increasing pleasure with the attained result (Ambrus et al., 2009). The dyadic connection is facilitated by the PA awakened by establishing an agreement, which brings commitment and sets the foundation for further interactions. PA also has disadvantages: it affects people's perceptions of their own performance, making them appear to be better than they are. As a result, studies based on self-reported outcomes may be skewed.

Negative Affect: Negative affect has a negative impact on the bargaining process at various levels. Although a variety of unpleasant emotions influence negotiating results, rage is by far the most studied. Even before the discussion begins, enraged negotiators want to adopt more competitive methods and cooperate less. Reduced joint results are linked to these competitive strategies. Anger disrupts the negotiation process by lowering trust, clouding judgment, narrowing focus of attention, and altering the major purpose of the parties from achieving an agreement to retaliating against the other side.

Furious negotiators stop paying attention to and are less precise in interpreting their opponents' goals, resulting in lesser shared gains. Furthermore, because anger makes negotiators' preferences more self-centered, it raises the risk of them rejecting profitable proposals. Angry opponents (or those who cry or otherwise lose control) are more prone to make mistakes, so make sure they're in your favor. Anger does not aid in the achievement of negotiating goals: it diminishes joint gains and does not increase personal profits, as furious negotiators fail.

Furthermore, negative emotions contribute to the adoption of settlement that has a negative utility function rather than a positive utility function. However, expressing negative emotions throughout a negotiation can be advantageous in some cases: properly expressed rage can be a powerful approach to demonstrate one's commitment, sincerity, and needs. Furthermore, while NA diminishes benefits in integrative activities, it outperforms PA in distributive activities (such as zero-sum). Seidner discovered evidence for the relationship of a negative affect arousal process in his work on negative affect awakening and white noise by observing the depreciation of speakers of other ethnic origins. Submerged antipathy toward an ethnic or gender group may, in turn, have a negative impact on negotiations.

According to studies, a negotiator's emotions do not always influence the bargaining process. Albarracn et al., (2003) proposed that emotional affect is caused by two factors, both of which are linked to ability (the existence of environmental or cognitive disruptions) and encouragement:

- Recognition of the effect necessitates a high level of drive, ability, or both.

- Determining that the affect is significant and crucial for the judgment necessitates a lack of motivation, capacity, or both.

Figure 2.14. Emotional intelligence.

Source:https://www.supplychain247.com/article/why_emotional_intelligence_matters_in_negotiations/vantage_partners.

Negotiations are only affected by emotions when one is high and the other is low, according to this hypothesis. When both motivation and ability are low, affect is detected; when both are high, affect is detected but dismissed as unrelated to judgment. This approach could imply, for example, that the favorable impacts PA has on negotiations (as discussed above) are only visible when either motivation or ability is low.

2.13. HOW THE PARTNER'S EMOTIONS CAN AFFECT NEGOTIATIONS?

Most of the research on emotion in negotiations focuses on how the negotiator's personal emotions affect the procedure. However, it's possible that how the other party feels are just as essential, as group emotions have been shown to influence processes at both the group and individual levels. When it comes to negotiations, confidence in the other side is required for the emotion to be influenced, and visibility amplifies the effect.

Emotions have a role in negotiation by conveying how one feels and thinks, preventing the other party from participating in damaging conduct and indicating the next actions to take: PA indicates that things should stay the same, whereas NA indicates that mental or behavioral changes are required. The emotions of the partner might have one of two main effects on the emotions and behavior of the negotiator: reciprocal/mimetic or complementary (Wu et al., 2012).

Delusion or despair, for instance, could lead to empathy and more collaboration. Most people reacted mutually instead of complementarily to partner emotions in a study by Butt et al., (2005), which simulated real multiple phase negotiations. Different emotions have been found to influence the feelings and strategies of the opponent:

- Pride resulted in the partners being more inclusive and compromised.
- The opposition's indignation led to lower demands and to allow for more in a zero-sum bargaining, and less favorable evaluation of negotiations. It caused the opponent's behavior to be both dominant and yielding.
- The negotiator's guilt or regret led to his assumption by the adversary, but it led him also to make higher demands. Personal culpability was related, on the other hand, to more satisfaction.
- Worry or deception left the adversary with bad feeling; however, the adversary's demands were relatively lower.

2.14. HOW TO DEAL WITH EMOTIONS?

- *Making emotions validate and explicit* – By proactively discussing one's emotions, a negotiation can focus instead of any scruffy feelings on the problem itself. Both parties must be able to share emotions.
- *Allowing for time to let off steam* – At some time throughout the negotiation, one of the parties may become enraged or frustrated. Allow the individual to express their sentiments rather than trying to avoid them. Sitting and listening, without giving too much input to the material, can be enough to help the person feel better. It may be easier to negotiate once the grievances have been released.
- *Gestures that are symbolic* – Considering that an apology, or any other simple deed, could be one of the most efficient and low-cost ways to alleviate any unfavorable feelings between people.

2.15. ISSUES WITH LABORATORY STUDIES ON EMOTION

Negotiation is a difficult interaction to master. It's tough enough to capture all its intricacy, let alone isolate and control only particular portions of it. As a result, most negotiation studies are conducted in a laboratory setting and focus on only a few topics. Although lab studies have certain benefits, they have significant downsides when it comes to studying emotions:

- Emotions are generally influenced in lab research and so are fairly 'cold' (not intense). Although those 'cool' feelings may be sufficient to produce consequences, they differ qualitatively from the 'hot' emotions commonly experienced during talks.
- People choose which agreements to participate in real life, which has an impact on emotional engagement, desire, and interests – but this is not the case in laboratory studies.
- Most lab investigations concentrate on a small number of well-defined emotions. Real-life situations elicit a considerably broader range of emotions (Weller et al., 2007).
- When emotions are coded by a third party, some feelings may be undetected because the negotiator sublimates them for strategic purposes. Self-report measures may be able to overcome this, however, they are often completed before or after the process, and if completed during the process, they may cause it to be disrupted.

Neil Rackham is a unique researcher who investigated and contrasted real-world labor management negotiation case studies to uncover the elements that separate the most long-lasting and satisfactory agreements. He discovered that the greatest negotiators asked more questions than the poor ones, listened intently, and aggressively sought common ground as well as mutually beneficial innovative ideas.

2.16. COMPOSITION OF THE GROUPS

2.16.1. Multi-Party

While talks involving upwards of two parties are less frequently examined, some results from two-party negotiations with more than two parties still extend. One such conclusion is that language similarity is common among the two negotiating parties in negotiations. Language similarity was still evolving through the three-party negotiations and results were particularly successful when the other parties' language similarities most gained from the negotiations.

Figure 2.15. Illustration of negotiator's roles to play in negotiation.

Source: https://www.expertnegotiator.com/tip/pay-attention-core-emotions-help-negotiations/.

2.16.2. Team

As a result of globalization, negotiations are becoming widely accepted in the form of teams. Teams can collaborate effectively to dismantle a complex discussion. A team disperses more knowledge and wisdom than a single mind. Specific roles team members must fulfill are writing, listening, and talking. The team's base of capacity reduces the bug and makes negotiations more familiar. Unless a team can make proper use of its full potential, efficiency can however, be impaired. A problem which occurs through solidarity is one factor in the effectiveness of team negotiations. Solidarity is a matter of reducing the utility of one team member (benefit) so that other team members can gain more benefit. This will probably happen when conflicts of interest rise. If the usefulness/needs of the negotiating opponent do not match the interests of every team member, team members start making concessions and balance the advantages they gain from their team.

It can feel like a cooperative approach, intuitively. However, while a team can seek cooperation or cooperation, the results can be less successful than they can be, particularly if integration is possible. Where various negotiation questions are of difference principle to each team member the integrative possibilities are possible. The lack of understanding of the interests and preferences of each member frequently misses the potential for integration. In the end, this leads to a poorer outcome for negotiations.

As a result, if each team member communicates his or her views before to the negotiation, the team will be more successful. This stage will enable the team to recognize and arrange their shared priorities, which they may consider when engaging in negotiations with the opposite party (Van Ginkel & Van Knippenberg, 2009). Because a team is more likely to discuss similar facts and shared interests, teams must actively seek out and include unique perspectives from specialists in many industries. Daniel Thiemann's research, which based attention on computer-assisted collaborative work, discovered that the Preference Awareness approach is an effective tool for generating knowledge about shared priorities and for assisting the team in determining which negotiating problems are most important.

2.17. WOMEN IN NEGOTIATION

Many negotiation methods differ between genders, resulting in differences in outcomes for various genders, with women often having less success in negotiations as a result. This is due to several variables, including the fact that it has been proven that women find it more difficult to advocate for them while bargaining. In comparison to other advocating women, self-advocating men, and other advocating men, many of the consequences of these studies have significant financial ramifications in addition to the social backlash suffered by self-advocating women in negotiations.

In addition to more particular topics like women as physician assistants, research in this topic has been conducted across platforms. The negative reaction to this type of behavior is since being self-advocated is regarded male, whilst being accommodating is seen more feminine. Males, on the other hand, appear to be unaffected by their lack of self-advocacy. Multiple studies have backed up this theory, including one that looked at applicants who were involved in a compensation discussion. According to this study, women who initiate talks are rated lower than males who initiate discussions. Men and women rated movies of men and women accepting a remuneration package or initiating discussions in another variation of this setup.

Figure 2.16. The difference between women and men negotiator.

Source: https://www.negotiations.com/articles/gender-interaction/.

Men had a lower opinion of women initiating talks, whereas women had a worse opinion of both men and women starting negotiations. Women were less likely to initiate a negotiation with a male in this study, expressing anxiousness, but there was no difference when the discussion was launched by another female (Bazerman & Moore, 2012). Research also backs up the idea that how people react in a negotiation is influenced by the gender of the other side. The use of deceit had no effect on the level of confidence amongst negotiating parties in all-male groupings, but it did in mixed-sex groups when the opposite party was utilizing an accommodating technique. There were various alterations in when individuals used dishonesty in their negotiation strategies in all-female groups.

2.18. ACADEMIC NEGOTIATIONS

The educational sector has a unique administrative system in which tenured faculty members live in educational institutions (e.g., departments) and are controlled by chairs, or heads. Deans of the school where their educational unit is housed oversee these chairs/heads. Faculty chairs/heads, and deans have minimal experience with negotiation because their PhD degrees are often in a highly specialized area based on their academic knowledge. The academic setting, on the other hand, consistently offers situations that require negotiation. Many professors, for example, are hired with the aim of conducting research and publishing intellectual works. Negotiating a "start-up" package for these academics is crucial for their success and potential promotion because their research requires equipment, space, and/or financing. Furthermore, department chairs are frequently placed in situations wherein they must negotiate with their dean on account of their unit, generally involving resource redistribution. Deans also head colleges where they must maximize limited resources such as research space or operational cash while also fostering student achievement, research achievement, and other factors.

Integrative negotiation is a style of negotiation that is commonly encountered in academic settings, and it emphasizes trust and long-term relationships between parties:

(1) completing your homework – defining your request in facts;
(2) realizing your significance;
(3) actively listening and recognizing what is being said;
(4) placing oneself in their shoes;
(5) asking – negotiation begins with an ask;
(6) not willing to commit promptly;
(7) trying to manage emotion; and
(8) remembering the principle of a "wise adversary." Several case studies of academic discussions can be found in the publications by Callahan et al., and Amekudzi-Kennedy et al. (Tang & Liao, 2021).

Chapter 3

Classes of Multi-Person Decisions

CONTENTS

3.1. INTRODUCTION

Decision-making is vital in each and every organization. However, it is considered to be the toughest parts that an organization has especially in their process of inventing new ideas. The process proves to be more challenging especially when a group is involved. The reason behind this fact is that, when a group is involved, each individual wants to be the one to make the decisions. It is by nature that an individual would always find it fitting to have their decisions taken into consideration. This is the reason as to why in most organizations, it is important that they get to have leaders. With leaders, they can be able to understand the decision making process (Sorkin et al., 2001). The leader will be able to define the process of decision making that the he or she needs to be used. In order to make the process smooth for the entire organization, the leader needs to announce his moves at the beginning of the discussion on how well they can go about the entire process of making decisions. Furthermore, the leader has the responsibility to explain to the subordinates of how much each of them is required to participate in the process.

Figure 3.1. An illustration of being a leader with subordinates.

Source: The Grossman Group.

There are different kinds of strategies that need to be taken into account when making decisions in a group setting. The factors that need to be considered just like any other factors have some advantages and disadvantages. The first thing that should be considered is that the decisions made need to be unanimous. This means that all the members that are involved need to agree with the decisions that are made without having any reservations (Beynon, 2005). When a decision is made unanimously, one can say that they can actually work very well with trivial matter however, when the issues are considered to be of high importance and with high pressure. As such, individuals who are involved in decision making with a group should understand that there are differences with the case of consensus. Individuals may agree with each other just because they need to be through with the matter.

Figure 3.2. Decision making in an organization. In most cases, subordinates are involved in the decision making process.

Source: https://www.forbes.com/sites/hbsworkingknowledge/2020/09/04/its-time-to-reset-decision-making-in-your-organization/.

With the case in which the individuals decide to have a consensus, an individual decides on something and the rest agree to with whatever decision has been made. With this case, not all the individuals get to agree with the decision made and as a matter of fact, they do not get to give their consent on a particular matter. This shows that there is no uniformity in this case. As such, it is not quite fair to the members or rather the subordinates in the organization. Ideally, in this type of decision-making, there are cases where the individuals have differing perspective but they all just agree with the matter and decide to live with whatever has been decided. Consequently, this type of decision making is seen to be one in which the decisions or rather the input of all the members need to be taken into account, valued, heard and even considered before the final decision to be made. What can be concluded regarding this matter is that, before a final decision is made, a leader needs to understand what the rest of the team are saying with regards to a particular matter before deciding on the decision made.

Majority rule is the other issue. This is a type of decision making in which more than half of the individuals involved decided to vote on the matter. This means that the final decision is dependent of the number of people that vote on that particular matter. It means that if more than 50% of the team vote on a particular issue, then it will pass as the final one. In most cases, this method is normally used by democracies and in rare cases used in organizations. With this type of decision-making, there are risks that are associated with them (Schulz-Hardt et al., 2002). This s due to the fact that, the individuals that do not get to vote in favor of the matter, they may refuse to be helpful in the future especially when the decision made plays a vital role in whatever is being done. The worst case of the matter is that, in that particular setting, that is the organization may be faced with certain division within the members of the staff. In most cases, it brings about that mentality of an "us" versus "them." It may even pin friends within the organization against each other, which may even lead to individuals resigning from the particular job.

Figure 3.3. An image of employees engagement in decision-making.

Source: SocialChorus.

The other case is with the expert decision-making. This case involves the involvement of individuals who have better knowledge of a particular issue than the rest of the team. With this case scenario, the leader is assigned with the duty of appointing individuals that are experts in that particular issue and further delegating them with the duty to make the decisions. In other cases, the appointment may be a small group that may not necessarily have expertise on the matter. In most cases, this method is considered to be very efficient when the matter that is in question does not involve the whole team. If it is however, adopted in the case where the entire group or rather all the departments in the organization are involved, then there will be those that will feel left out of the matter and would want to get out of the matter or out of the employment entirely.

The other one is the executive decision making. This is whereby the leaders are left either the role to make their own decision. In a layman's language, the leaders make the call. In most cases, the decisions that are normally made tend to be executive in nature which is always what should be given the fact that most decisions are made for the good of the entire organization and not just one or several departments. The biggest issue in this case is that, in most cases, the amount and the kind of participation that is expected from this kind of decision-making. As such, the decisions made are not what it should be. In most cases, what actually makes the decision making to be considered the best is when there is a highly participative decision making. The approach is considered to be very critical especially when the organization is dealing with the mission and the vision of the organization. The advice that can be given to the leaders is that, they should make use of the minds of their subordinates. Some of them tend to have spectacular inputs that can put the organization at an A+ position in the competitive environment (Song, 2009).

The last type of decision-making is the default one. In this kind of decision-making, the made decisions are normally made by action. In the most likely scenario, the case in which there is inaction, the conclusion is normally forced. This decision making process is considered to be a powerless form and in most cases, organizations try their best to avoid the process. Decision-making is a vital process and thus should be treated with vital importance. There are the helpful decision mechanisms that a leader should put in mind in order to be successful in their works. In the process of making decisions, it is with no doubt that, each and every person wants their voices to be heard. In order to show inclusion in decision-making by the individuals involved there are some factors that the leaders need to take into account.

One factor is that; the leader needs to use polling. This is where individuals make decisions without any other members having to poke their noses on whatever issues. This process also helps leaders to determine the feelings of their subordinates without requiring anyone to commit himself or herself in a particular issue (Schulze & Newell, 2016). This process involves the leaders asking the members involved of what they may feel about a particular issue. A leader may ask a question that has a number of options and asks them of those that are okay with a particular option. In such a case, there are no commitments and all individuals will feel involved in the process. The individuals will know that they have a purpose in the particular organization and that their feedback in a particular matter is being valued.

Figure 3.4. Illustration of leader and subordinates exchanging ideas.

Source: Business News Daily.

The other issue that a leader should understand is that, they need to be able to assign accountability to the individuals that are involved in the process in which a decision has been made. It is vital to the subordinates to fully understand what is expected of them and how they are going to be held responsible for what they have done and what they are needed to do. Such things include the due dates of performing a particular issue and the budgets that they are given to take care of a particular issue. It is very important for the leaders to ensure that they have been able to assign the responsibility to every person especially in their areas of expertise. This will help ensure that decision-making process becomes participative for all the members involved instead of it being delegated upwards to the leaders.

Conflicts are very common in a particular environment that a group is involved. Human beings are prone to making mistakes and when the mistakes are made, they get to refuse any form of correction from their colleagues, which then lead to cases of conflicts in the organization. According to a researcher, the words provided have proven to be very true and very useful to the society. He says that, if something can go wrong, then it will and as such, on organization should always be ready for the same. The leaders need to ensure that there is a conflict escalation mechanism in place for two reasons. The first one is a mechanism of resolving the conflicts that exist between the peers (Sari, 2008). This means that there needs to be a mechanism that will help work out the conflicts that may occur between the individuals. By resolving the conflicts that exist between the individuals ted to lead to individuals not to work together, which is exactly what is required of them in order to ensure the success of the organization. The other reason as to why there needs to be a conflict escalation mechanism is to ensure that the leaders in the organization have the knowledge of what is happening in the organization especially when there are conflicts formed between the subordinates. It is very important for the leaders involved to understand the actions that are taking place in their organizations. Through this, they can be able to come up with mechanisms to ensure that the organization does not fall because of the same.

Figure 3.5. Conflict resolution in an organization.

Source: SlideShare.

In order to make sure that there is peace and harmony in the organization, there needs to be a conflict escalation mechanism. This mechanism is considered to be quite helpful especially since leaders get to know what is happening in the organization and devise ways to deal with other issues.

With a conflict escalation mechanism, the leaders have the capacity to fully understand the actions of the individuals that are involved in the conflict which will help them know whether it was a misunderstanding or there were cases of gross misconduct within the organization. The escalation procedures are normally built on a case-by-case basis. This means that the case of the individuals involved are followed to the latter to ensure that there are no cases of cheating and blaming of the individuals.

Decision-making is quite easy especially when only a single individual is tasked with the process. In the case where a group is involved, it is quite difficult. However, it does not mean that it is not doable. It rather means that the process may prove to be difficult and a lot of work needs to be put to ensure the voices of all individuals is heard and that it is taken into account (Saaty & Peniwati, 2013). In the case in which a group is involved in the process of decision-making, there are classes of multi person decision making. It is where decisions are made and are involving a group of individuals as seen. The classes include:

- Individual decision-making in a group setting;
- Hierarchical or bureaucratic decision-making;
- Group decision-making or one-party decision-making;
- Multi-party decision-making or negotiation.

All these classes involve making decisions by the group of individuals in the group or a single person in a place in which the entire group is present for the show.

3.2. INDIVIDUAL DECISION MAKING IN A GROUP SETTING

Figure 3.6. Image illustrates the importance of individual decision-making.

Source: Moodle ISQ.

When an organization is involved in individual decision-making, then it is as simple as it looks. In a group decision-making, the decision is normally made by a single individual. When a single person is involved in this important process, it proves to be quite easy. This is due to the fact that; individuals need not ask others for assistance or need to consider the inputs of others. In the past decades, there have cases of individuals pronouncing that there have been shifts towards groups instead of individual decision-making. Taking for instance the case of key financial institutions such as the Bank of England, the decision making process normally involves the groups of individuals in the organization. Suggestion from researchers is that, there needs to be adoption of group decision making especially for the case of the governments. In such situations, the decisions normally made are known to affect the entire society or nation and thus there needs to be representatives to put out their word regarding what needs to be done.

Figure 3.7. Individual decision-making.

Source: Insights for Professionals.

In a group, what constitutes an individual decision-making does not involve the entire group or even more than a single person. Ideally, this type of decision-making is considered to be cost effective and in a way, it is very quick mainly because it does not require any form of gathering. With this type of decision-making, there is no need for schedules to be made for the purpose of trying to make a decision on the strategy that best suits the individuals of the society (Saka et al., 2008). This means that the instances in which individuals are called for a meeting or even sent emails does not exist for this kind of decision-making. With this case, the individuals that are involved tend to as their leaders of best way to go about a particular thing and further think on the same. By doing this, it makes it easier for the organization to have a clear picture of the individual which is a good thing as in the process the organization has the capacity to fully understand their employees.

There are certain advantages that are attached to individual decision making especially in a group setting. When a single individual is involved in the process, the decisions made are normally prompt unlike when the entire group is involved. A group is normally dominated by a good number of individuals in the organization, which then makes decision making very time consuming. Furthermore, in the process of assembling the members involved and also settling down tends to consume a lot of time. In a way, it can be said that when a group is involved, mobilization and settling down may take up to half of the time that there is. Ideally, when decisions are made, individuals are normally held accountable for whatever the decision they decide to make, how they act upon it and their performance after the decision has been made.

Figure 3.8. An image illustrates the disadvantage of individual decision-making.

Source: Forbes.

When a group is involved, it proves to be quite hard to hold a single person accountable given the fact that when everything goes wrong, all of them will deny of even having an opportunity to get involved in the entire process. Apart from the fact that individual decision-making saves time, it also saves money as in the process, the single person will be able to think logically and make prompt decisions. Knowing that the decision-maker would be held accountable if the decisions that results bad impact for the organization. Anything with a pro also tend to have cons and just like group decision making, there are cons to individual decision making. With the case of an individual decision-making, the research on a particular matter may not be exhaustive. This is due to the fact that it is only a single person delegated with all the duties of research and decision-making. In a group, the individuals will be able to make decisions based on complete information as the duties regarding the research can be delegated to different individuals. When a single individual is individual, he gets to only use their intuition regarding a particular matter while the group has different vies concerning the matter (Risco & Duffy, 2011). The phrase normally says that two heads are normally better than one and what can be agreed is that many heads are much better than two are. Due to the fact that a group has many views, the approaches that are used in the process may result in a much better decision-making process. When the group is involved, the individuals have the capacity to fully understand the competency of their colleagues and their core competency. It is during this process that all the members involved are able to get a full picture of what an individual is all about and what their strengths are. In the process, they can be able to understand the person that can be asked to run point on certain particular issues. When an individual is involved in h decision making process, they will not be able to take into consideration the views of the other members in the organization while when the entire group is involved, the views of each individual is taken into account.

Decision making in an organization is very important given the fact that there needs to be the right kind of information and the ability of all the individuals involved to synthesize what has been obtained and further make sense of the same.

In understanding the process of decision-making, there have been a number of scholars from different disciplines that have been trying to make sense of the same in order to make the process easy and efficient for the groups that are involved in such a crucial aspect in the organization. Different groups just like different individuals tend to have different interests with regard to a particular aspect. In the process in which the scholars try to make sense of the decision making process, the aspect is normally studied as a group phenomenon in order to help fully understand the best approaches that can be helpful for organizations in the decision making process. There are a number of concepts that need to be taken into account when a single individual is involved in the process of decision-making (Reynolds et al., 2009).

- *One of the aspects is of the Dominant Incentive.* In an organization, the one thing that an individual wants is to have more health benefits, to maintain the status quo, to make more money, to raise their own status, to protect themselves and in the process the organization and find the best partner. In other instances, it may prove to be quite difficult to fully understand the concept of dominant incentive when it comes to an individual in the organization. In most instances, this can be easily identified when individuals are communicating with each other and how they feel about certain particular aspects. In line with the same, individuals may not be fully aware of what they actually want which means that they find it difficult to understand their own dominant incentive.
- *Rationality and rational choice is the other aspect.* Rationality is where lone behaves in a manner that shows that they are working towards a particular goal. For a person to have goals in their minds, they tend to normally have an idea of what the end may be like. In most cases, the assumption is that most human beings are considered to be rational, as they tend to pursue their own personal goals or group goals in the case in which a group is involved. Ideally, most of the goals are not as obvious as one may think and thus may need some form of research and experience in order to be able to identify them. The goal that an individual has may prove to be rational but the way they go about it in order to achieve the goals that they have in mind may not be rational. In the process of making decisions, wanting to put the organization at the top is a rational decision. Hurting the members of the organization in the process of ensuring the success of the organization is also rational but may not be considered as an ethical process. This is what happens in most instances as individuals are trampled by others in the name of wanting to make the organization a better place. Most individuals believe that making an organization a better place and sacrificing some of the members of the organization is something that are interrelated while for the case of others, they tend to be mutually exclusive. What individuals should have in mind is that, rationality does not actually mean that there

needs to be full consideration of ethics as long as it helps in the achievement of the goals in the organization. In the process of understanding the behavior of others in the organization, rational choice tends to be used as the guiding assumption. The reason behind is that, if in the case where individuals were assumed to be irrational, then ideally, there would no need to study them. In most instances, individuals are normally seen to be behaving in a rational manner even though they are normally guided by irrational factors.

- *Framing is another aspect that is considered in individual decision-making.* In most cases, how a particular concept is described is normally seen to influence how individuals think about something. Every aspect can be framed in different manners basing on the attributes of a particular event or an activity. Framing can be best described in the political field where opponents tend to describe a particular concept in many different ways. Most research has shown that framing is a tool very powerful that it can be able to persuade and shape the opinions of an individual and the public at large.

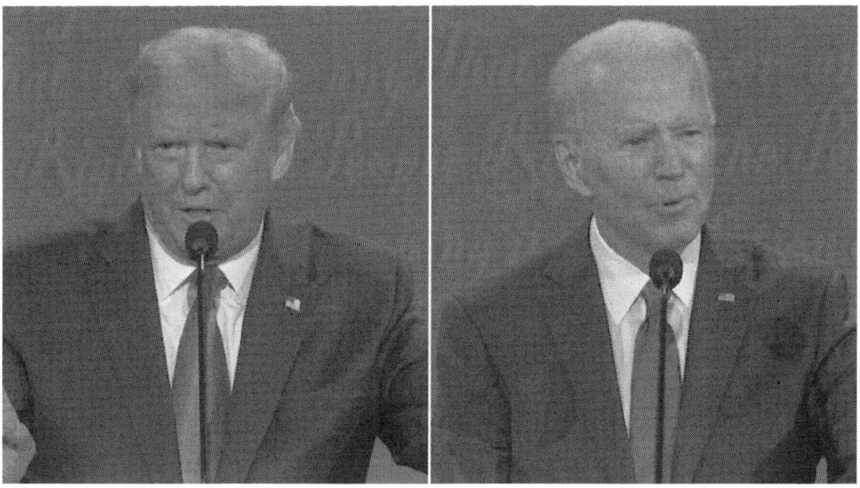

Figure 3.9. An image of two opponents that best describe the framing aspect.

Source: CNN.

Cognitive miser is another important aspect that needs to be taken into account when the organization is involved in an individual decision making process. This is normally used to describe individuals who will defend the first thing that comes to their mind without even doing a proper research on the same. In the process, they do not get to evaluate the possibilities of the decision that they make. In most cases, what they normally adopt is the one that is considered to be good enough. In a way, almost all individuals are considered to be cognitive misers (Reinalda & Verbeek, 2004). Ideally, it would be quite hard to find individuals are evaluating every step of their lives. However, cognitive misers are considered to be very problematic in the process of decision-making. The individuals in a group setting that are unwilling to follow the basic steps of making decisions instead of weighing the alternatives tend to contribute to poor decision-making process.

- *Another aspect that is important in the decision making process is with the case of group thinking*. In most cases, group members tend have a notion that they are right and they need not question their ideas. The case of group thinking tends to occur when there is an insulation where making decisions concerning particular policies and the input received is from outside members. This normally occurs when the group does not have the norms in which there needs to be a methodological process in the process of decision-making. With the care of groupthink, there are a number of errors that normally occur such as incomplete survey of alternatives and objectives, a failure to examine the risks and reprising the initially rejected alternatives, poor information search, selective biasness in processing the information at hand and a failure for the individuals to work out some contingency plans.

On hand, individual decision-making may seem as the best and simple process but individuals should be cautious of some of the advantages that are attached to the same.

3.3. HIERARCHICAL OR BUREAUCRATIC DECISION-MAKING

In most organizations, or rather in most settings, a hierarchy is normally involved. This is normally suitable given the fact that a hierarchical chain of command especially in the division of labor tends to be very effective. In most cases, the individuals that are ranked higher in the hierarchical chain tend to set the principles that guide decisions, help in constraining and focusing the operational tasks that are normally carried out by the subordinates. This mode of decision-making is a cornerstone in the modern decision making process. As such, it is mostly adopted around the world especially by human organizations that are normally independent of ownership size and purpose. In such organizations, the decision-making process normally takes place in different multiple levels. They then tend to operate with the information provided on different degrees and on different time scales.

The reason as to why hierarchical decision-making process is preferred as it deals with most of the cognitive limitations that exist in the case of individual decision-making process. As such, there tends to be an effective organizational response given the fact that the individuals in authority always hold the fold and the rod. With this kind of decision-making, there is always an effective and adaptive response. However, this process tends to promote feedback ambiguity, which then complicates the process of experiential learning. In the case in which the decisions made take the wrong turn in the organization, it is not clear whether the reason behind such failures are the disturbances that are occurring within the vicinity or it may be because of the mistakes of the individuals at the higher level. Ideally, it proves that when the high-ranking individuals are involved in the decision-making process, it is quite hard to have individuals that need to answer for the actions that have been committed. In most cases, the failure of a strategy that has been made by the individuals high up in authority tend to be blamed on accidents and as such proves to be quite difficult to assess the errors that occurred and led to the failure of the same. Despite the fact that this type of decision-making is responsible for relieving the effects of individual cognitive limitations, they tend to increase the ambiguity of the feedback that need to be provided and further spoils the chance for the subordinates to gain a learning experience from the same.

This class of decision-making is not unique in most organizations, it is one in which most organizations see fit to use in making decisions given the fact that it would be easier for the subordinates to follow the rule provided and in the process saves on the time that is needed when the staff is involved. This decision making type tends to have some characteristics. With it, the knowledge that is used in the process tends to one of quality and precision (Rassin et al., 2008). This is due to the fact that, more is expected of the leader and in most cases do extensive research on a subject matter before deciding on the final decision. Another aspect is that, there is normally a clear planning of the same and as such, there are normally backup contingencies in order to ensure that the objectives of the organization have been met. Within the organization, there is normally a broad span of control and the authority tends to be centralized. The leaders always ensure that the policies and the procedures that are normally used to ensure the success of the organization are elaborated to the subordinates in order for them to understand their duties as they work together towards the attainment of the goals. In order to make the process a success, there needs to be an effective communication system where there are normally lengthy communications that are provided for the individuals. They tend to be lengthy in order to ensure that the strategic plans and the vision is well communicated. In the process, the information regarding the progress of the individuals towards the attainment of a particular goal is communicated and the logical explanations provided. This show how the hierarchical decision making process tends to be inclusive and ensures that the systematic process is known to every individual in the organization.

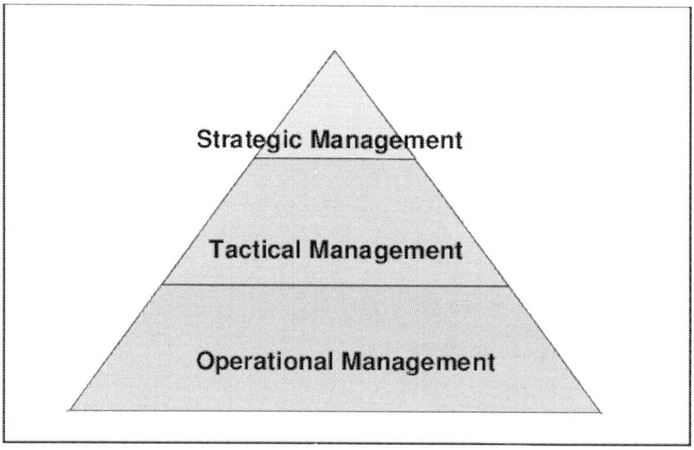

Figure 3.10. Illustration of hierarchical decision-making.

Source: https://www.researchgate.net/figure/Management-hierarchy-based-on-decision-making-required_fig2_225809480.

Just like in hierarchical leadership structures, decisions made in a hierarchical manner normally establishes a clear chain of command. In such a situation, each of the functional departments are required to develop their own functional plans in which the plans that are brought about need to be in line with the strategic goals of the company. In order for action to be taken, there needs to be layers and layers of approval and the leaders tend to organize the employees in a manner that they are in the capacity to perform specialized activities (Pérez et al., 2010). In such cases, there are normally cross-functional roles and responsibilities that ensure that the existence collaborations between different departments. The final decisions made are then made solely by the leaders and they do not seek any form of input from their employees. In most instances, this mode of decision-making brings about lack of understanding within the department and the employees tend to feel left out from the decision making process and the organization at large. As such, they tend to portray lack of job satisfaction, which in turn leads to poor performance by the employees.

Bureaucratic way of leadership has been in most organizations in achieving objectives as well as organizational goals. The rules, regulations, procedures, and standards involved in decision, making are efficiently put in place to ensure achievement control being the main mechanism used. Control is mainly used to ensure that the staff are well behaved and conduct themselves in a good conduct at the work place. The rules and regulations in a bureaucratic kind of decision-making are normally put in writing such that they are bound by the government and the rules of the land and any administrative system. The rules are rational and hierarchical in terms of coordination. The structure in bureaucratic decision-making is well defined in terms of the existing linkages in relationships that exist between senior and junior staff in any organization or institution. It also denotes the existing social relationships in the structure of an organization thereby bring about order and stability of leadership. The rules put in writing in a bureaucratic institution are binding to all and are all followed in the day to day running of the business .the rules and procedures are first formulated through a systematic procedure then implemented.

Past studies have however, reported that the bureaucratic form of decision making are mainly found in the public organizations as the private organizations are more inclined to other forms of leadership and decision making. Unfortunately, one of the challenges that are involved in the bureaucratic kind of decision making is that they create objects that lead to inflexibilities in any situations at the workplaces. In a large scale organization especially the admiration and management using this kind of decision making cannot easily adjust upon any changes in the way of bunnies as they tend to be slow in adjusting decisions due to the rules that have to be followed. This system creates inflexibility in solving solutions in the organization promptly (Patalano & LeClair, 2011). Additionally, in a large-scale enterprise the challenge may be encountered in controlling, managing and coordinating of the huge tasks involved with the involved complex organizations rules and regulations. The bureaucratic decision-making is placed at the shoulders of the owners of the business or in the administrator's hands in the case of a public institution who have a legal right in controlling an organization or an institution. The private business and or public organization is further divided into other forms of authority and power relations in the company that is mainly entitled to personnel according to their education and training, ability and skills that one has, specialization and profession that one has in form of expertise within the organization as well as the experience that one has in the line of duty that he or he has been called upon to perform .the kind of bureaucratic decision making has however, dominated the today's organizations as have proved to be the best in terms of the most universally acceptable and globally established form of decision making way of mass management in especially decision making.

The greatest advantage that the bureaucratic decision-making and leadership holds is that they revolve around the establishment of rules and organizations in an organization or institution. Therefore, the likely hood of all the staff including all the senior and junior staff to be treated equally is very high. This is because they are all governed by the same rules and regulations. Most organizations do pledge to avoid any kinds of favoritism, discrimination of all forms including race, gender as well as status or position of any staff in the organization and also all forms of prejudice are also prohibited. In several studies the bureaucratic decision making puts in place the ideas that are given out by the personnel in an organization without any form of discrimination. The rules that are laid down by the owner of a business or administration entitled to be leading public institution are binding to all thus, the decisions that are put in place are adaptable by all. The decision-making however, lacks any form of flexibility and lacks the tendency of turning means to an end according to the rules laid down. The decision-making process follows all the rules and thus the decision to be made can be seen to follow the procedures in place.

In conclusion, the form of bureaucratic form of decision making followers all the laid down rules and regulations in an organization and intuitions. The rules are binding to all the decision makers in the organization or any said institution.

3.4. GROUP DECISION MAKING OR ONE PARTY DECISION-MAKING

In every aspect of management, there has to be decision making and these are in various stages. The whole process of decision-making is very complex and there are many stakeholders that are involved and there are also several factors that need to be taken into consideration (Nutt, 2006). The decision can be made either by a group or individuals. The main question that needs to be asked is whether decision made by a group or those that are made by an individual.

Figure 3.11. Group decision making.

Source: Growth CPR.

Individuals can be consulted on their expert advice on management decision whereas in some instances the board of directors to make decision on behalf of the company or organization. In another example, the community may make decision as a group when making decisions on the natural resources in the area.

In the recent past, there has been a shift from individual group decision to more of using groups in making decisions. Example include big institutions such as banks and also some governments have preferred to use groups rather than use individual experts in making decisions that are science related. When decisions are made by multiple individuals then there will always be opposing views. This is because most of the time an individual is psychologically biased. A decision can sometimes be exacerbated because it involves some politics. In some instances, some decision has to be made very fast due to the circumstances such as when there are natural calamities.

In some instances, some group decisions can be without close interaction and these can be quite different from those where individuals are face to face. There are sometimes individuals who are known to groupthink. To groupthink is whereby an individual decides to base their decision on those presented by the group rather than their individual judgment because they majorly think of harmony, unity and agreement of the group rather that there to be discord among them. There might be individuals in a group who might be referred to as egocentric, i.e., individuals who think that their opinion and/or views are believed by many members or most of the group members. There are several characteristics of individuals that groupthink. These are:

- Think that they might become invulnerable. This is common in most members of the group as it can create optimism and this would encourage them to take extreme risks hence they tend to keep to themselves (LeClair, 2010).
- They downplay negative information and sometimes even warnings.
- They avoid from raising some opinions because they think that this may make them reconsider what they had already assumed.
- Belief in inherent morality. This may make some of the members to do some action that may not be ethical or moral hence they end up ignoring them. Pressure from members of the group especially when the person is raising any argument or opinions that may be against the groups' commitment.
- They tend to self-censor. They downplay their own arguments and do not want to express their counterarguments or the doubts they may have.

Groups that may have individuals that may be self-appointed mind guards in that they put down in order to protect the beliefs of the group. They immediately shut down the thoughts that may deter the groups' way or course of action.

As most people think, that two heads are better than one. In the late 1920s, a psychologist from Germany known as Max Ringelmann decided to determine whether individuals put in a group put out the same effort as when they worked individually. He decided to use a tug of war on athletes and they first worked individually where they used an average of 63 kilograms but when worked in pairs they released 53 kilograms and when they were three it drastically reduced to only 31 kilograms.

Figure 3.12. Dr. Max Ringelmann. A German psychologist who carried out experiment on the effect of individuals in a group and individual setting.

Source: quartz.

This then shows that individuals would tend to give less when they worked as individuals (Leclercq, 2018). This then can be explained by the fact that some individuals think some of the members are not putting in enough effort and for some it can be seen that if there is any failure from the group then no one will directly be blamed. This is mostly referred to as social loafing. This is a culture that is not common in most societies and it is common in the west especially countries that are mostly individualistic such as the United States of America and Canada. In countries that are mostly communal based such as china, the social loafing does not occur mostly.

In most cases, the process of decision-making is very fundamental and in the past most of the decisions was held by individuals or people who held high positions in the society. There has been significant change in the last few decades. This has been accelerated by the fact that groups have become popular because groups have been seen to perform better than individuals do.

Group decision making should be differentiated from concepts such as teams, teamwork and self-managed teams. In most of the cases decision making the groups making decision can be informal in nature and sometimes they are formal with a defined set of rules and a target. The process that is used to arrive at decisions can be structures with steps and stages or unstructured. Some factors that can influence decisions in a group include the size, purpose, structure, demographic and its composition. In a group, it is composed of different groups where; there is a group leader in charge of the running of the group, members of the group who have individual responsibility and are accountable. In a group, they discuss, make decisions and will delegate other duties as compared to a team who discuss and decide and they do work instead of delegating.

In a group, there are different methods and procedures that are used. The procedures most groups commonly use include: brainstorming, Delphi technique, nominal group technique and dialectical technique.

- *Brainstorming.* Involves a group of people verbally giving their ideas, opinions and views on the course of action they should take. The session commonly referred to as the 'brainstorming session' is usually unstructured. The issue or situation they have at hand is described in detail to the group members so that they can all be brought to speed in understanding it. The leader of the group would then give members opportunity to raise their ideas. The members are allowed to air their ideas and after every member has given their idea its then time to evaluate each and every idea. It is then known that brainstorming provides best when providing ideas but in the evaluation, it does not offer much.

Brainstorming provides individuals with opportunity to air their ideas but there are individuals who are hesitant and do not want to give their ideas because they fear judgment from fellow members or they do not want to be ridiculed by the others. In recent years' members of particular groups have been sending their suggestion through electronic mail (e-mail) where they send their views anonymously. This then offers the members to give ideas that are unique and creative without fear of ridicule or judgment (Mustakallio et al., 2002).

- *Dialectical technique.* It is a type of decision making which considers going through all the available alternatives. It involves even splitting the group into opposing sides which can then debate the advantages and disadvantages of any solution or decision that has to be made. Similarly, there can be a group member who can be referred to as the 'devil's advocate,' and this requires that one member researches and brings to fore the disadvantages of a particular decision if they make it. In this version of group decision making it means the group can discuss the possible side effects of a decision.

Figure 3.13. Nominal group technique where individuals present their ideas in form of writing before debating them.

Source: KAMA group.

- *Nominal group technique* which is essentially structured and members are required to come up with a detailed list of ideas, views and/or opinions in form of writing. Every member of the group comes up with their ideas in private. After they have completed coming up with their ideas they then present them one at a time and are recorded on a board. At this point, there is no criticism of any idea that has been brought up. After they are all listed the group discusses all the listed opinions and is arranged in terms of preference. Research conducted has shown that the nominal group technique is efficient in coming up with a high number of decision that are good and of high quality.
- *Delphi technique* where this is a type of decision-making used by groups to make decision when members of a group are not in the same location. In this type, the members are chosen because they are experts in a particular field and are related to the problem they are tasked to decide. The individual members are asked to provide ideas and different solutions to the problem in successive stages (Beekun & Westerman, 2012). The ideas can be provided through different means such as e-mails, fax, an online discussion room etc. after each and every stage the members are allowed to ask questions after which the ideas are raked and rated based on

the groups preference. After a number of rounds and stages, they can then come up with the best decision.

The group discussion making process cannot be said to be always worse or better than individual decision-making. In many senses, a diverse group may have to overcome difficulties or social barriers in the early stages of discussion in the group and with this reason; they can slow down in decision-making. Although some research has shown that in groups that are diverse if and when they are managed in the right way these types of groups tend to come up with the more variety and high quality decisions.

Group decision making has some pros and cons. The pros include: in a group setting, it takes advantage of the strengths and expertise and experiences of its diverse members. The group can generate a wider number of alternative ideas and they will also be of high quality and with this, the group can reach greater solution as compared to individual decision.

The group decision making help the members to understand the best course of action to be taken. This is because the members of the group could have been involved in coming up with the decision in use. This then brings the sense of ownership from the members of the group.

There are some disadvantages to group decision making. Groups take a lit bit longer. They are slow in coming up with decisions.

The most common con in group decision is groupthink. This then means that the opposing views of a majority opinion are mostly shot down and are not fully discussed or debated.

Polarization of members within a group. This mostly takes place when a group has to make a very risky decision but if they were asked individually, they would not make the same decision. This may come up because in most instances members of the same group do not feel responsible or accountable for any decision that the group will eventually make.

Individuals can sometimes play a very pivotal role in decisions being made by a company or organization. The individual decision-making has some advantages; the decisions made by an individual are always prudent. The decisions made by a group always involve risks because individuals in a group know that consequences of the decisions are not severe but for an individual they always practice caution. Most companies and organizations when making timely decisions will rely on individual decision-making (Bolaños et al., 2005). The cons in individual decision-making may include: the individual may have limited knowledge and information and if available, it may be incomplete. The solution that an individual may come up with may be incomplete and hence can also be inaccurate as compared to a group with more knowledge and information at their disposal.

From the points illustrated above both group and individual decision-making have their advantages and disadvantages. In most instances most organizations and companies rely mostly on individuals rather group decision making, as they tend to have a lot of setbacks. For any individuals they end up preferring individual decision-making as it results in sound decision and more accountability. The groups can sometimes come up with absurd decisions, which can be a waste of time and resources to an organization.

3.5. MULTI-PARTY DECISION-MAKING OR NEGOTIATION

In this, types of negotiations there are several parties involved, i.e., more than two. A good example is when people are sitting at a lunch table and as an individual you are trying to decide on where to go, at the table there are individuals who don't eat French fries, another individual is a dedicated vegan, and another individual wants stake while there is another individual who says they are good with anything that is offered but when offered anything they say no. now try and imagine those individuals as countries trying to negotiate some treaty of sort. This means there are more than two parties involved in the bargaining room (Mukherjee et al., 2016). There are many challenges in such types of negotiations this involves a lot of information is in play, coalitions start forming, social dynamics are involved and procedures become more and more complex.

Figure 3.14. A multiparty negotiation in progress.

Source: UK in a changing Europe.

When dealing with a large group of individuals in multi-party negotiations there is a lot of information you have to deal with. In this case, every part has brought in their desired outcomes, strategies, perceptions and their interests into the negotiation room. With all these they have brought in their evidence for where they stand, expert opinions, projection of what could happen, facts that each party has researched even the figured will be added. With all this information at the ready and with the number of parties, this could mean that things at the negotiation room could get complicated quite easily.

In most instances, individuals involved in negotiation processes are recommended to keep spreadsheets also referred to as "payoff matrix" before negotiations begin. The different parties can be arranged in rows whereas the issues and interests are arranged into different columns and as changes occur while the negotiation is in progress the individual can change or update the matrix to indicate whether there has been any change.

At some point as the negotiations progress, there are coalitions that will be formed in order to reiterate a common purpose. The formation of coalition is good for negotiators that are weak and can link with larger or better negotiators in order for them to gain some power and to some extent have their say. Within these coalitions that form there will be intense cooperation and even competition. Some coalitions may try to poach some members from the other coalitions and this may make some coalitions paranoid when they lose their members, as they know their information will be leaked.

In these cases, it involves managing a large group of individuals and this can be pretty challenging under most if not any circumstances. This is because everyone in the room would like to express himself or herself and with everyone bargaining for time then there needs to be rules and a set format for everyone to follow (Martinsons & Davison, 2007). It will all depend on the arbitrator to decide whether he/she will allow everyone to give an opening statement or have an open discussion where it is random or allow it to go round the table in an order. The arbitrator should also decide on how decisions are to be made whether by majority rule, unanimity, or a consensus.

In every party of negotiators, there is a pecking order and there is status. The status can bring authority into play and when authority is used, it could result to a power struggle and the main agenda of the negotiation could be lost.

The people that are involved in the negotiations all have their own different agendas and they all try to maintain a unified direction. The negotiators will face a lot of tactics and some may become unethical as everyone tries to drive their point home.

According to Massachusetts institute of technology there are three issues that make multi-part negotiations more complex than two party negotiations and these include coalition formation, management of issues and the fluctuating nature of the negotiators commonly referred to as Best Alternative to a Negotiated Agreement (BATNA). If one prepares for these three, then an individual will be well prepared for success in a negotiation.

Choose the coalitions wisely. In the midst of the negotiation process, it may be difficult to be heard and under such conditions, it might be best to collaborate and join forces. This brings to fore that, there is strength in numbers but in some instances, these coalitions can become unstable and someone may end up being left out and the partner can decide to go for their own. This means that the negotiator should leave an open mind as it means one should be able to reach out across party lines and keep communicating with others. This simply means a negotiator should plan on how and when to meet with other coalition partners so that one can get full information and have a chance to talk to other parties this means one should be able to be flexible.

How one manages, the process is very vital. When managing a group of parties whether 4, 50 or even 600 negotiators how these parties interact are very vital. This can be very complicated as the more the parties the more complicated it becomes as it can be easy to deal with only one party. This can make a manager to be appointed to oversee the whole process (Kugler et al., 2012). The manager will be required to come up with the agenda, setting the rules to be followed, to summarize the understandings of all parties and he/she will communicate any decisions to the outside parties. If the groups are too many or the number of people too large this can lead to breaking the group into smaller parties so that they can develop preliminary proposals so as to arise them as the main agenda.

The third and last is calculate the BATNAs. As everyone is entering into any negotiation with an idea of the best negotiated agreement. With this in mind, it helps a negotiator to stand firm when being offered any alternatives that do not reach anywhere close to the goals the negotiator has set.

There are several challenges in multiparty negotiations and the first is dealing with coalitions in that some coalitions might come together and pull together their resources in order for them to affect the outcome of the decision that is made in order to favor them. They can also be used to reduce the number of conflicts but in that, the stronger party will suppress these of the inferior member of the coalition.

Voting and majority rule are very crucial in multiparty negotiations. Voting is majorly carried out to oversee and collect what individuals prefer on alternatives to the issues they have raised and the alternative that has the majority becomes the choice of everyone. Although the use of majority rule brings democracy and the most will have their way this type of decision-making tends to not consider the preference of individuals. Sometimes some negotiators may decide to use the concurrence rule r commonly refer to as unanimity rule where the members or negotiators have to agree before coming up with the final decision. This type of rule is more efficient and they will come up with the best decision although most of the time it consumes a lot of time. In some cases, there is consensus agreement where parties agree publicly to a particular settlement although there might be some members of the party that have a varied opinion.

In some cases, there is communication breakdown because most of the time some of the individuals take communication to multiple parties for granted. There is private caucusing where individuals within the different parties discuss issues among themselves. This causes problems as the individuals involved in the caucuses cannot follow the proceedings and also they cause disturbances due to the discussions they are carrying out. They generate a lot of noise (Kulcsár et al., 2020).

During the communication there is biased interpretation where instead of the members of a different party having an open mind and listening to the idea they misinterpret meanings of statements and believe that most of the words and phrases being used are said against them or to discourage the message they are trying to pass across.

There are indirect speech acts, this is brought about when an individual is speaking to the head of the negotiations but whatever they are saying is directed at the other party they have a dispute with. This mostly leads to many negotiations to breakdown and parties to depart because of protecting their dignity.

There are several key strategies to know before heading to a table to negotiate with multiple parties. You need to understand the people who will be at the negotiating table, i.e., carry out research on the individuals or organization so as to know the type of language to use so as not to use offensive language.

Use brainstorming wisely so as to get correct information and ideas that are helpful and not waste time in the initial stages. Stay at the table when the meeting is in progress so as not to miss any progress or decision that can be made.

In some cases, in multiparty negotiations there can be a no-agreement scenario. Due to many parties, being involved and not all will feel listened to or their issues addressed especially if an agreement has to be unanimous. Most negotiations involving multiple parties need to discuss what would happen if there will be a no-agreement situation so as the negotiations would not go in vain. Some of the ways they can use to address the situation is to look for a facilitator who will break the ties and act as the ultimate decision maker or in some cases they can use the Delphi technique or in some instances thy can decide to do a secret ballot where the majority decision will carry the day.

Figure 3.15. A two party negotiation. There are fewer individuals involved and takes less time.

Source: The business journals.

On the other hand, we have two party negotiations, which involve two parties or two individuals of opposing sides negotiating in order to formulate agreements or treaties on issues that they are disputing.

In multiple party negotiations there are vices that could greatly affect the process and these vices include: intolerance. An individual on the negotiation table has to be tolerant to every opinion that another individual is raising even though you do not like the opinion. This means the person has to be intelligent and handle the situation calmly while raising any objections and present any argument without any hatred.

An individual should always keep their emotions in check. Due to negotiations taking long periods, it can make individuals to become impatient and this brings about emotions that can near boiling point. Individuals can decide to move out of the room and take a 5 min break and breathe in some fresh air (Hwang & Lin, 2012).

An individual need to prepare in advance and have adequate knowledge and information. Lack of preparation can lead to lack of credibility and reduce trust in what you bring to the table.

In conclusion, multiparty negotiations have many hurdles and hence many people prefer negotiating as only two parties as decisions are easy to come by and it takes less time. The multiple party negotiations need careful thinking, a lot of planning and preparation and a lot of elements need to be considered before the whole process can even begin. The multiple party negotiations mostly occur in countries but two party negotiations occurs between organizations or companies.

Chapter 4

Group Decision Making Problems

CONTENTS

4.1. INTRODUCTION

The action of choosing a choice from a variety of choices by a specified number of people is known as group decision making. According to Henry Mintzberg (2011), one of the most important managerial activities is decision making, and Herbert Simon (2013) identified this phenomenon as a core of management. Dedication, backing for the organization's goals and the skill of the team all contribute to increased decision effectiveness. Personality trait, group interactions, strategy, immediate environment, and availability of information are all factors that influence decisions, according to the descriptive model (Huczynski, 2013).

The goal of this approach is to determine which component has the biggest influence and how they interact while making a decision. In contrast, the behavioral theory (Huczynski, 2013) emphasizes the importance of decisions in an individual's behavior. The group can make better decisions by gathering, comparing, and assessing a number of options before selecting the best one. Some employees, on the other hand, make decisions based on the first option, which is satisfactory, and after they have completed their investigation. The mechanism they employ is known as the satisfying strategy.

Figure 4.1. An image illustrating effective group decision-making.

Source: http://www.free-management-ebooks.com/news/effective-group-decision-making/.

As per Huczynski (2013), decision-making can be influenced by certainty, risk, or uncertainty. The phase between the alternative and its consequence is known as certainty. Employees are certain that all results will be helpful to the organization, and they must choose the most advantageous one. However, because the majority of decisions involve some level of risk, it's critical to predict the possibility of it occurring based on the members' collective knowledge and experience. The most difficult decisions are those made in the face of ambiguity, and they are frequently related with new, unknown aspects such as new markets, new technology, or new target customers.

Personal choices can differ significantly from those made in groups. This potential for variance in outcomes is one of the reasons why collective decision making is appealing. Individuals make a collective decision from the options presented to them in a circumstance known as group decision-making. The decision is then no longer attributed to any single group member. This is because the outcome is influenced by all people and social group processes such as social influence. Individual decisions are frequently different from those made by organizations. There's a lot of discussion over whether this distinction leads to better or worse decisions. Decisions made jointly are more effective than decisions made by a single individual, based on the current concept of synergy. Group decisions are influenced by factors that influence other social group activities. Furthermore, when individuals make decisions as part of a group, they have a propensity to favor discussing shared information over unshared information (i.e., shared information bias).

On a daily basis, we all make personal decisions, and we all understand that some decisions are more challenging than others. We encounter some problems when making decisions in groups that we do not experience when making decisions individually, but we also stand to profit from some group decision-making advantages (Napier & Gershenfeld, 2004). Group decision-making can appear to be fair and democratic, but it's really just a ruse to hide the reality that certain members of the group or the group leader have already made up their minds.

Group decisions also take longer than single decisions and can be burdensome, if certain group members fail to do their work divert them into self-centered or unproductive roles or miss meetings. Group decisions are also difficult for groups to take place. However, on the other hand, group decisions are often more informed because through discussion and debate all members have a shared understanding of the problems. The common understanding of the individual can also become more complex and profound because the group members are exposed to a range of points of view, so that their own perspectives are expanded.

Figure 4.2. Image illustrates decision-making in groups.

Source: https://www.researchgate.net/publication/341458831_Techniques_of_group_decision_making.

Synergy, one of the primary advantages of group communication that we covered previously, also benefits group decisions. Most groups don't have a set strategy for making decisions, assuming that they'll figure it out as they go. This can result in unequal involvement, social loafing, rash decisions, lengthy debate, and a slew of other bad outcomes. So, in this section, we'll study certain practices that will help us make better decisions and some particular approaches that will assist us in making a final selection.

Before a group can reach a decision, it must first brainstorm potential solutions to their issue. Although most people do not follow the recommended steps of brainstorming, it is the most widely used strategy. As you may know, brainstorming is the process of quickly generating ideas without evaluating them. For brainstorming to be productive, according to the inventor of the word (Osborn, 1959), the following four guidelines must be followed:

- It is unlawful to evaluate concepts.
- Crazy and outlandish ideas are welcome.
- The goal is quantity, not quality, of ideas.
- It is encouraged to present new combinations of ideas.

Group communication academics have proposed extra processes that precede and follow brainstorming to make it more of a decision-making process rather than an idea-generating tool (Cragan & Wright, 1991):

- Performing a warm-up session for brainstorming – Some individuals are more hesitant than others about publicly sharing their ideas, and a warm-up practice can help alleviate fears and prepare members of the group for task-related generating ideas. Anyone in the group can start the warm-up, which should only last a few minutes. To get things going, someone could ask, "What else would our band be named if we established a band?" or "What other uses could a mailbox serve?" The first warm-up in the previous examples stimulates the group's abstract creative impulses, whereas the second concentrates on practical and tangible ideas.
- Perform the actual session for brainstorming – This meeting should run no more than thirty minutes and adhere to the four brainstorming criteria described before. The facilitator could urge participants to build on one other's ideas to ensure that the fourth rule is followed.
- Remove ideas that are duplicate – After the brainstorming process, members of the group might reject concepts that are the same or quite similar (without evaluating them).
- Evaluate, organize, and clarify ideas – Check to determine if any ideas need to be clarified before evaluating. Then, in some organized method, try to theme or group thoughts together. Because "outlandish" concepts are encouraged, some recommendations may need to be clarified. It may be deleted if it becomes evident that a notion does not have a solid foundation and is too ambiguous or abstract to be defined. However, it may be prudent to save off-the-wall ideas that are difficult to categorize in a miscellaneous or "wild and crazy" category rather than discarding them.

The nominal group methodology involves a four-step procedure that incorporates generation of ideas and evaluation, with the goal of eliciting equal contributions from all members of the group (Delbecq & Ven de Ven, 1971). This strategy is beneficial because it incorporates all members of the group in a methodical manner, which eliminates the problem of uneven involvement during talks. This strategy can also assist prevent instances of social loafing because everyone contributes to the debate.

Follow these steps to apply the nominal group technique:

- Individually and silently listing ideas;
- Creating a huge list of ideas;
- Clarification of ideas as required;
- Taking a secret vote to rank the acceptance of ideas by the members of the group.

Have group member's work silently in the same place during the first step to write down any suggestion they have for addressing the task or problem they are facing. It shouldn't take more than twenty minutes to do this task. Anyone leading the discussion should encourage participants to use brainstorming tactics, which means they shouldn't assess ideas as they come up with them. To avoid distracting others, ask group members to remain silent once they have completed their list.

Figure 4.3. Illustration of how groups members work together.

Source: https://www.benpham.net/management/problems-in-group-decision-making/.

The facilitator walks around the group in a consistent order in the second stage, asking each member to share one idea at a time. The facilitator writes the suggestion on a master list that is visible to everyone as it is presented. Keep track of how many times each concept comes up, as it's possible that one of them deserves greater attention. This approach should be repeated until all of the ideas have been discussed. When asked to share one of the thoughts, some group members may start to alter their list or self-censor. It is good to encourage members of the group to switch lists with somebody else so they can share ideas from the list they receive without fear of being personally criticized. This will reduce people's nervousness about sharing their ideas and ensure that each suggestion is shared.

The moderator should mention that members of the group can now seek for clarity on concepts on the master list during stage three. Do not allow this discussion to devolve into a debate about ideas. To avoid an unduly protracted conversation, go from person to person asking which ideas need to be clarified, and then go to the originator(s) of the idea in issue for clarification. Participants rank the appropriateness of the concepts on the master list using a voting ballot in the fourth step. If the list is lengthy, ask members of the group to rank only their top five or so selections (Herrera et al., 2005). The facilitator then takes the secret votes and goes through them in a random order, noting the order in which each suggestion was ranked. The highest-ranking suggestion should then be considered and chosen. The nominal group methodology does not take a group all the way to a decision; instead, it prepares the group for a roundtable discussion or another method of evaluating the merits of the top ideas.

4.2. PROBLEMS IN GROUP DECISION MAKING

4.2.1. Groupthink

Groupthink is a phenomenon in which people seek for agreement while also ignoring their own drive. Because they are frightened of upsetting the group's consensus, members do not criticize the group's views. Because only the smallest number of risks and choices are considered, the group loses the potential to make the best judgments. Cohesion is often connected with favorable outcomes, but it can also have negative implications. Individuals must write down their opinions on a subject and rate them on a one to ten scale before the meeting starts, as per Victoria Medvec (Berger 2014). This will help them avoid being affected by others afterward.

Groupthink is a psychological phenomenon that happens in a band of people when the group's drive for harmony or uniformity leads to unreasonable or inefficient decision-making. In a group, cohesion, or the desire for it, can lead to a tendency among its members to agree at any costs. As a result, the group is able to reduce dispute and achieve a decision without doing a critical analysis. Although groupthink is a social psychology concept, it has a wide range of applications and impacts literature in organizational theory, political science, management and communications studies, as well as essential parts of aberrant religious cult activity.

Groupthink is often claimed to happen (more widely) in natural groups inside a community, for instance, to clarify the lifelong differences in mentalities of those with opposing political opinions (like "conservatism" and "liberalism" in the United States political context) or the alleged advantages of teamwork vs. solo work. However, this group homogeneity of ideas may be best described by the group's collective confirmation bias rather than conscious group decision-making. William H. Whyte Jr. invented the word in 1952. Irving Janis, a Yale University research psychologist, was responsible for the majority of the early groupthink study. In 1972, Janis released an influential book, which was revised in 1982. Janis cited the Bay of Pigs tragedy (a 1961 attempted invasion of Castro's Cuba) and the 1941 Japanese attack on Pearl Harbor as his two main case studies. His groupthink paradigm has been tested and revised in subsequent investigations (Escobar & Moreno-Jimenéz, 2007).

Individual originality, individuality, and independent thought are lost as a result of groupthink, which encourages individuals to avoid addressing contentious subjects or alternative solutions. An "illusion of invulnerability" is created by the unstable group dynamics of the "in-group" (an inflated certainty that the right decision has been made). As a result, the "in-group" considerably overestimates its own decision-making talents while considerably underestimating the ability of its opponents (the "out-group"). Furthermore, groupthink can lead to actions that dehumanize the "out-group."

Figure 4.4. In 1972, social scientist Irving Janis coined the term "groupthink" to explain inferior judgments founded by a team as a result of group social constraints.

Source: https://corporatefinanceinstitute.com/resources/careers/soft-skills/groupthink-decisions/.

When little to no innovative ideas or justifications for improved policies, outcomes, or arrangements is brought forward in group interactions, it can be cause for concern. (McLeod et al.) Because group activities and group initiatives in general make it incredibly easy to pass on not delivering valuable thoughts, groupthink is often referred to as a group of "yes men." Selecting teams from more varying backgrounds and even combining men and women for groups have all been tried in the past to combat group thought (Kamalnath). Many people believe that groupthink is detrimental to businesses, organizations, and workplaces. Most senior-level occupations require employees to be self-sufficient in their thinking. Outstanding CEOs and decisiveness have been found to have a beneficial relationship (Kelman). Groupthink also prevents a company from progressing and inventing if no one ever speaks up and suggests a better way of doing things (Eden & Ackermann, 2001). The potential of groupthink influencing decision-making is influenced by antecedent factors like group cohesion defective, group structure, and situational context (e.g., community panic).

There are certain symptoms of groupthink. Irving Janis proposed eight signs suggestive of groupthink to make it testable:

- Type I – Overconfidence in the group's strength and ethics:
- Excessive optimism and risk-taking are encouraged by illusions of invulnerability.
- Unquestionable faith in the group's morality, enabling members to disregard the repercussions of their conduct.
- Type II – being closed minded:
- Warnings that might threaten the group's beliefs are rationalized.
- People who oppose the group are stereotyped as weak, wicked, bias, spiteful, powerless, or ignorant.
- Type III – pressure towards a uniform front:
- Ideas that depart from the apparent group agreement are self-censored.
- Silence is seen as agreement, creating the illusion of unanimity among group members.
- Any member who doubts the group is subjected to direct pressure to comply, which is couched in terms of "disloyalty."
- Mind-guards are self-appointed members who keep dissenting information out of the organization.

To prevent groupthink, Janis proposed three antecedent conditions:

- **High cohesiveness in the group** – The key component that leads to groupthink, according to anis, is cohesion. Of course, disjointed groups can make poor decisions, but they do not suffer groupthink. In a cohesive group, members refrain from speaking out against choices, avoid disagreeing with one another, and endeavor to keep the group nice. When a group's cohesiveness reaches a point where there are no more differences among members, the group is primed for groupthink.
  - *Deindividuation* – Individual freedom of expression becomes less vital as collective cohesiveness becomes more vital.
- **Faults in the structure** – Groupthink requires cohesion, but it is made more likely when the group is arranged in a way that prevents information from being communicated and when the group makes decisions carelessly.
  - Insulating of the group: can lead to the formation of unique, wrong perspectives on difficulties that the group is dealing with, which can lead to flawed solutions to the problem.
  - Lacking leadership that is impartial – Leaders can entirely control the group discussion by pre-planning what will be addressed, allowing just specific questions to be asked, and soliciting the opinions of just specific members of the group (Dyer et al., 2008). When leaders disclose their ideas on a topic before the group debates it together, this is known as closed style leadership. When leaders use an open style of leadership, they keep their opinions to themselves until later in the conversation. It has been discovered that groups led by a closed-style leader are more biased in their assessments, especially when members have a high degree of certainty.
  - Lacking norms that require procedures that are methodological.
  - Members' social backgrounds and ideologies are similar.
- Contextual context
  - External dangers that are highly stressful: High-stakes judgments can cause tension and anxiety, and group

members may respond irrationally to the decisional stress. Members of a group may justify their action by exaggerating the favorable repercussions and downplaying the unfavorable ones. In order to reduce the amount of tension in the circumstance, the group will make a speedy decision with little to no debate or dispute. According to studies, groups who are under a lot of stress are more prone to make mistakes, lose sight of the big picture, and utilize procedures that haven't worked in the past.

- Recent failures: can contribute to low self, leading in group consensus for fear of being judged incorrectly.
- A great deal of difficulty in decision-making activities.
- Time constraints: members of the group are more concerned with efficiency and speed than with quality and accuracy. Furthermore, time constraints may cause group members to ignore critical facts related to the topic of discussion.
- Moral dilemmas.

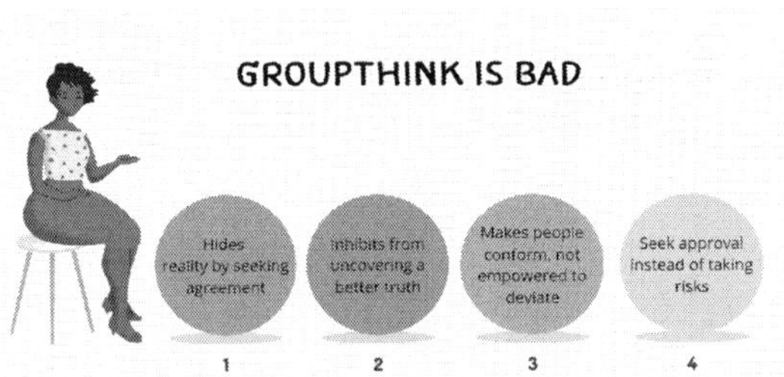

Figure 4.5. A fixed attitude can cause leaders and managers in positions of power to reject any information that contradicts their authority, resulting in blind spots.

Source: https://www.techtello.com/avoid-groupthink/.

Although all three of these variables may be present in a circumstance, they are not necessarily present, even when groupthink is present. Janis felt that a high level of cohesion was the most significant antecedent to groupthink and that it was always present when groupthink occurred; yet, he also felt that high cohesion did not necessarily cause groupthink. A tightly knit group adheres to all group norms; whether or not groupthink develops is determined by the group norms. Even in a highly homogeneous group, groupthink is unlikely to emerge if the group supports individual dissent and alternate problem-solving solutions. This suggests that high cohesiveness will only contribute to groupthink if one or both of the other antecedents are present, with situational context somewhat more likely to create groupthink than structural flaw.

The groupthink phenomena appear to be based on a series of implicit and generally restricted assumptions, as Aldag and Fuller (1993) observed:

- The basic goal of group issue solving is to increase the quality of decisions.
- Problem solving in groups is thought to be a reasonable process.
- Advantages of group problem solving:
  - A diversity of viewpoints additional information on possible options.
  - Improved decision-making accuracy.
  - Bias dampening is a term used to describe the process of reducing biases.
  - Effects of social presence.

It has long been assumed that organizations with a high ability to collaborate will be able to solve problems more quickly and efficiently than individuals. Because groups have more resources, they are better equipped to store and retrieve knowledge and come up with more potential solutions to a problem. The disadvantage of group issue solving is that it takes longer for groups to reach a resolution and forces members to make concessions with one another.

However, it wasn't until Janis' study that anyone seriously explored how a tight-knit group could compromise the group's capacity to make good decisions. Tight-knit groups might seem to make superior decisions since they can reach an agreement quickly and with little effort; yet, this decision-making method may erode the members' ability to think critically over time. As a result, many people believe that combating the impacts of groupthink is critical (Di Fabio et al., 2015).

Janis claims that decision-making groups aren't always doomed to groupthink. He proposed methods for avoiding groupthink, including:

- Leaders should designate each team member as a "critical evaluator." This allows each member to openly express their concerns and reservations.

- When assigning a work to a group, the leader should not give an opinion. To prevent significantly influencing the outcome, leaders should avoid attending many of the group sessions.
- The organization should form multiple separate groups to work on the same issue.
- All viable options should be considered.
- Outside of the group, each member should discuss the group's ideas with trusted persons.
- Outside specialists should be invited to meetings by the organization.
- Outside specialists should be allowed to speak with and question group members.
- At least one member of the group should take on the position of devil's advocate. For each meeting, this should be a different person.

In order to avoid groupthink decisions, the devil's advocate in a group may ask questions and provide insight that contradicts the majority group. According to Hartwig's research, the devil's advocacy strategy is extremely effective for group problem-solving. It permits conflict to be used in the most effective way possible for discovering the optimal solution, avoiding the need for members to go back and try again if the first one fails. To uncover and assess different solutions, Hartwig advises combining the devil's advocacy strategy with other group decision-making theories such as the functional theory.

Figure 4.6. Groupthink isn't just a problem in large-scale business choices. Smaller ones can also be affected.

Source: https://www.jabra.com/blog/groupthink-kills-collaboration/.

The basic notion behind the devil's advocacy strategy is that by facilitating somewhat controlled disagreement, not only can groupthink be reduced, but also problems can be solved.

The Abilene paradox is a concept that is similar to groupthink and is another phenomenon that is harmful when working in groups. When companies fall victim to the Abilene paradox, they take activities that are in direct opposition to their stated goals, so defeating the same goals they are attempting to achieve. The Abilene dilemma can be caused by a failure to convey one's desires or beliefs (Davenport, 2009).

The Watergate scandal is an instance of this, as stated in the Abilene paradox. A meeting was held prior to the scandal to discuss the situation. One of Nixon's campaign aides was undecided about speaking up and offering his opinion. It's possible that the incident could have been avoided if he had expressed his displeasure with the group's choice.

Other methods for avoiding or preventing groupthink include:

Following the failure of the Bay of Pigs invasion, President John F. Kennedy used "vigilant assessment" to avoid groupthink during the Cuban Missile Crisis. He welcomed outside specialists to express their perspectives at sessions and allowed group members to examine them thoroughly. He also encouraged group members to talk about potential solutions with trusted colleagues in their respective departments, and he separated the group into sub-groups to break up the cohesion. Kennedy stayed away from the meetings on purpose, so he wouldn't have to express his own viewpoint.

Introverts can be mute in meetings with extroverts, according to Cass Sunstein; he advocates openly asking for every person's perspective, either during the discussion or later in one-on-one discussions. Sunstein cites research that shows groups with a high level of internal socializing and pleasant chat is more likely to make poor investment judgments due to groupthink than groups of investors who are strangers and more open to argue (Dalal & Brooks, 2013). To avoid group polarization, which occurs when a discussion with like-minded people leads to a result that is more radical than any of the participants advocated before to the conversation, he suggests forming diverse groups that include people with a variety of viewpoints. Sunstein further points out those persons who argue for a cause in which they do not genuinely believe (in the position of devil's advocate) are significantly less effective than those who argue for a cause in which they really believe. Dissenting individuals or a group like a Red Team that is intended to pursue an alternative strategy or aim "for real" can do this.

4.2.2. Escalation of Commitment

The concept of escalation of commitment is when people display their devotion to behaviors that have had unfavorable consequences in the past. This propensity manifests itself in situations involving waiting, such as economic investments or gambling. The findings of the dangerous shift stress that this phenomenon is more obvious in groups, because people can persuade opponents to their beliefs, have support from others, and the decision-making duty is shared among the other members.

Escalation of commitment is a human behavior trend where an individual or group faces more bad consequences as a result of a decision, action, or investment yet refuses to change course. The actor continues to act in irrational ways that are consistent with earlier judgments and actions.

The sunk-cost fallacy is a term coined by economic experts and behaviorists to define the rationale of greater investment of money or effort in a decision based on the total prior investment ("sunk cost"), despite new evidence indicating that the long term cost of preceding the behavior outweighs the maximum outcome (Cheek & Goebel, 2020).

Figure 4.7. Commitment escalation is a well-known issue. We've been trained not to give up just because something is difficult.

Source: https://www.organizing4innovation.com/how-to-stop-3-tips-to-prevent-escalation-of-commitment/.

Similar behaviors are described in sociology as unreasonable escalation of commitment or commitment bias. "It's never too late to make the right decision," "In for a penny, in for a pound," "Throwing good money after bad," and "If you find yourself in a hole, stop digging," are all proverbial pictures that illustrate the occurrence and the mindset that underpins them. Barry M. Staw initially characterized rising commitment to a selected course of action in his 1976 paper, "Knee deep in the great muddy: A study of escalating commitment to a selected course of action." Barry M. Staw initially characterized rising commitment to a selected course of action in his 1976 paper, "Knee deep in the great muddy: A study of escalating commitment to a selected course of action."

Researchers studied factors, conditions, and causes of escalation of commitment in studies influenced by Staw's work. Other studies of situations and how people approach challenges and make decisions were introduced as part of the study. Some of the first study was inspired by occurrences that occurred as a result of these phenomena and served to explain it.

Many cases of escalation of commitment to a problem have been studied and monitored by researchers over the last few decades. Three aspects are used to explain the heightened conditions. To begin with, a situation has a significant investment of time, money, and people in the endeavor. Following that, prior conduct leads to a point in time when the project has failed to meet expectations or is in a cautious decline. Finally, these issues all force a decision-maker to make decisions between pursuing a project till completion while incurring additional expenditures, and terminating the project entirely.

Researchers also argue how the increase in engagement is seen in two different categories. The necessity to increase resources is linked to expectation theory. Many researchers believe. "In that regard, policymakers assess the likelihood of further allocations of resources to achieve the objective as well as the value of achieving the goal (i.e., incentives minus costs) and generate, thus, a subjective expected utility associated with the decision on the allocation of additional resources."

The next step in the escalation process is self-justification and rationalization, which involves determining if the leader's action made good use of resources, whether the resources were used to effect positive change, and ensuring themselves that the decision they made was correct. To make a final decision, leaders must balance costs and advantages of any problem. Whether the decision is what others believed in is important for assuring the leader that he made the right choice regardless of the final outcome.

There are numerous other forms and theories of psychology research carried out on the topic. Many people believe that situational development and resource allocation are the greatest ways to assess and test what researchers have done so far to explain this behavior. Other studies have discovered factors that contribute to de-escalation of commitment, the polar opposite of escalation of commitment. The significance of accounting and mental accounting is discussed in this study to explain the elements that impact if commitment escalation or de-escalation is more likely to happen (Charness & Sutter, 2012).

The process of self-justification is part of the group leaders and managers' commitment decisions and can therefore lead to increased levels of commitment. "One explanation for why people intensify loyalty to their previous investments" is this mentality. Managers make decisions based on their previous actions. Managers are more likely to remember and apply knowledge that is consistent with their behavior in order to make consistent decisions in the present and future. If a group member or an outside party notices the manager's inconsistency in decision-making, the manager's leadership role may be altered. External influences like as society, peers, and authority have a substantial impact on a manager's perspective of what aspects are realistically important while making decisions.

The natural reactions and complexities involved in making that decision in a risk-taking situation are described using prospect theory. Prospect theory argues that different degrees of affluence, such as people, money, or time, influence how people make decisions. The way one interprets a situation depending on costs and advantages was of special interest to the researchers. The context in which the problem is presented is critical for comprehending and considering the likelihood that the scenario will either work in your favor or against you, as well as how to prepare for those changes.

"Prospect theory, according to Whyte (1986), provides a psychological framework for explaining rising commitment to a failing course of action without relying on self-justification processes (Fiegenbaum and Thomas, 1988, p. 99). "Prospect theorists argue that one should adopt this technique when the stakes are low enough to have an impact on the project's result. To guarantee that they do not fail, the person may increase their resources to make sure that they triumph. Researchers "Davis and Bobko (1986) observed no influence of personal accountability on continuing commitment to the prior course of action in the optimistic frame condition," despite the fact that this theory appears plausible. As a result, in a higher-responsibility circumstance, the escalation of commitment will be smaller.

Figure 4.8. In the theoretical method, there is temporal model of escalation.

Source: https://study.com/academy/lesson/escalation-of-commitment-definition-examples-quiz.html.

According to Frits Heider's attribution theory, "attempts to provide causal explanations for events and human behavior." The locus of causation and stability are two methods of investigation used in this theory. The relationship between internal features of an individual, such as intelligence levels and attention seeking, and exterior space, such as weather forecasts and task complexity, is reflected in the locus of causation.

Control aspects play an important role in how a management defends a decision. Managers will explain why they made a decision to a particular point of view by describing the relationship between internal and external elements. Managers may rationalize their conduct by claiming that the situation was beyond their personal control, or they may assume that no one else could have made the decision (Colombo et al., 2003). According to research, "an employee's willingness to engage in the negative emotional behavior known as escalation of commitment is likely to be influenced by the sort of attribution made by an employee across these dimensions." Identity has a significant role in how we navigate the world. The social identity idea is based on private ideas and beliefs as well as the influence of others. Researchers have discovered that people establish linkages between their use of groups and their own self-perception, which encourages them to maintain their social position and protect it when it is threatened.

There is also the aggregate method. "Rather than the ordering of effects throughout time, the aggregate model emphasizes the accumulation and balance of forces." The model is general and can provide an excellent understanding of how micro and macro factors define the impacts, whether positive or negative. Rather than what experts have identified as the standard, this model is based on the context. There is no procedure to follow, which is advantageous to researchers since it allows them to grasp a problem more clearly and comprehend the wider picture. Project, psychological, social, and structural factors all have a role in the desire to keep investing in failed propositions.

The original agreements and choices made at the start of a project are referred to be project drivers. This comprises the project's overall qualities as well as the first financial costs. Decision risks, potential cost information, and information acquisition have all been linked to escalation of commitment in a negative way. Positive connections have been discovered between choice uncertainties, positive performance trend information, and reported preference for the initial option.

High expenses of terminating or modifying the purpose of the activity, the possibility for financial gain upon conclusion, and the project's elaborate structure can all contribute to an escalation of commitment, making it difficult to abandon the project. Avoiding the behavior can be accomplished by preventing future monetary loss, prospective savings, and having readily available alternatives. Situations where stopping an action costs more than finishing it resulted in decision makers being caught in their present, costly habits, according to Teger and subsequently Ross and Staw's research.

The internal views on the behavior and details related to the project are psychologically determining. This can include cognitive factors, personality and emotions related to elements of the project. Among these, sunk costs, investment time, decision making experience and expertise have been shown to show positive ties with increased commitment, self-efficiency and trust, personal responsibility for the first step, ego threat and proximity to the final project, whereas expected regret and positive information framing have shown negative links.

Hope and the assumption that one can influence what will still be beneficial outcomes leads to continual self-justification of activities. People increase their early personal investments in the hopes of improving existing results. In a case study by Staw, giving business students altered responsibility for initial decisions and their consequences resulted in the strongest commitment to greater actions and resources when the original decision was made directly by the student with negative consequences. People take greater risks in these situations in order to avoid more issues

(Brodbeck et al., 2002). This is especially more frequent when people perceive current events as having unstable rather than steady thinking, or when they are unwilling to confess mistakes. They expect the situation will thereafter settle or improve. Confirmation bias can also contribute to an increase in commitment since people are less likely to see the negative consequences of their choice. If the results are identified, however, they might be attributed to unanticipated occurrences that occurred throughout the project.

Sunk costs are sometimes perceived as rising commitments. When the amount invested is bigger and cannot be recovered, the desire to avoid total loss of those resources and maintain impression control motivates ongoing investment rather than withdrawal. In addition, because invested resources can include time, the proximity of a project's completion provides similar consequences. Due to the clarity of completion goals at certain points, projects are given more value when they are early or late in their development. Risks are more likely to be taken at these points than they are closer to a visible halfway in a project.

The assumptions and impact of various persons or groups on implementation are referred to as social determinants. Among these, group identification or cohesive strength has been shown to have the greatest impact on intensification of commitment, whereas public judgment of choice and opposition to choice from others has little bearing.

Individuals in the surroundings exhibit themselves with caution. They are primarily concerned with their organization's appearance of competence, not with themselves and what they believe is correct and competent. Escalation of commitment refers to the process of making a choice, which can be done by a group or an individual. Managers are in charge of deciding the fate of a project that a group of individuals has been working on.

A manager who wants to pull a team out of a development is anxious that members of the team would think the manager is incompetent, not because the plan failed. Policy opposition, employment uncertainty (Fox & Staw, 1979), and audience size were among the variables studied in this phenomenon (Rubin & Lang, 1981). When these realistic variables are present, all of them demonstrate an increase in commitment. The face-saving effect refers to this mental and emotional reaction. Individuals in positions of responsibility are continually checking themselves to ensure that their behavior and beliefs are in line with the expectations of their audience. The public perception of one's social identity can determine one's fate. A team, for example, can determine the level of devotion and personal connection to a project or idea. Members of the team frequently say things like "that project is Bob's baby" or "yeah, we had the same idea." Both extremes are critical in determining how people perceive and assess a situation, particularly one that has failed.

Figure 4.9. Political decisions during the Vietnam War and, more recently, Brexit are seen to have been influenced by escalation of commitment.

Source: https://www.emergingrnleader.com/avoiding-the-escalation-of-commitment-problem/.

Supervisors are in charge of leading a group of people through difficult difficulties to a solution. Although the negative sides of commitments are frequently explored in more depth and relevance, there are numerous social benefits. Persistence is an example of these phenomena. A manager's role is to save a project on the point of disaster, yet with tenacity, a manager can be rewarded for converting a terrible project into something amazing (Caemmerer et al., 2021). Turning around a team to accomplish something successful earns you rewards. When managers stay focused on their objectives and motivate their employees to produce properly. The environmental and cultural elements and assets of the development's entire vision are referred to as structural determinants. According to the limited research that has been done on them, agency issues have the greatest impact on commitment escalation.

There are macro-level aspects that affect a team's organizational structure and decision-making process. Individuals in a group context with specified roles and functions make decisions, which then have an influence on the decisions made as a result of team interaction. Institutional inertia is a factor that influences commitment escalation. Individual views and behavior vary regularly; hence the status of a group is also unpredictable and controlled, according to this phenomenon. "Organizations have very imprecise sensory systems, rendering them largely immune to environmental changes." This is one component that influences how difficulties are handled. When a group of people is involved in communication, decision-making, and change, most of the tasks fail to be completed due to a lack of consistency in the group. This happens in events like policy changes, court judgments, and processes.

This problem can also cause disaster for a company if it is overly connected to a policy, train of thought, or image and is unable to modify it. "On occasion, a project, product, or policy might become so inextricably linked to the organization's beliefs and purposes that it becomes nearly unimaginable to imagine abandoning it." The demise of Pan American World Airways, better known as Pan Am, is a prime illustration of this occurrence. With hundreds of staff, Pan Am was a well-known airline and hotel. Airline policies were deregulated as the business changed, and Pan Am's financial situation deteriorated. To stay solvent, the corporation had to make cuts over time. The firm decided that maintaining their image as an airline was more essential than having a successful firm, so they eliminated all of the assets that were actually generating the most cash in order to preserve their image as Pan Am.

Chapter 5

Formal Models for Group Decision Making and Negotiation

CONTENTS

5.1. INTRODUCTION

The fact that individuals can be able to reach an informed decision collective is considered as an important aspect in civilization, which is very important to individuals in a particular nation and an organization at large. It is normally recommended that individuals use a formal procedure in order to make better collective decisions. As a matter of fact, a collective decision making can further e improved through a process of a systematic approach. If the collective is in contact with a good group contact, then this can be very helpful in making the right decisions (Caemmerer et al., 2021). The professional field whose main aim is to understand, develop and implement the ideas that are useful in a collective group to improve their process of decision-making is what is known as group decision and negotiation (GDN). This field involves the development and study of various factors and methods that can assist the groups or the individuals that are within the group as they try to work together towards attaining collective decisions. In order to ensure that there is the success that is needed in the organization, individuals need to be included in the process of decision-making. Ideally, making decisions in a group has proven to be quite hard, costly and time consuming. As such, it is required of the involved members to find out strategies that will ensure that individuals are able to make collective decisions in harmony without having to go against each other.

Figure 5.1. Individuals in a group making decisions collectively.

Source: Reference for business.

The main aim that GDN plans is to ensure that the individuals in the group are provided with a number of procedures that will be very useful in improving and further optimizing the collective decisions that are made by the group. The spectrum within GDN is very wide such that it caters for the tactical, psychological, strategic and the social issues that are normally faced by individuals within the organization and the organization at large. They are considered as very important aspects especially in the process in which they need to come up with collective decisions (Wu et al., 2012). Ideally, the field consists of all the techniques, procedures, and a support system that has been designed for the sole purpose of ensuring that the negotiation process becomes a success and that ensure that the decision makers cooperate in making decisions dealing with even the complex issues in a more efficient and effective manner. The reason as to why GDN is considered as a very good approach when going about the collective decision making by individuals is due to the fact that it is formed from a combination of different fields including, political economy, systems engineering, information systems, operations research, computer science, psychology, social psychology, social choice theory, game theory, system dynamics among various other fields. All around the world, researchers are looking at the same field showing how much interest this subject matter has attained all around the world. As a matter of fact, this field of study is very crucial in promoting the field of research as it contributes to the same literature.

In most instances, decisions that are involving he important sectors in a particular country tends to take into consideration the use of negotiations given the fact that, group decision making is the way to go with such issues (Weller et al., 2007). Taking for example in the United Nations, which is a worldwide body. This body acts as a center of negotiation given the fact that it aims to achieve and maintain international peace. Apart from that, it is tasked with ensuring the security of all individuals in the world, ensure that there have been friendly relations fostered between countries and further ensure that there is international harmony and cooperation. However, the negotiations tend to involve not only the national governments but also the regional ones, non-governmental organizations that are the cornerstone of developments in most countries, among other fields.

Figure 5.2. The United Nations representatives having a meeting.

Source: The United Nations.

In addition, the governmental organizations and the corporate tend to always negotiate in order to forge certain group decisions for the sole purpose of ensuring that they can be able to develop policies and come up with the best strategies so as to ensure the success of a particular strategy. When dealing with decision-making, negotiations tend to be very useful especially at individual levels and have been seen to work miracles in the international organizations and corporate ones. In the industrial period, everything is being done to ensure that there is ease in everything that is being done.

Figure 5.3. The e-negotiation systems.

Source: qinyu2015-WordPress.com.

In fact, negotiations have not been left behind given the fact that, there have been electronic communication system that have been developed including the e-negotiation systems, sophisticated computerized group support systems (GSS). Apart from this, messaging systems have also been developed which have helped the process of decision making faster and easier especially for individuals that are in no capacity to meet in person.

In the process of making decisions collectively and introducing negotiation in the process, what is normally seen is that there is unity and diversity. This helps in promoting international development as individuals work together to attain a particular goal. In fact, most scholars find it appropriate to distinguish between negotiation and group decision making. Well, looking at the two, negotiation aims at ensuring that there is agreement within the organization especially when there are some forms of misunderstandings.

Collective decision making on the other hand is a vital factor that is considered in the process of attaining certain organizational objectives (Van Ginkel & Van Knippenberg, 2009). Scholars claim that, group decision is normally involving a decision problem that is seen to be shared by two parties and in which all the parties involved need to make a choice concerning the particular issue and they need to be able to take responsibilities on whatever choice that is made. For the case of negotiation, the parties involved are required to make a choice on a particular aspect or in the process may make no decision at all. In general, one can easily say that with the case of a group decision, it is considered as a generic process while negotiation considered as a specific process.

What distinguishes the two is the fact that with the negotiation process, there are normally possibilities that a decision might not be made in the end unlike with group decision making. It is not only the outcomes that show the differences but also the existence of common ground, the number of individuals participating in the process and the types and modes of participation. In meetings, technology has allowed for individuals especially managers to have access to devices that allow them to communicate with each other and their subordinates. It involves all forms of communication including those that cannot be heard or even seen by individuals that are within the group. In the past decades, it has been seen that there have been developments in the communication systems that have allowed for group meetings, decision-making and negotiations among groups. The mechanism is a group support mechanism, which has been designed to ensure that there is better running of the groups by use of personal digital assistants otherwise known as PDAs.

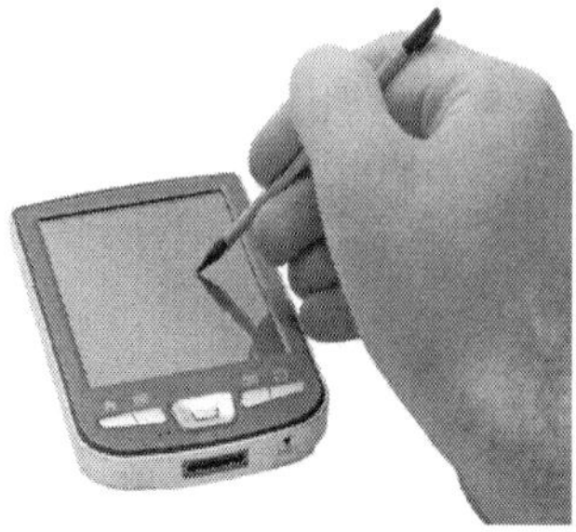

Figure 5.4. A personal digital assistance.

Source: Impermanence.

Various modeling approaches can be very crucial in influencing the hard and complex decisions that need to be made within the group. Hard decisions are described as those decisions that can have dire consequences if not approached carefully. With modeling, a group is well within their capacity to go about the same especially in the process of forming their problem decisions. The scope of the matter is that, with careful consideration of the decisions that individuals make, then individuals can be able to go about the process with better approach to a particular problem. In GDN, what needs to be taken into careful consideration is the fact that, emotion plays a vital role though has been given less consideration. Under emotions, there are certain fields such as ethno-methodology, neurology and linguistics go far away to help understand the process of face-to-face negotiations as in the process, and one can be able to understand the language of an individual and their feelings towards a particular aspect. Through this, one can be able to fully understand how a person feels about a particular issue and how they react to particular aspects in life. Apart from the fact that emotions are crucial with the case of face-to-face negotiations, they also go a long way in using computerized technology in negotiations and group decision-making.

In the process of decision-making, an underlying aspect involves that of the choice of the individuals that are involved in the decision making process. The game theory of non-cooperative and cooperative is given a level of consideration. To ensure that there are fair divisions, the choices that individuals made are analyzed in a game theoretical manner so as to ensure that the decisions of all the parties involved are integrated into a collective choice. For over two decades, there have been the existence of Group Support Systems and have been in use as a way of facilitating negotiations so as to ensure that the process id efficient and effective (Tang & Liao,

2021). Through the process, it will ensure that the decision making process ensures that there is increased group productivity, better collaborative work between the colleagues, anonymity among individuals and further form a basis for visual interactive modeling. In the current times, there has been increased use of the same as they have helped in promoting the negotiation process so as to ensure that the organization moves towards a more strategic direction that will ensure the attainment of the organization's objectives. Initially when GSS was being developed, it was done by scholars that had the interest in the field of information and communication technologies.

Figure 5.5. GSS is a group support system.

Source: Covisian.

One support system includes the meeting works. This system uses a modeling approach that works with a number of criteria for decision making which in most cases are seen to be conflicting. The working of this approach is that it combines a modeling approach with a good record keeping, attention, and consensus generating measures. When dealing with very important decisions, the multi-criteria method is normally used where the decision makers tend to make use of different alternatives. With the use of multi-criteria, there is the chance that decisions recommendations will be generated which then offers support, which helps ensure that the decisions made are of quality, ensures that there is improvement in the communication among the members and theta the implementation process becomes simplified. A researcher once wrote of a use of a GDSS known as Group Explorer (Sorkin et al., 2001). This system was useful in promoting what is known as soft negotiation where the process is meant to be qualitative and more importantly aimed at improving the negotiation process. With soft negotiations, the main aim is to ensure that there is a positive shift with the social and psychological understanding of all the actors that are involved in the negotiation process. The main reason individuals are involved in the decision making process is so as to ensure that they can be able to reach an agreement and change the thinking of the members involved.

The GSS have been very helpful in ensuring that cooperation's are able to reach some difficult decisions and help in informing GDN. Research is done to fully comprehend the effects of the GSS in the process of converging the ideas of individuals as it translates them to knowledge that can be useful in the decision making process.

5.2. ECONOMIC MODELS OF BARGAINING

Since the dawn of time, bargaining has been an aspect that has been of interest to the economists not only because of the fact that in each and every transaction negotiation is considered as an important component but because of the fact that bargaining is considered as the opposite of perfect competition when thinking about markets. Individuals that are involved in the bargaining process may be as low as two people to as many as an uncountable number may. The parties that are normally involved normally try to reach an agreement in which case it may leave both individuals better off or in other circumstances, they may not get to reach an agreement at all (Schulz-Hardt et al., 2002). Since the 19th century, it was claimed that it is important to model the individuals that are involved in the trading process by how they are initially endowed.

Figure 5.6. Bargaining is a common aspect in the market.

Source: Stuff Expat Aid Workers Like.

Indifference curves are also used in modelling and are often considered to be adequate in determining the effective equilibrium especially in a market place. However, they would not be efficient in determining the outcome of the bargaining process however, if a contract curve is used, there is a chance that the outcome of the bargaining process can be determined.

Game theory was developed in the past and with its dawn upon time, there were attempts made by economics to determine the models of bargaining that would help in predicting the various outcomes. John Nash in 1950 came up with two influential approaches, which would help in predicting the outcome of bargaining. The outcome would be based on the bargainer's preferences given due to the expected utility. He considered a simple model of strategic choices that faced the individuals that are bargaining. His approach of analyzing bargaining by use of complementary models focused on the outcomes on the spirit of cooperative game theory. He told of a more detailed strategic model in the spirit of non-cooperative game theory, which has influence on the game theory. How the work of Nash has taken involves the connection between the bargaining theory and that of competitive equilibrium markets (Song, 2009). This is done by the examination of markets models where the agents meet and have the negotiations transactions. The option for the agents is returning to the market in the case of disagreements. There are however, shortcomings that are seen to come with the classical game theories of classical models that help in explaining some of the disagreements that exist due to the fact that there exists mistakes that take place in the negotiation process by the bargainers. One way is the incomplete information models, which can be very helpful in trying to remedy some of the mistakes that accrue from the actors during the bargaining process.

It shows how positive probability of disagreements may be inescapable at equilibrium. This is especially when other actors are unaware how the other agents value the transactions. Different actors tend to vale transactions differently and thus it is important to make sure that all the rest understand how they feel about transactions. What is known by most individuals is that whenever the actors are able to reach an agreement in the time when there are gains from trade, they should understand that they are not making as much as they should (Schulze & Newell, 2016). The logic behind this is that if individuals are seeing that they are gaining at the time when the entire nation is gaining from trade then it means that in normal circumstances, the trader does not get to gain as much as they should during other periods. Even though bargaining is considered as a normal thing, the fact of the matter is that, there are many transactions associated with the same. Taking for instance, during the bargaining process, individuals tend to consume a lot of time and loses much. On the other hand, the trader tends to lose a lot of money given the fact that they do not get to have the kinds of profits that they were expecting.

Figure 5.7. Trader and consumer negotiating about a product.

Source: Agate Travel.

There are many game theoretical models of bargaining that depend on information that is normally difficult to observe in the field. Such information that tends to be hidden in the market includes the bargainers' detailed information and the preference of individuals over time. There has however, been growth in the economics field and as such, economists have come up with laboratory testing that has helped testing the predictions of some of these theories. There are those quantitative predictions that have received support from the models that are currently in existence that have however, performed quite poorly as predictors. In the recent time, the lack of predictions has led to new and different forms of theories that are in line with coordination and learning of the adaptive behavior of individuals.

The game theory is considered to be a branch of game theory that deals with some of the problems that accrue due to the process of bargaining. In this case, the parties tend to bargain over the division of goods. The solution to the bargaining problem means that individuals need to determine how such divisions are going to take place. There are the example of the simple and the more complex application of the bargaining theory whereby it is used with regards to the field of politics, sociology and economics. Essentially, one may also follow an axiomatic technique to bargaining problems, that is, postulate a few axioms regarding ability solution, after which inspect its lifestyles and homes on account of the followed axioms. One can also follow a unique technique to bargaining problems, known as the dynamic or strategic technique, which entails the illustration of a good deal as a non-cooperative sport and the research of answers from a few of the equilibria of the sport.

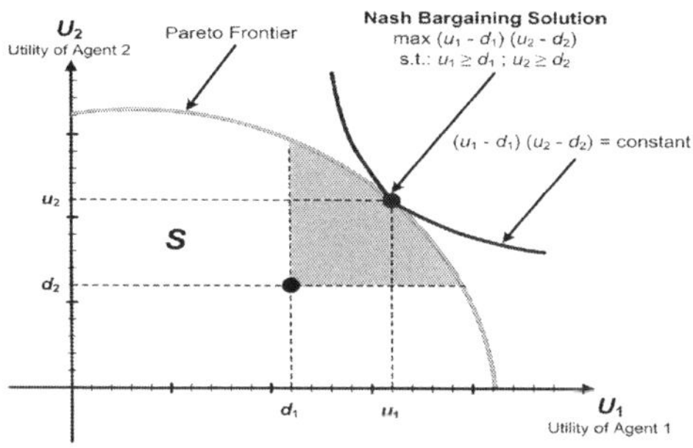

Figure 5.8. Nash's bargaining solution. The model was established in order to deal with problems that are encountered during the bargaining process.

Source: ResearchGate.

In defining bargaining, there are those that understand the definition in a different manner. When two individuals are involved in a bargaining scenario and have the possibility to collaborate for mutual advantage in multiple way then it is considered as the bargaining process. Under any such definition, almost all-human interplay may be visible as bargaining of one aspect or another. To say something significant at the subject, it is essential to slender the scope of the inquiry. We comply with Nash in assuming that the two people are surprisingly rational, every can as it should be, evaluate his or her dreams for numerous things, they are considered to be the same in bargaining skill (Sari, 2008).

In addition, we anticipate that the system with the aid of which settlement is reached is each uncomplicated and unambiguous. This lets in the bargaining trouble to be modeled and analyzed as a non-cooperative game. The goal of the sort of non-cooperative concept of bargaining is to discover theoretical predictions of what settlement, if any, can be reached via way of the bargainers. One hopes thereby to provide an explanation for the way wherein the bargaining outcome relies upon at the parameters of the bargaining trouble and to shed mild at the fact that the number of the verbal ideas which are used while bargaining is mentioned in everyday language. However, the concept has most effective peripheral relevance to such questions as: What is a simply settlement? How might an affordable arbiter settle a dispute? What is the socially most efficient deal? Nor is the concept in all likelihood to be of greater than heritage hobby to folks who write manuals on sensible bargaining techniques. Such questions as "How can I enhance my bargaining skills?" and "How do bargainers decide what is considered to as jointly feasible?" are mental troubles that the narrowing of the scope of the inquiry which is designed to exclude.

Figure 5.9. Illustration of successful bargaining.

Source: Medium.

Cooperative bargaining principle differs specifically in that the bargaining process is left unmodeled. Cooperative principle consequently has to perform from a poorer informational base and as a result, its fundamental assumptions are always summary in character. As a consequence, cooperative answer principles are often hard to evaluate. Sometimes they will have multiple feasible interpretation, and this may result in confusion if distinct interpretations which are not truly separated. In this aspect, we observe Nash in adopting an interpretation of cooperative answer principles that attributes the equal simple goals to cooperative as to non-cooperative principle. With these facts, ideally we can say, in recognition to the interpretations wherein, to cite Nash (1953), to the bargaining problem, they are considered as complementary where each and every concept facilitates and justifies in order making it clear to other actors. In the manner especially with regards to what we should say on cooperative answer principles isn't applicable to interpretations that are looking to cope with questions like the ones given above which can be mainly excluded from the study. It should be noted that one should no longer see cooperative and non-cooperative principle as rivals. As a matter of fact, the issue is that there may actually be an experience wherein cooperative principle is "too general;" but similarly there may be an experience wherein non-cooperative principle is "too special." Only hardly ever will the very concrete methods studied in non-cooperative principle be located in practice. According to Nash, his claims are that "one cannot represent all possible bargaining devices as moves in the non-cooperative game. The negotiation process must be formalized and restricted, but in such a way that each participant is still able to utilize all the essential strengths of his position."

Even if one makes excellent judgments in modeling the necessities of thc bargaining process, the result can be too bulky to function a device in applications, wherein what is required is a fairly easy mapping from the parameters of the hassle to an answer outcome (Saaty & Peniwati, 2013). This is what cooperative idea supplies. Nevertheless, which of the numerous cooperative answer standards is suitable in a given context, and the way needed for it to be applied? For solutions to such questions, one may appearance to non-cooperative idea for guidance. It is on this experience that we see cooperative and non-cooperative idea as complementary.

5.3. GAME THEORETICAL MODELS IN FORMAL MODEL OF DECISION MAKING

Past studies have revealed that most organizations both private and public use game theory in making rational decisions in their day-to-day relationships interactions. Game theory has proved to be better in that it places particular emphasis on market profit standardization in the today's market competition, unlike the traditional economic management, which only focuses on a single enterprise of profit maximizing given the recourse constraints. The traditional economic management does not put into practice the competitors that an enterprise faces in a given market. Evidently, game theory is more applicable in the today's business as it is faced with many market competitors as the market becomes more globalized. The strategies used by different leaders or business owners in attaining their equilibrium conditions are the kinds tat equalize profits in decision making processes. The competition that exists between different companies within a market is what encompasses the different strategies used in game theory. Every competitor in the game makes a decision in a competitive decision making game process to maximize his or her own profit. The firms carefully analyses the competitors strategies so that the firm can come up with the ultimate decision on the strategy to pick.

The game theory provides guidance in enterprises in coming up with competitive strategies in their decision making processes. The subjects of the decision-making are the competition participants in the game. In the game, each participant analyses the strategies that are likely to be taken by their fellow participants, the consequences for the strategies chosen and predict their next move in creating their defense in order to identify their best strategy. This then allows the firms to be assured of making maximum profits given their constrained resources and the choices of strategies made by the other enterprises. The game theory is of a competitive model.

The world of business is constantly changing thus policy makers in the organizations and or institutions need to make imperative prompt decisions constantly so as keep up with the competition. The availability of relevant information in the process making decisions to the benefit of the company makes it easy for decision makers in an organization. With incomplete information, the decision-making process is very dynamic involving the competition decision-making partners. One of the games model used is for example the prisoner's dilemma model. The model creates an understanding of the business in making decisions in the business or organization among the partner's relationships collectively (Saka et al., 2008). The prisoner's dilemma model is also known as the classic game .it represents the situations found in a law and order circumstance. The episode is of two suspected to be criminals for a crime they committed together. They are put in separate rooms by the police officers and they are told to confess in exchange for a lighter sense for the suspect who confesses first while if the other does not confess while they do confess then they go free. The sentence is even heavier if the two of them do not confess .the playoffs for the prisoners dilemma is represented by the number of years in prison. The said criminals who are rational would then seek for an option that would maximize their utility thus chose the best for only oneself without considering the other party. Rationally it would be expected that both the prisoners confess even though cooperating with each other would lead to a lesser prison sentence given that the suspects in the situation is always at a better chance confessing. This is because if no one confesses they would be given more time in prison while if one confesses then he or she goes free while the other faces more years in prison. Additionally, both prisoners have been given a dominant strategy thus they have no rational circumstance or excuse that would force them to change their decision. In a business situation, the prisoner's dilemma model put in place would lead to a situation of Nash equilibrium.

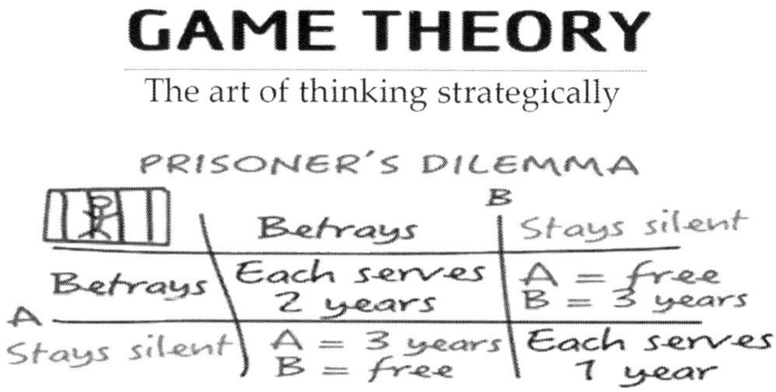

Figure 5.10. Prisoners dilemma in game theory. The model has been used in the process of making decisions in many sectors since time immemorial and has been useful in enhancing cooperation among the parties involved.

Source: StudiousGuy.

The prisoner's dilemma model in game theory has been used for time immemorial for making decisions in many sectors. For example, the situation is used as to enhance cooperation on arms among individuals in a given area in controlling pollution to the environment. Although the pay offs of the game change occasionally because the parties involved will not always be faced with dominate situations. The main limitations of the game theory models in decision-making processes are inclined to the perceived and assumed rules in the game. The game always assumes that people or the parties involved in making the decision on the better strategy to choose are rational and intelligent. This is however, not the case as human beings are limited by circumstances such as the bonded will power that would make them not be rational at all times. The limited information may have one to speculate about the unforced circumstances, which would make not be rational in choosing a good strategy.

The other limitation in the game theory is that it assumes that all parties measure pay offs the same way. For example, it assumes that a one-year prison to a mother who has just given birth to baby is the same to a 40-aged woman with no family. This is thus not applicable to the two parties, as the mother would choose a strategy so that she gets to raise her child at her home while the other might not care, as much, after all it would be one year. The game theory also assumes that there is no communication between the parties while as in the real circumstances the parties involved in the same completion often collude and form relationships for the benefit of their businesses in especially protecting their stay in the market. Lastly, the game theory only consider a situation with limited number of participants normally two or three while in the real world of business the parties involved are very many. Thus, it brings a challenge in using the game theory models as the basis for decision making in organizations and or institutions (Ambrus et al., 2009).

The uses of game theory in organizations in making decisions can be both independent and interdependent. The mainly concerned attribute is whether the outcome would depend on two or more players. This would be due to the nature of the situation where no single decision maker has full control of the issues surrounding a decision that has to be made. Moreover, the relationships that exist within an organization or any social situation all fall within the ambit of the game theory situation every day.

The use of classical models in decision-making processes is used in the situations that do not require collaboration of efforts or the interdependent decision-making. During the interdependent decisions making processes the decision makers make decisions based on the influence of others. This is however, different from the use of game theory models where the model is constructed around specific choices of strategy to be appalled where the outcomes and consequences are clearly known.

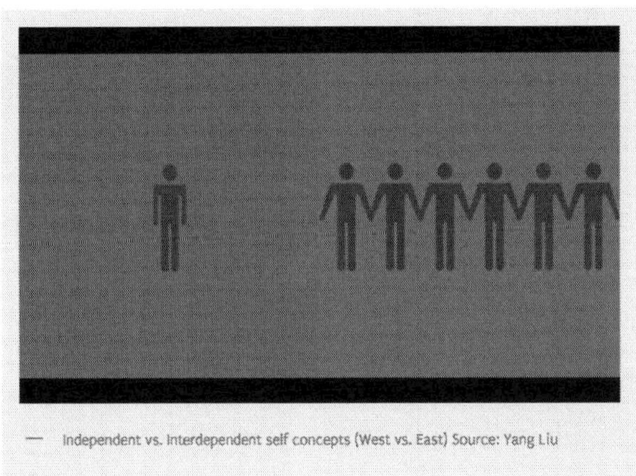

Figure 5.11. The concept of independent vs. interdependent decision making.

Source: The Fearless Heart.

For instance, in game theory model, a situation the considers two cyclist cycling in opposite direction and about to hit on one other head on collusion, it is in the interest of the two cyclists to avoid any form of collusion as the collusion will hurt them both severely. The cyclists are however, faced with only three strategies, which are to move to the right, to cycle towards the left or to collude in the case that they choose to maintain the direction (Bazerman & Moore, 2012). Thereby given the situation, as the players do not know the strategy that the other party is likely to take there is a quick need to the decision to first collude to make the best decision that would favor both of them. The players in the game need to quickly signal their intentions to each other. However, the interests of the players may be opposed are the players doing not come in to an agreement. In a business, setting two companies involved with making the same product would have to consider whether or not to reduce prices without knowing the move of the other company. If the turnover would increase for one company due to it choosing to engage a strategy it would lead to a loss or gains to the other competitor. Thus is he or she reduces the price and he or she increases her customers it would mean that the other company would lose some of its customers to this other company. This in game theory can be termed as a zero sum game where the game is non-cooperative. This is because the players do not conceal their intentions. Many companies would make a decision like such so as to push others out of the market. This would help them have a large market share as compared to their competitors.

Another category of game theory in decision-making processes involves a situation where the decision of the parties involved is partly opposed and partly coincident. The situation brings forth the idea of mixed motive game. This may lead to the parties sharing in a common language, which may be seemingly technical.

In game theory, a pure strategy may be in which the player has all the information on the game in response to any circumstance of the game. In the situation if a player would select a strategy without prior knowledge of the other parties' intentions or strategy the players' pure strategy are equivalent to purely his choices alone. While if the player has selected a strategy subsequent to the other player's strategy with the knowledge of what they are to choose as their strategy then they are termed to are more than in other choices involved. As in mixed motive game, the party has two choices that would be to either concede or refuse to the agreed situation. One party would have to make its decision after the other party has chosen a motive so that their pure strategy is in line with the strategy that the other party had chosen. Although the choices that exist in a mixed game theory involve about four choices to be involved in the two choices, to choose one choice or the other choice and lastly to not to choose any choice at all one party must choose head of the other. In companies, the decision making processes that relies on this game theory model in making decision often make informed decisions as they are aware of the consequences and the move of their partners. It is very likely that a company would consider all its gains and losses of a certain kind of decision and thus be able to make an informed good decision.

Consequently, in a game of complete information the players involved knows their parties moves and the pay offs to them and their partners. Additionally, the players known are that their partners have complete information of themselves. This would be compared to a game of chess. On the other hand, a game of imperfect information is in sequential thus the players do not have knowledge on what their partners are going to choose as their strategy (Risco & Duffy, 2011). In decision-making processes if the policy makers or the decision makers have complete information on their competitor next move or already moved move, they are likely to make adjustments to benefit from the knowledge that they have unlike when the decision makers in an organization do not have the knowledge. In decision making processes the persons involved in the decision-making or the management they ate often advised to search for as more information as possible so that this would be reflected in choosing the best strategy. The decision making process though a game is thus highly dependent on the available information. The available information gives room for prediction of the limitations and challenges that would be associated with choosing a specific strategy and thus lead to choosing of the optimal strategy.

5.4. AGGREGATION MODELS OF GROUP DECISION MAKING

Various aggregation methods can be used to make decisions in solving problems. In a management, process decisions have to be made when dealing with world problems. The "multiple criteria decision making (MCDM)" is one of the knowledge areas that is fast growing and has been used widely in many disciplines. Many researchers have used the MCDM criteria to make decisions as it is a branch of operation research. The MCDM procedure can be used to solve both qualitative and quantitative criteria. MCDM problems can be divided into two major subtopics, i.e., continuous and discrete. Out of the two, there are two major categories, i.e., the Multi objective decision making and multi attribute decision-making. In the multi objective decision making it is made in a continuous manner as its decisions involve a large number of alternatives whereas the multi attribute decision making has a limited or reduced number of alternative hence it becomes generally discrete. MCDM helps the individual making the decisions choose the alternative that is best based on the alternatives provided by the criteria.

There are four steps that are taken to make it more efficient and the decisions to be more rational. The first step involves structuring the decision process, choosing the alternatives and formulation of criteria. The second step involves comparisons among the different criteria and the weight of each criterion. The third step involves application of judgment to the different criteria and evaluating them. The last and final step is calculating the best criteria before making the final decision. They are then ranked and the best alternative decision is chosen. To some individuals the MCDM can be divided into two phases, i.e., the first phase is referred to as the rating phase and this involves aggregating the values for each criterion for each alternative is then made. The second phase is ranking of the alternatives using the global consensus degree of satisfaction.

In every decision that has to be made the weights of each alternative is very important as it is used to measure in totality the preference of the alternative that will be best. It can then be seen that aggregation is the prerequisite for the decisions that have to be made. Aggregation can then be defined as the process of combining several scores by using an aggregation score so as to come up with a global score and make the best available decision. According to Detyniecki, he defined aggregation as "a mathematical object that has the function of reducing a set of numbers to a unique representative value." Xu defines aggregation as process that involves gathering of information for multiple uses. Omar and Fayek defined aggregation in terms of decision making as a process that involves combining the values of a set of attributes into one value that will represent the entire attributes that were first described. It can then be seen that aggregation is very vital.

In instances where there are several decision makers, it is assumed that there are a definable number of alternatives as well as experts. Each expert is known to have their own opinion and ideas. In this instance then the values are not represented in numerical values but in terms of linguistic terms.

There are several aggregation methods that have been put in place and are being used so as to choose the most preferred and desirable solution.

Aggregation methods are many and choosing the best method is hard. The aggregation methods can be divided into basic operators, which include average or arithmetic mean, harmonic mean and geometric mean. The other is classical operators, which include, power aggregation operator, linguistic aggregation operator, prioritized average operator, hybrid aggregation operator, Bonferroni mean (BM), and fuzzy operator.

5.4.1. Basic Operators

Geometric mean operator is a traditional mean operator, which proposes that information is aggregated on a given ratio on a measurement scale in MCDM models. There are authors such as Wu who defined geometric aggregation that were families as being trapezoidal. Many authors defined their own geometric aggregate methods.

The arithmetic mean operator: Involves using scoring techniques, which may include weighted aggregation operator which bases on multi attribute theory. The most common aggregation operator is the order weighted averaging (OGA) operator. The OGA operator adds a parameter between the maximum and the minimum, the arithmetic average and median which is original to Yager. This operator has been widely used because it is able to show linguistic models in form of aggregation. It has been used in various disciplines such as data mining, decision-making, image processing, engineering, neural networks and expert systems. In some instances, the information may not be precise and they can also be vague and this can lead to it becoming hard to analyze with the crisp numbers. This then leads to the use of another approach that is able to use the uncertainty, which leads to the use of fuzzy numbers. The use of fuzzy numbers then it is able to analyze the real situation and provide a fuzzy value.

Intuitionistic Fuzzy Ordered Weighted Averaging (IFOWA) and Continuous Ordered Weighted Averaging (C-OWA) have been combined and used to diminish the fuzziness in order to bring preciseness in the making of a decision.

The harmonic mean operator. Harmonic mean can be seen to be opposite of the arithmetic mean of reciprocal, which is traditionalistic average, which can be used to provide an aggregation, which lies between the maximum and minimum operators. It has been a widely used tool to accumulate the central tendency data, which in most instances is in numerical values. Most researchers view the harmonic mean as a method of solving aggregation in the decision-making challenges.

Figure 5.12. Carlo Emilio Bonferroni; he developed the Bonferroni operator.

Source: https://www.slideshare.net/scottstgeorge/contemporary-problems-in-ancient-climates.

Bonferroni mean (BM). Bonferroni first introduced it. It is regarded as an extension of the arithmetic mean. It is different from the other means, i.e., arithmetic, harmonic or geometric because the BM mean shows the interdependent of individual criterion as compared to the classic means whose individual criterion is independent. The mean as defined by Bonferroni mean operator is the most suitable as it aggregates crisp data can seize the interrelationships that have been expressed among the different criteria. Since its introduction, it has received attention from various researchers and several practitioners. Some scientist such as Xia combined the Bonferroni mean and geometric mean and came up with Bonferroni geometric mean, which can show the interrelationship between aggregated arguments.

Power aggregation operators. First introduced as power average (PA) operator that in turn uses a non-linear weighted average aggregation tool and a power ordered weighted average (POWA) aggregator that provides the aggregation tools which then allows the arguments to exactly support each other in the process of aggregation (Reynolds et al., 2009). The weighed vectors in PA and POWA will depend on the arguments that have been inputted and this will allow arguments that are being aggregated to reinforce and support each other. In comparison to the other aggregation operators PA and POWA, bring information together regarding the relationship between the values that are being combined. In the recent years, these operators have been receiving attention in the field of literature.

Fuzzy integral. There are several types of fuzzy integrals (FI). The most common and well-known fuzzy integrals are: Choquet and Sugeno integral.

- *Choquet integral*. This was first introduced by Choquet. It is then defined as a sub additive to integrate functions or sometimes a supper additive. It is a way that has been seen to be very useful when measuring the utility that is expected of an event that may be uncertain. Many authors have proposed the use of the Choquet integral as it extends the OWA operator as it takes into consideration how the various criteria are interacting. It can also be applied in the fuzzy environments.
- *The Sugeno interval*. It is one of the fuzzy integrals and was introduced by M. Sugeno in 1974. This integral proposes that it could cypher an average value with the use of a fuzzy measure of some function. The Sugeno integral only uses functions that are weighted maximum or minimum.

Hybrid aggregation operators. It has been proposed for use by several authors. It is very important to contemplate more than one aggregation operator, as this will allow a wide range of fuzzy aggregation operators to be used in a bigger range to solve problems and come up with the best decisions. This led many authors to come up with combined aggregate operators so as to come up with ways to select the best decision.

Prioritized average. This type of aggregator has a lot of interest from scholars. In situation that are practical in nature individual tasked with decision making have to consider different criteria priorities. Based on this Yager then developed prioritized average operators where the criteria priority is modeled from the weights that are associated with the criteria depending on the higher priority criteria being satisfied. This type of operator has several advantages over the other operators, e.g., it does not require that weight vectors are provided and when this operator is being used, the only thing that is necessary is to understand the priority given to the various criteria.

Linguistic aggregation operator. Decision making by humans is known to be too complex or its definition is too weak hence, it cannot be represented by a numerical value. The available information has always been seen to be vague or not precise and therefore makes it hard to analyze in terms of numerical values. Such a situation can then be solved by using a qualitative approach, which is the linguistic variable to aggregate the information that has been fused. The linguistic aggregation operators are only offered in situations where information provided cannot be assessed in numerical values.

The most common method that has been used is the Choquet integral, closely followed by linguistic aggregation operator then the arithmetic average operator with the Sugeno integral being the least used among the different methods. Among the aggregation operators, the aggregate mean has received a lot of attention from many scholars and since its introduction by Yager (1988), the OWA provided parameters for the arithmetic mean. Depending on various factors, many aggregation operators have been used in decision-making (Reinalda & Verbeek, 2004).

Choquet is the most common currently because this method can represent different interactions among criteria, i.e., interaction ranging from negative to positive. This method can also in future be improved or in some instances extended to take into account a combination that has been weighted of both knowledge and data.

From the methods above it can be noted that the methods are, independent from one another but in the real sense the criteria of all the problems it can be seen that they are interdependent and are interactive. In most instances, there is some kind of interaction among the preference of the individuals making decisions. In order to understand how different human beings come up with their decisions then it would be natural to apply the fuzzy measures, as it does not assume, there is additivity and independence in the criteria of decision-making.

In order to tackle the said problem, the Choquet integral is a tool that is powerful enough to solve the MCDM problems. In the model, the criteria can be interdependent; to define a weight a fuzzy measure is used on the combination of the criteria this then makes it possible to come up with a model that is able to show the interaction among the different criteria. The Choquet integral can also provide an accurate users' rating based on the correlated inputs and it can also be a very important tool to be used in measuring the utility that is expected in an environment that is uncertain.

5.5. TACTICS MODELS OF DECISION-MAKING AND NEGOTIATION

A group that is effective is characterized by the use each and every member of the group. This may include the use of members' resources, efficient use of time that has been awarded. When it comes to quotes that are always inspirational working together or bringing people together for a common goal is very common, quotes such "no man is an island," "there is wisdom in crowds," etc. It can be noticed that many of the achievements that have been made by man was not made by a single person but by a group of people who pulled together for a common goal, though working, as a group is not always easy but the results are always the best.

Figure 5.13. J. Richard Hackman: A psychologist from Harvard university and he put forward five conditions for groups to prosper.

Source: Scrum Inc.

Putting together a group of people is not as easy as expected. It is not as simple as just choosing individuals and putting them in a room an expect them to come up with a solution. There are several considerations to be taken into account so as to come up with an effective group. As set by J. Richard Hackman who is a professor of social and organizational psychology at Harvard university put forward that there are five conditions that are needed in order for group to become effective; the conditions include:

- The team has to be 'real.' In simple terms, Hack was referring to the group having a specified leader, a purpose and a goal that is unchanging. The members should be the same always. When a team is real with each other they get to bond, know, and understand each other. This will then instill confidence to the members and bring trust among members (Rassin et al., 2008). This will ring a sense of accountability to the members of the group so that everyone understands that they play a role in the decisions that will be made by the group.
- The team needs to have an enabling structure. Just as everything in life requires direction then as team they need to be structured

so as to be successful. The direction will then empower every member of the group to do their work to their best. When everyone works to achieve their goal as set in the group then the time taken can be less and the group becomes effective in coming up with the best decision.

- The team needs to have a compelling direction. As every teams puts their effort to their work but do not have direction then the work being done becomes pointless. This then means that every member of the group should work towards a particular goal and should all be actively pushing each other to achieve the set goal.
- The team needs a supportive organization. A team that has been set up to make decision is always under an organization or a company. This means that the organization within which a team or group has been set up needs to be in support of the teams goals or objective. This may include infrastructural or financial support to the order for them to work hard to achieve them. When teams are denied the support then they will feel frustrated, they will not be effective, and this may weaken their motivation to achieve their goals.
- The team needs expert coaching. This simply means that the individuals that are part of the team need to understand that they are going to work with others. It is known that individuals like working individually with their own set goals hence members in a group need to understand that they'll be working together to achieve a similar goal and the input of everyone is vital.

The techniques and/or tactics that are used can provide a group of individuals a structure that they need to put aside their egos and focus to come up with the best decision for the company or organization. The tactic that will be used will depend on the dynamics of the team. What the team is trying to achieve will also determine the tactic that can be used. In most instances, it is advised that a team tries all the tactics until they find the best fit for their team. The tactics do not determine the outcome or decision to be made but rather these tactics act as the mechanics that help the team to come up with the best decisions. As they go through all the tactics it allows the members of the group to go through a problem from different angles and find the best that works for them.

The following four tactics that are mostly used in order to come up with the best decisions.

1. ***The Delphi method.*** It is also referred to as 'iterative convergence.' This is a tactic that will depend on the expertise of a group to assist in coming up with decisions that are complex to the company or organization. This tactic involves collecting, organizing, then reviewing and revising the opinions of a group of individuals that have not actually met. The members are not physically present at the same venue. The ideas and opinions are provided through the use of questionnaires.

   The steps involved in the Delphi technique are; to solicit input from members. This involves the solicitor to solicit for information from the members of the team. Through the use of email, mail and/or fax. The members after receiving the mail then brainstorm through the question and then give their opinions and ideas on the survey. Upon completion of the survey, the members send back the filled questionnaires back to the coordinator via the way they received the questionnaire. The input from members is then summarized. The coordinator after receiving the opinions and ideas from the team members, he/she then compiles the ideas and it is done in such a way that the anonymity of members is always maintained. After summarizing, the coordinator then sends the compiled ideas to the members of the group (Pérez et al., 2010). The members will then revise, refine and prioritize the inputs that had been given earlier. This will also involve the members giving the ideas that have more strength than the others have and give the weaknesses. When prioritizing they state why and give reasons for each idea and they can identify new ideas. When they have finished they send their reviewed work back to the coordinator. The coordinator compiles the ideas again and step three to five are repeated until the members do not have anything to add. If the members come up with a consensus and agree on a decision, then the exercise is finished but if there is, no consensus then the members is asked to rank or rate the decisions. After which the best-ranked or best-rated decision then becomes the decision of the group.

   As this method requires members to work independently this method promotes accountability from each member, equalize participation from each member, decrease social loafing, it also eliminates the bias effect by the dominant members, it also prevents impaired communication which arises from unproductive disagreements, avoids logistical problems arising from trying to assemble people in the same physical area, it also provides for anonymity of members and this reduces pressure to conform and also decrease evaluation apprehension.

Research shows that members who have used the Delphi technique appear to be more satisfied. Although it appears to get results this tactic tends to use a lot of time and with the use of mail or fax it reduces interaction among members.

2. ***Stepladder tactic.*** The stepladder tactic is a technique that staggers members from entering a group. It facilitates both evaluation and generation of ideas similar to Delphi and nominal technique. The stepladder tactic allows members of the group to come up with the final decision as a group. The stepladder tactic starts with only two members where the two members discuss the problem and present the ideas to each other, when the two members feel they have understood each other a third member is then introduced. The new member then presents their ideas and a discussion that is preliminary starts. A fourth member is then introduced into the group, presents their ideas and then takes part in the preliminary discussion. The same procedure continues until the last member joins. The group members work together and come up with the final decision.

This technique has four ground rules that each member has to adhere to. These include,

- Each individual gets enough time for individual problem solving. Every member of the group before joining the discussions gets enough time to research on the problem, and ideas that can help in decision-making and also come up with the best decisions.
- It requires the members joining to speak first. As a new member joins the group, he/she has to present all the ideas and opinions before they hear the ideas from the core discussion (Patalano & LeClair, 2011).
- Disusing time is more. There is adequate amount of time for members to discuss as more members are added. This allows the group members to discuss ideas that a new member gives.
- Delay the final decision until all members have given their final

inputs. This requires that all members be in before the group comes up with the final decision.

As all members are required to give their input immediately after joining, it allows each person to give their opinion and this breeds accountability, and reduces biasing effect. As the group is required to wait until the final member joins then this allows the group not to come up with decisions prematurely. Members of a group who have used the stepladder tactic it allows the members to feel friendly towards each other and feel that they've collectively come together to come up with a common decision.

Figure 5.14. Brainstorming session: Member of a group coming up with ideas.

Source: Wework.

3. ***Brainstorming.*** This type of tactic involves coming up with ideas and opinions to explore before coming up with the best solution. Members meet to generate alternatives as they are instructed to come up with as many ideas or opinions as possible. Brainstorming doesn't come up with the decision but rather it comes up with alternatives that can later be considered, discussed and evaluates so as to come up with the best decision. They have their own group rules, which include,
   - All judgments should be suspended. Evaluations and criticisms of any ideas during brainstorming need to be avoided.
   - Allow members to freewheel. Members should be allowed to express their ideas freely no matter how insignificant an idea may seem. Ideas even those that are impractical or considered to be risky to the organization should be listened to and they are also expected.

- Members should emphasize on the quality but not on the quantity. All ideas should be expressed and this will encourage members to move past their favorite ideas thereby increasing the range of ideas.
- Encourage on creativity that is pooled and synergy among members. Allow members to build on other's ideas. The members should feel free to build on the ideas of other member's idea or suggestion.
- Ignore members that tend to show seniority. Members should behave as if every member of the group is of the same rank. The members should feel relaxed, uninhabited and have a cooperative atmosphere.
- Ensure that all members are heard. Ensure that all members have participated so as to ensure no one is left out.
- All ideas should be recorded. Any and every idea that every member has brought up should be recorded to ensure it should be discussed (Nutt, 2006).

The main purpose of brainstorming is to bring about divergent thinking and produce many ideas and opinions over a short period of time.

4. ***The nominal group tactic.*** This tactic allows for both generation and evaluation of ideas. This allows the group to come up with the final decision unlike brainstorming which deals with only generation of ideas. The steps usually followed in nominal tactic are;

Figure 5.15. Nominal group tactic. Members' present ideas and the facilitator record them on the flipchart.

Source: RCN.

- Ideas are written in private. After the problem has been well understood by the members, then silently and privately the members generate ideas in form of writing. The members are not allowed to discuss at this point.
- Reporting of ideas are taken in turns. Members of the group take turns in reporting of their ideas. They present their ideas one at a time while a facilitator records them on a flip chart or a board. At this point also, there are no group discussions.
- Discussion of ideas. Members start discussing the ideas that have been recorded. Members then criticize, clarify and even defend the ideas.
- Members vote on the ideas. After discussing, the members vote on the ideas. Each members votes anonymously and privately.
- The group's decision is calculated. The groups votes are calculated mathematically based on the earlier votes. The final decision is then determined (LeClair, 2010).
- The structured nature of the nominal technique tends to limit creativity of some if not all members. Research has shown that members from this tactic tend to feel less satisfied after a decision has been made.

Chapter 6

MCDM and Negotiation Support

CONTENTS

6.1. INTRODUCTION

Negotiation is the process by which two or more people come together to make a decision together. It is communication among two or more persons or groups who seek a mutual understanding. There is a frequent need to negotiate when similarly sought after resources are incapable of fulfilling all parties or when relative preferences are divided between concerns. Negotiation is used when it is neither feasible or practical for a person to act independently in order to resolve disputes. Everybody negotiates, ranging from partners trying to select where to go to dinner, energy-environmental stakeholders, legislative elected representatives, international diplomats. Negotiation research has traditionally been done in isolation in a variety of domains (Leclercq, 2018). However, in the last four decades, negotiation has become a distinct field of study. It was understood, for example, that negotiators could not rely solely on game theory. Professional economists especially those that use game theory often seek equilibrium outcomes resulting from strategic interactions between completely rational players who are completely aware of the game's rules. However, this search has frequently failed to yield didactic theory and practical recommendations for negotiators. There may be multiple possible equilibriums or solution in real-world circumstances involving genuine negotiators, with no evident method to pick among them postulated.

In addition, one or more of game theory's axioms may be broken. An opposing party, for example, could respond irrationally. Alternatively, all players may not be totally aware of the game's rules or the utility functions of opponents. As a result, it's possible that you don't know what movements or results are feasible, or that you don't know what the other party is thinking. Negotiation analysis made progress against this challenge by lowering rigorous strategic complexity expectations (e.g., completely rational participants aware of all the laws of the game) and stating that imaginative use of often simple mathematical analytics might be helpful in a variety of ways.

Negotiation studies has had minimal formal engagement with the nearly four-decade-old area of multi objective analysis (commonly known as multi-criteria decision making, or MCDM). MCDM usually focuses on a single decision-maker who chooses autonomously between options whose results (typically supposed to be known with assurance) vary on two or more "targets," "criteria," or "features." Many multi-objective decision-making challenges can be expressed as linear, integer, or nonlinear mathematical programming issues, in which a product of a vector of choice variables must be optimal while remaining within a realistic range. The focus is on options on the region's outskirts, known as the efficient frontier (Q, R, S, T, and W; *see* Figure 6.1), where concurrent wins in all targets or for all stakeholders are not conceivable.

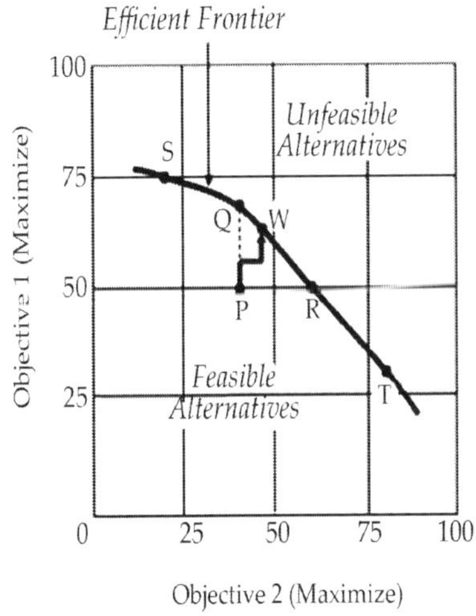

Figure 6.1. Tradeoff Curve (Pareto or efficiency frontier) between two objectives or the interest of two parties.

Source: https://www.eolss.net/sample-chapters/C14/E1–40–04–05.pdf.

6.2. MULTI CRITERIA DECISION MAKING TECHNIQUES

In general, common decision-making processes involve eight steps. The first step in the decision-making process is to choose an appropriate decision-making approach that suits the problem type in order to attain the aim and goals. To choose the optimal solution, they must be compared based on different sorts of difficulties and their benefits and drawbacks must be highlighted (Mustakallio et al., 2002). The prerequisites of a decision should be stated in the second phase based on expert opinions or any other technological constraints. Goals must be defined in the third step, and the most crucial component is that goals must be seen favorably. The forth step is defining alternatives. Alternatives or options include the techniques which alter the initial environment into the more favored condition.

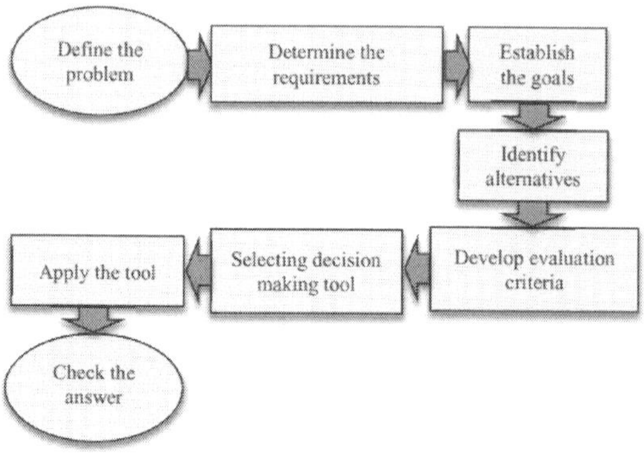

Figure 6.2. General decision making process.

Source: https://www.sciencedirect.com/science/article/pii/S2212827115009403.

Often, none of the options are ideal for achieving objectives. By weighing the various options vs a set of criteria, the optimum option for the goals can be determined. These factors aid in the differentiation of alternatives and the selection of the most relevant one depending on the desires of the decision maker. Identifying and evaluating the criteria is the next phase in the decision-making process. Some specialists have reached an agreement, and some criteria requirements have been presented. While established parameters have these requirements, distinguishing between the alternatives and picking the correct one is easier and more accurate when the established goals are given. The following are the detailed specifications: (i) the option is non-redundant; (ii) capable of encompassing all objectives; and (iii) useful and operational.

The choice technique should be chosen in the next stage. There are a variety of decision-making strategies, the most prevalent of which will be discussed in the next section. In the last stage, choices should be weighed against criteria to determine which is the best option.

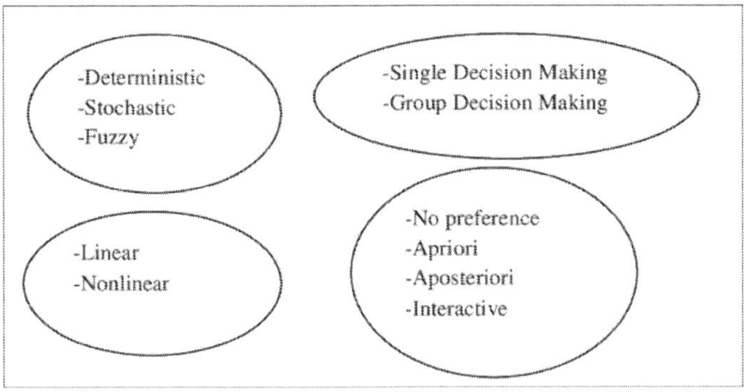

Figure 6.3. MCDM approaches.

Source: https://www.researchgate.net/publication/312212912_A_Survey_on_Interactive_Approaches_for_Multi-Objective_Decision_Making_Problems/figures?lo=1.

6.3. MCDM OVERVIEW

Interactive MCDM approaches are frequently used to find solutions, in which the decision maker is aided in finding and investigating the efficient frontier by examining a series of alternatives in a step-by-step manner. While initial negotiation research focused on simple mathematical evaluation, multiple-objective decision-making employs advanced computer-assisted analysis to uncover the most optimal frontier. One way that multiple-objective decision-making can contribute to negotiation is by assisting negotiators in identifying and mutually investigating this area. Multi-objective mathematical models of a country's energy economy, for example, can have tens of thousands of objective functions and are commonly used in policy debates to explain tradeoffs between goals like economic development, environmental control costs, employment, and air pollution emissions. Another method to multiple-objective decision-making emphasizes the necessity of assisting a decision-maker in considering his or her principles in relation to the objectives, measuring those values if feasible, and adapting them to the decision or negotiating problem at hand (Mukherjee et al., 2016).

To assist decision-makers, a range of techniques and theoretical concepts have been established. In value quantification, there are seven distinct tasks that can be recognized. The first is of a qualitative nature. The targets or criteria of interest must be determined, as well as attainable levels or degrees of consensus on these criteria (which may be a continuum). Second, a suitable value model for scoring and merging the various difficulties is found. Later in this chapter, we'll go through a few different value models that could be used. The third phase entails defining accessible alternatives and measuring their effectiveness against the objectives. This can be done when subjective probabilities exist, representing the individual's assessment of the relative probability of alternative possibilities. When important ambiguities exist The fourth to seventh objectives are quantitative. The fourth phase entails "value scaling" of the individual criteria – is to provide relative values to the relevant level of each of the various objective(s) to the individual decision-maker (or agents of a particular party in the negotiations). Fifth phase, i.e., weighing criteria, addresses value-addresses and indicates how much achievement one would want to give up for a certain improvement in each other objective

Sixth, to establish a multi-criteria model that combines the criteria or "amalgamates," the Decision Maker utilizes the value and the weights to classify the options. Some approaches produce a scalar acceptability index (a value function as it is sometimes known), which can be used to rank the alternatives. Additionally, systematic comparisons of alternatives incorporate other ways of fusion, giving partial or complete rank ordering. We provide a more comprehensive type of value quantification methods later in this chapter. The seventh stage is to apply the multicriteria model to classify the alternatives and then analyze the sensitivity of these outcomes. Experts have indicated that at three rounds of negotiations, MCDM methods to describe and explore the effective boundary and quantification values may serve useful roles:

- *Initial evaluation and screening of impacts among many choices*. At this first step, decision alternatives are developed by technical employees that assist a negotiations process and subject to preliminary review. They can either work with a specific negotiating party or with a neutral facilitator or sponsor. Multi-target analysis is beneficial at this phase for structuring the comparisons of options and sifting out alternatives that are clearly inefficient or lack exclusionary parameters (such as physical infeasibility, or violations of budgets). However, it is possible even at this point to make critical value judgments. As a result of this phase, the negotiations and stakeholders will have a "short list" of possibilities and early description of their tradeoffs and uncertainties. This step can also record the screening process, which enables external stakeholders in the course of producing and screening choices to assess the premises and valuation judgments made.

- *Structure and evaluation "within interest."* The second phase is intended to enable individual parties to form a cohesive perspective on alternatives in a negotiation or policy procedure. Since members of a special interest group share values, talking about a group's assessment can often make sense (Martinsons & Davison, 2007). However, even if group members have prevailing issues and a basic idea about its objectives, their views on specific valuation issues, such as the degree of their willingness to trade off particular quantitative criteria are difficult to be specific and universal. Multi-objective analysis can be useful in various ways: allow individuals to generate and systematically articulate value assessments which can comparison alternative measures; acquire understanding into the significance of the varied opinions and approaches to the problem.
- *Negotiations and decision making "between interests."* Once members in a process grasp the compromises and take an initial position on the options, communication and negotiation between the parties will be the next phase. At this step, the purpose of multi-objective analysis is to find probable compromises and agreements, to analyze the causes of any discrepancies and to document the findings of the process. This approach gives an opportunity to discuss trade-offs and uncertainty systematically. The MCDM aims in particular to help parties focus during the negotiation process on their key objectives and interests.

Because the parties at least share these aims partially, such a focus has often been found to lead to satisfactory agreements rather than to "placement negotiations." In the positional negotiations, each party argues that it prefers a certain alternative to alternatives chosen by the other parties. MCDM can find options that almost all groups have found appealing on the basis of their goal and assist explain why they disagree with other choices, as the case study given later. The purpose of multi-objective analysis at each of these steps is not to calculate the "correct" reply. Instead, participants must develop insight and understanding to offer suggestions and choices effectively. In consequence the following features are needed for an MCDM-based process.

- Simplicity and clarity: the method and calculating algorithms should be understood by users; 'black box' methods and extra complications should be minimized.
- Feedback: MCDM approaches can help people better perceive the situation, examine their sentiments, establish a consistent and justifiable system of values, and grasp the consequences of those values for the decision when they are unsure of their specific priorities. MCDM approaches are most effective when promoting learning and making it possible for people to change their judgments. Users should therefore be able to swiftly and conveniently analyze the impact of alternative value judgments on the results.
- User control: Stakeholders despise procedures that solicit value judgments and other contributions and then analyze them, announcing results without allowing users to reflect on and alter their inputs. People dislike feeling out of control, particularly when their inputs are shaky. All suggestions and decisions should be the product of careful consideration by users; MCDM methods should support rather than supplant that consideration.
- Effective participant communication: in a structured group context judgments, like criteria weight or subjective probabilities evaluating the impact of alternative criterion, may be debated so that ideas and viewpoints can be shared efficiently. Issues can be presented and either solved or clarified the grounds for differing opinions (Kugler et al., 2012). Structured debate such as the methodology of the Nominal Group provides for an anonymity in the sharing of individual judgments and discusses them in ways that encourage the participation of all groups and deter more aggressive people from dominating their decisions.
- Patience: There is much time to ensure that people comprehend and are confidence in the process when engaging with many stakeholders.
- Various approaches: ample empirical evidence suggests that (a) different methods of multicriteria evaluation are more suitable for different persons. Therefore, no single approach of eliciting the value for all should be adopted.

By looking at the problem in many ways with the support of more than one approach, users acquire the best insight, satisfaction, and confidence and then perform the hard work necessary to reconcile contradictions between the outcomes.

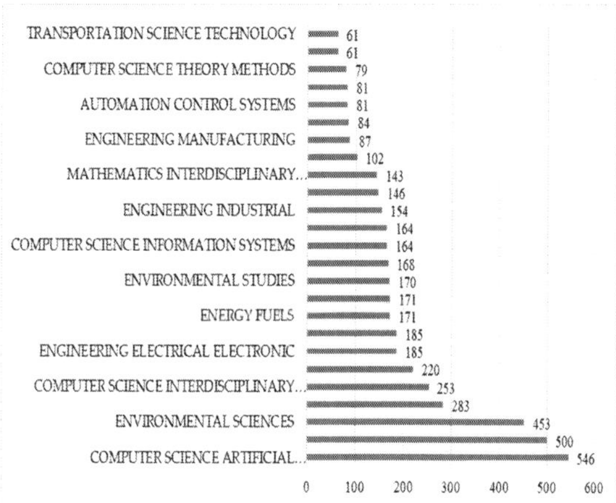

Figure 6.4. Number of articles on the application of MCDM methods in various fields of science and technology.

Source: https://www.mdpi.com/2073–8994/11/3/350/htm.

Certainly, a variety of other real-world concerns contribute to guarantee that the negotiating and dispute resolution process remains artistic. Creativity, expertise, and strong intuition play a role that can never be superseded by increasing analysis or formal processes. A well-negotiated solution should not only be efficient but also seek to incorporate fairness issues. It should be prudent to portray the most essential experience and knowledge. It should be stable, which could imply a fair settlement at least possible and renegotiation options if a side is unable to comply with its own commitments. Such stability depends on relations, so excellent settlements should aim to maintain friendliness between the parties.

Finally, competent negotiators distinguish between people and this problem and evaluate it on its grounds (that is, founded on the primary goals that the parties are concerned with). They seeks, rather than starting negotiations, to find and focus on the core interests of the parties. As indicated, MCDM methods are used to help parties develop their core purposes by stressing the quality of objectives; qualified facilitators use their capacity to measure, empathize and explain. To sum up, potential users of negotiated MCDM tools have to acknowledge that analytical techniques can play a valuable role in many negotiation issues, but these tools are by themselves not enough to assist litigants reach effective, properly designed or sustainable agreements. In the following several parts we discuss some general approaches to multi-criteria methods of negotiation and resolution of conflicts. First, we provide approaches that formally quantify each party's values in the negotiations (Kulcsár et al., 2020). We then describe techniques emphasizing mathematical description and analysis of trade-offs between distinct parties' interests, where their values have not been specified specifically. The next item is a review of the need for electronic and multi-objective negotiation support systems and a synopsis of the case study showing how multi-objective analyzes are used successfully in negotiations.

6.4. MCDM APPROACHES TO QUANTIFYING PREFERENCES OF INDIVIDUAL PARTIES IN NEGOTIATIONS

We turn to MCDM techniques, which explicitly generate scalar values. The basic objective is to examine the intricate compromises, which commonly define negotiating situations, from an individual party perspective. These approaches may be used, as indicated in the introduction, to preliminary screen alternatives, to prioritize interests and to alternate assessments as well as to identify possible compromises and reasons for conflicts among the parties. For example, during multilateral negotiations, the parties may be ready to reveal their value functions to a third party, an intervener, who might then use them to seek an effective agreement or compromise.

To achieve this, weighted-sum value and utility functions can be employed and applied subsequently in this chapter for a simplified climate policy scenario. A understanding that many people do not arrive into discussions with hard and fast-foot beliefs on what specific compromise measures are desirability is essential to the successful implementation of these strategies (Hwang & Lin, 2012). Therefore these strategies should be employed in order that the possibilities may be explored and their overall priority crystallized into particular judgments on value that can be used to classify alternatives.

Figure 6.5. 30–31 July 2015, New York, USA – The United Nations Institute for Training and Research (UNITAR) New York office organized a workshop on multilateral negotiations with a specific orientation towards protection of civilians (PoC).

Source: https://unitar.org/about/news-stories/news/leveling-playing-field-multilateral-negotiations-protection-civilians.

These MCDM approaches seek to enhance decision quality through explicit, efficient and effective choosing with risks, multiple criteria and multiple interests. This is tried in three different ways:

- by communicating tradeoffs between objectives and associated uncertainties, so that negotiating parties can comprehend alternatives' positives and negatives;
- by pushing the debate away from alternatives and towards fundamental goals.

Group decisions and negotiations are sophisticated and structured multi-person procedures. Due to shifting information, participants' aspirations, preferences and methods, these are dynamic in nature. In addition, decision-makers seldom comply with conventional rational behavioral theories. You do not want to expose your true interests and change your techniques over time. A vast volume of research has been driven by the significance of group decision making and negotiations (Herrera et al., 2005). At one end of the scale, behavioral researchers analyzed individual behaviors in prescribed environments for exceptional situations or aspects, in order to determine the relevance of certain components to the whole process. Formal efforts to comprehend collective decision-making and negotiations have, on the other hand, used different forms of mathematical or logical representation.

However, these efforts have frequently been so abstract that they are hardly used in particular situations in the real world. While the conduct approach tries to detect a specific, widespread rationality, the formal method assumes a generic rationality that can be deployed to specific problems. This paper provides an overview of formal models for group decision making and negotiation with a special focus on those that can be used in developing computer-based support systems.

6.5. FORMAL MODELS FOR GROUP DECISION MAKING AND NEGOTIATION

Conflict resolution initiatives with theoretical frameworks are many. The two classics are business and game-theoretical models and use the concept of utility.

Figure 6.6. Group decision-making is a sort of participatory process in which several persons acting together examine problems or circumstances.

Source: https://www.referenceforbusiness.com/management/Gr-Int/Group-Decision-Making.html.

6.5.1. Economic Negotiation Models

Economic models are linked to pioneering specialists and treat negotiation as a converging process over time that encompasses a range of proposals and offers. These models imply that participants' efficiency depends and are defined and known from the beginning and that a compromise zone exists, can be established and consistent over time (Gati et al., 2011).

In addition, the economic models address talks on a single, consistent and constantly divisible item, such as money. The importance of the time as a negotiator is stressed by an influential piece of economic models. Negotiations are a routine discovery process in the Cross model. The participant begins with a set of assumptions that, on the basis of experience, he tries to correct. The procedure creates solutions that guide the behavior of the participants given correct values. The model provides the same conclusion as the Nash solution if the players are identical. The Cross model and Rao and Shakun's (1974) approach seek to provide regulatory guidelines for the making of concessions. But this technique is based in part on Cross model, although we deal with both prescriptive and descriptive parts, scenarios with numerous criteria and "non-rational" parts of the participant's behavior.

6.5.2. Game–Theoretical Models

The second type is game theory and extensions. Game models presuppose that players' numbers and IDs, and alternatives and utilities are defined and understood, that participants are entirely streamlined and communication is conducted exclusively in the model and that the form or content of a reward matrix cannot be modified. While game theory investigation has produced valuable insight into negotiation and negotiation strategy processes and outcomes, constrictive presumptions and computational problems in all but the linear case underpinning this framework have intended that it is hard to develop and implement appropriate mathematical structures. These restrictions are embedded in the fundamental method. "There is sometimes highly riddled and unclear responses from game theory," one expert says.

Figure 6.7. This is the first form of game that Game Theory aimed to solve, where two people confronting one other during which whatever one person wins, the other will lose

Source: https://medium.com/@sabinelea/game-theory-in-negotiation-84dda8f4f707.

6.5.3. Aggregation Models

A different technique, widely employed, identifies the variety of variables behind the conduct of participants and seeks to build a rule of decision(s). One assumes that each user's utility functions are static and can first be individually evaluated and aggregated by calling upon the concept of utility independence. This premise reduces the negotiations process to the preference definition and then combines them for each participant and for the entire group. For compromise, the collective utility function generated (improver or multiplicative) is used. Specific group decision-making processes (e.g., project or scenario assessment, common model building) may be using the utility aggregation approach but not in traditional business situations when the participants have contradictory objectives, display strategic behaviors and retention preference and other information. It was challenged for the presumption of independent utilities and a general group-consensus function was presented in the literature that does not presume that each member has a von Neumann-Morgerstern utility function. Others do not need to establish a group utility or consensus value, but rather employ rules of decision stated for different ways.

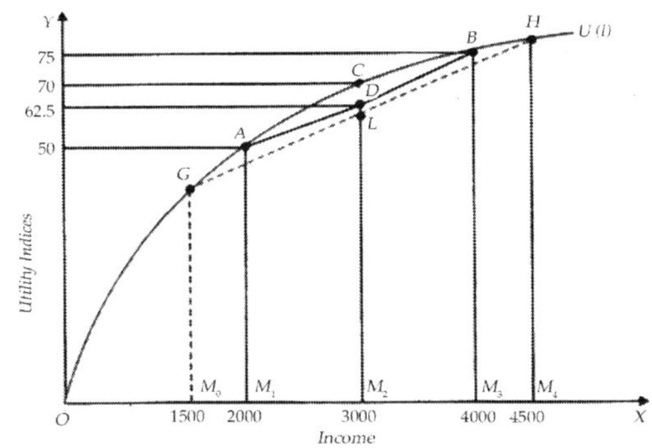

Figure 6.8. It may be noted that marginal utility of income of a risk-averter diminishes as his income increases.

Source: https://www.economicsdiscussion.net/articles/utility-theory-and-attitude-toward-risk-explained-with-diagram/1384.

An example is the classification by each member of options and then determination by means of expanding contracting operations of the many alternatives of settlement alternatives. Experts propose a new expansion method based on a reference method for targets/values (Forbes & Milliken, 2008). One assumes that participants begin with lower choices and that the process of negotiations consists of a contracting method with participants selecting the direction of changes. Each member can switch from a poorer to a better alternative by means of the Isermann model such that concessions are unneeded. Ranking is the mechanism for collective decision and is another example of the classification.

6.5.4. Tactics Models

Models that concentrate on negotiating methods have been established through labor analyzes and international negotiations. There are no limiting assumptions on tactical models for utility-specific models. You do not presume that the information is complete or that utilities and alternatives are provided from the beginning and are reliable. The method is regarded as one of the most significant qualities for manipulating these feats of the negotiating scenario. In manipulative models, the officialization is low. You cannot set forth results or try to describe negotiation as game-theoretical models with complete resolve. Heckarton sees these traits as shortcomings and they are actually used to replace, examine or verify the process using a model.

This is not, therefore, the scenario if the model is a device to support a member of the group or the mediator, if the present negotiation scenario is analyzed and tactics checked and defined. We consider manipulative models beneficial because we are interested with latter. The tactical models allow "non-rational" behavioral characteristics that arise in negotiations. Negotiation, for example, need communication between the participants, but what is said depends on communication.

Compromises can depend on the starting point rather than on any underlying collection of values because of communication union. It also implies that players are not immune to strategies of other players, although they perceive their own action as sensible (Escobar & Moreno-Jimenéz, 2007). Another result of communication's significance during these procedures is that one member's admissions rely upon other players' concessions. There are other actions that are also not traditionally reasonable, because interaction between actors is vital to negotiation and negotiation as a way to decide.

Since players consider such messages to be (minimum) partial or wrong, their own action in the classic sense is probably unreasonable. Models of tactics suggest that decisions, and hence concessions, are based on time, context and strategy in negotiations and negotiations. We can determine a fallback decision that they will not accept, even if the precise utility functions of the players are known. This is because the choice was reached without consideration of the technique of negotiation: abilities to persuade: arguments, the ability to utilize negotiating measures, and the knowledge of how and when to use them.

We also ignored the impacts of learning; that is, changes in problem and player awareness. The tactical model of the negotiating process was presented by Kersten and Szapiro centered on accessible information to both actors and mediators. The fluid character of negotiation, different player tactics and the presence of secret and revealed objectives and interests are taken from this model. This study extends this technique somewhat and concentrates on the issues of aiding the negotiators in determining their compromises.

6.6. MCDM AND NEGOTIATION SUPPORT

6.6.1. Group Decision Support Systems (GDSS) and Negotiation Support Systems (NSS)

The NSS is a group-based support system (DSS) for negotiation that attempts to enhance the efficiency of the negotiations and to manage conflict of opinion. In early times, most NSS was based on an autonomous computer. The first reference of online NSS in 2000 was that it has become a hot topic in the EC field. An extensive online communications and negotiation platform for all businesses may be created by NSS, and a great deal can be minimized in terms of transport and telecommunication.

Negotiation support systems are an industry of group decision support systems (GDSS) in which individuals, whether departments, organizations and countries, are involved in the process of reaching an agreement on a given topic. Comprehensive findings are available to prove the efficiency of group support systems for decision making (Eden & Ackermann, 2001). For example, these studies suggest that GDSS can help groups make better quality judgments, enhance the range of choices they evaluate, boost involvement, and lessen undesirable characteristics of group work such as group thinking. Most of these outcomes are acquired in an American environment, based on American group processes' traditions and culture. It is an open topic whether or not these results carry on in multicultural negotiations. The number of transnational groups from diverse cultures is increasing as marketplaces develop. These meetings have as their objectives:

- submissions and briefing;
- strategically planned;
- sharing of information;
- management of crises;
- agreement or negotiation of the treaty;
- solution of cooperative problem.

The cost and duration of transactions can be considerably lowered by negotiating over the Internet, which just became a global communication platform. The Internet allows companies and people to interact, conduct out different trade operations and offer value-added services. Nevertheless, contract negotiations are sometimes still carried out manually without computer or only by e-mail support. The biggest challenge here is its slowness that is aggravated by cultural, ego and pride concerns.

First used in the 1960s to facilitate negotiating were computer applications. The 1980s saw the development of computer-based NSS and they were generally utilized for training and research in the academic world. The main elements of NSSs are as follows:

- a formal description of the negotiating activities with regard to decisions and results;
- a technique to characterize the probabilities of results associated with this;
- a model computing methodology for evaluating predicted alternatives of choice values.

The NSS usually supports negotiators in assessing situations, developing and evaluating options and implementing decisions. Most NSS do not, nevertheless, consider contract formation as an outcome of the negotiating process, which we regard as the main purpose of e-commerce negotiations. NEGOTIATOR, for example (Bui and Shakun, 1996), aims to aid negotiators in moving their separate objectives and opinions to increase the probability of a consensual solution. It facilitates adaptation of problems by the sharing of information, concession and reorganization of problems. NEGOTIATOR nevertheless just assists the negotiators to decide without any assist to other negotiating bodies such as contracts. It can anonymously conduct negotiations, assess the fairness of an offer and examine the background of a negotiation. INSPIRE facilitates negotiated communications through exchange of messages, but also offer direct interactions with web services across distinct entities.

In the artificial intelligence arena, negotiations were regarded completely automated utilizing negotiating software agents. The intelligent software officers in this technique interact with other agents and decide on behalf of their owners in accordance with pre-programmed tactics with or without learning. Negotiating strategies software agents based on game theory and the heuristics have been developed and evaluated.

Combined discussions have been researched from the perspective of workflow management. The combined negotiation is a process in which a user participates simultaneously in multiple negotiations. They have built a combined negotiation support (CNSS) system that enables the user to coordinate all the conversations. They have demonstrated the functional needs of the CNSS and produced CONSENSUS prototypes using the MQSeries of the commercial WfMS-IBM. The users define the integrated negotiating process at design phase in the CONSENSUS structure. Every individual negotiations on the combined negotiation process are then allocated to the software agents and the procedure is then executed.

The effect of several other negotiators' qualities such as their domestic culture, image or fear of losing reputation have been studied in the empirical investigations. Rudolf (2007, 2009), who explored whether inclinations contained in a model directly affect behavior and results, conducted one study on our research question in this context. Another set of experiments employed to assess the consequences of framing effects on negotiation results by using differences in utilities functions to achieve gains and loss. Some viewed the relationship between preferences and procedure of negotiation as a feedback mechanism and examined the effects on preferences of processes.

6.6.2. THE SPACES WHERE DECISIONS CAN BE MADE

The models described in the previous section are intended to describe and analyze group decisions and procedures for negotiation. Although some were computerized, they were either by chance or limited to a very particular context. Discussions are underway on the utility and breadth of use of GDSS and NSS. These solutions, are built tested and empirically verified with their underlying theories and procedures. Consequently, assumptions cannot be established in response to queries like: How much can GDSS be used for the decision-making of actual world groups? Is the NSS more problematic than the NSS? Can malfunctioning negotiation tasks be encouraged? and so on.

Decision-making on multiple-criteria (MCDM) is one of the most dynamic study areas, geared at understanding and supporting decision-making, group and negotiation in general. MCDM offers group decision frameworks and support for negotiations. The architecture can be structured around places in which individuals can decide, analyze and compare choices by individual or group. Keeney and Raiffa (1976) and Kersten can find more about the topics covered here (1988).

Figure 6.9. The ministers of foreign affairs of the United States, the United Kingdom, Russia, Germany, France, China, the European Union and Iran negotiating in Lausanne for a Comprehensive agreement on the Iranian nuclear programme (30 March 2015).

Source: https://en.wikipedia.org/wiki/Negotiation.

6.6.3. The Decision Variable Space

Decision variables are the particular actions taken, discussed and decided upon in the event of a compromise. Based on the, scenario the amount of the choice variable can be gross or fine. For instance, the total number of sprockets manufactured within one month or the total period of manufacturing for a product class may be. In mathematics programming, the decision variable is the known idea where the x vector is a vector for the choice variables. A resolution or a settlement proposal are the factors of decisions coupled with the variables of their worth which are evaluated at any time.

The decision-making process of a group can therefore be simplified to an interchange of decisions and negotiation amongst the Group members – a comparable interchange of offers for agreement. There are possible and implausible decisions inside the space of choice variables. In the continuing instance, there are a set of limitations allowing the feasibility of a selection to be determined, and the viable alternatives may be listed in the discrete case. If these limitations are accepted by all parties in the decision-making process, they are called harsh constraints, in that are binding on each person.

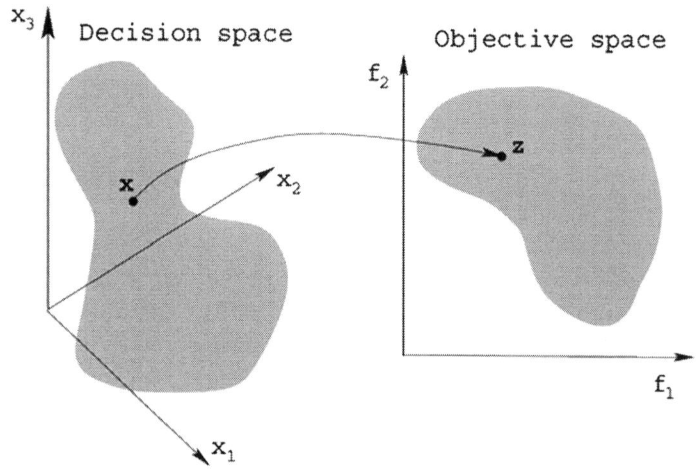

Figure 6.10. Representation of the decision variable space and the corresponding objective space.

Source: https://www.researchgate.net/publication/220888531_Multi-objective_Differential_Evolution_Approach_for_Optimal_Control_of_Water_Resource_Systems/figures?lo=1.

Mostly during pre-negotiations, harsh limits are commonly mentioned when the parties identify the definitions or potential values of a given decision variable. The objective nature of the space variable selection is an important characteristic. The actors in the procedure are only linked by a choice; the decision-making space provides the basis for building further spaces. Participants disagree in the assessment of a conclusion, yet objectivity for understanding a conclusion is the necessity for good negotiation or group choice (Dyer et al., 2008).

For some issues, it may well be hard to identify or not to discriminate between decision variables. A decision on a major company's management strategy frequently requires too many decision variables to make successful decisions. Even with more straightforward difficulties, like in the instance of union/management pay discussions, it may be tough to differentiate between a decision and a target.

6.6.4. The Objective Function and Weight Spaces

The objective function space is a further area to explore. Through modification of the selections, objects in this space are achieved using objective functions. It is generally a smaller space than the choice variable space, which enables analyzing and evaluating different alternative choices simpler. Whereas the objects in the space for decision are neutral, they can be assessed when translated into the space for objective functions. For instance, we can state that one is preferable than another since it is higher and we want to have the highest valuc attainable. Such a declaration on the values of a decision variable cannot be constructed. Implementing the objective space enables a quasi or efficient decision to be defined.

A quasi decision is a practicable one for which no other practicable decision provides higher values for one or even more objective variables We should note that a decision is or is not undominated, but we must analyze in the objective space of the function. The third space is the weight space, which is the space of the linear positive weights. Weights are used to add objective function values to a single value that determines the goodness or usefulness of different alternatives (Beynon, 2005).

This unit is referred to as the utility function. The size of the weight space has a link to the objective space of the function. This relationship varies with the type of utility function employed to express a certain decision maker's preferences. This value, for example, may be linear or multilinear with weights allocated to each objective function, as well as its multiplication or exponential. The weight space in the basic, linear case is identical to the objective function space; a single objective weight is provided so that the dimension equals the objective function space. In this situation, weight space may be a size less than the objective function space, since any collection of weight can be standardized without loss, cf generality.

In single decision support systems, both objective function and weight spaces are often used. For example, VIG supports the target function space whereas TRIMAP and VISA assist decision-making using weight.

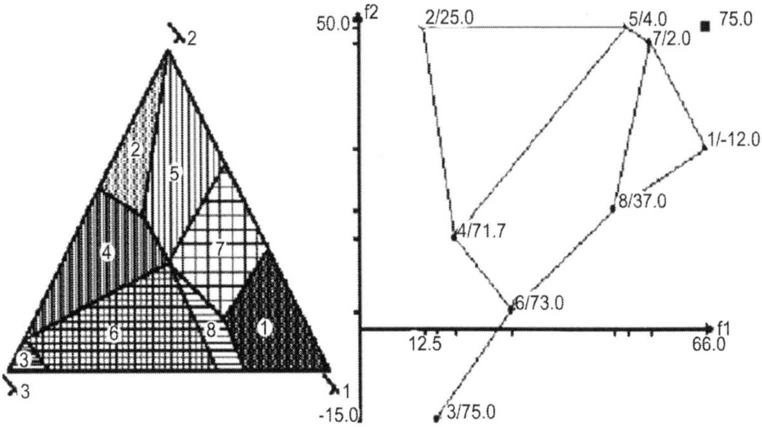

Figure 6.11. Graphs produced by TRIMAP, decomposition of the weights space and projection of the objective function.

Source: https://www.researchgate.net/publication/46189840_A_Study_of_Highways_Performance_with_a_Molp-Dea_Model_and_an_Interactive_Tri-Criteria_Linear_Programming_Package_Trimap/figures?lo=1.

6.6.5. The Party Utility and Weight Spaces

The three spaces examined relate to one party's difficulty of decision or multiple criteria. Due to the many agents, the party utility and weight areas are introduced. The space of the parties has as many degrees as parties and one dimension relates to one member in the Group decision or portion of the negotiation process. This dimension alludes to a particular individual or party's utility function. The objective function space as well as the party space are analogous. A idea akin to the non-dominated (effective) solution can thus be introduced. It is the ideal solutions for Pareto in the party area.

We say that the approach is optimal for Pareto when and only when there is no alternative where every party is at least as well off and at least one party is better off. Optimal solutions from Pareto in talks are regarded ideal. Pareto efficiency suggests the most economically effective allocation of resources, but does not imply equity or fairness. An society is said to be in the optimal state of Pareto when there are no economic reforms that can make a citizen better without leaving one person worse off. If a solution is not optimal for Pareto, then one or more parties may be able to negotiate benefits free of charge for the other partners.

This is achievable if the utility functions are completely exclusive and this premise reflects reasonable conduct of the parties, i.e., one party's rise in its utility does not entail another party's reduction. Extending the connection between the numerous purposes of an individual and numerous individuals, we may construct the party weight space. Remarks mentioned with regards to the (individual) weight space do apply there. The party weight space may be added, if we were to suppose a public utility function (social welfare function) or a "supra decision maker" as experts like to claim (Di Fabio et al., 2015).

In the hybrid support systems "MCDM/voting," the party weight space can be utilized. In MEDIATOR, for instance, the party utility space is employed and further described in Raiffa (1985). Be aware that the cartesian sum of objective function spaces can also be used, rather than utilizing explicitly the party utilities space (it is called the Cartesian product). In the former situation, everyone knows the dimensions of collective decision-making and negotiation, but a negotiating party knows only one's own subspace in that second scenario. The accessibility to all data would be provided only through the computer (as a facilitator or mediator).

An expansion of VIG from individual decision to group or negotiation is an illustration of an Objective Function Spaces support system. NEGO is also an example. The preceding factors and the geometric spaces series, maybe of several dimensions, that result in one dimension super utility or welfare function from a neutral decision space are often acceptable since the available methods to NSS and GDSS design do not remain restricted. There should be only one presumption, namely the economic reason of the persons or parties concerned.

Hence, one specific cases incorporate the aspirations which may cause the objective functions ,he utility functions to be defined for the aspiration levels intervals (Davenport, 2009). The reservation prices (the lowest/highest acceptable values), shifts in negotiation tactics, and context dependent concessions can also be introduced. the paradigm is, however, that a Pareto optimal solution is desirable, and that the decision problem can be expressed as a problem of identifying acceptable Pareto optimal solutions.

6.7. ELECTRONIC MULTI-CRITERIA DECISION-MAKING SUPPORT FOR GROUP DECISION MAKING AND NEGOTIATION

The study aims, one of the concerns, to define the sort of computer-based information systems capable of supporting group decision making and facilitating negotiations. In the first section, some conceptual framework frames for GDSS and NSS are discussed and summarized in the literature. The second section gives instances of the application of systems in the domain of group decision-making and support for negotiations.

6.7.1. Conceptual Frameworks for GDSS and NSS

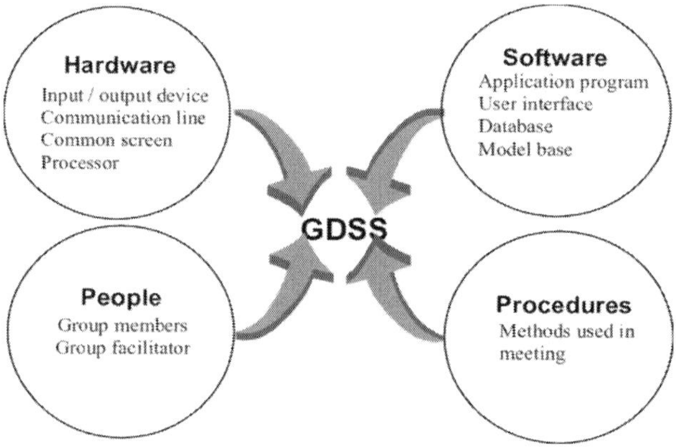

Figure 6.12. Components of GDSS (DeSanctis and Galluple, 1987).

Source: https://www.researchgate.net/publication/285512221_Improving_the_implementation_of_VM_studies_in_Hong_Kong%27s_construction_industry_--_A_GDSS_Approach/figures?lo=1.

GDSS was classified into 4 distinct areas: decision making room, decision room, local decision-making networks, linked decision rooms and remote decision-making networks by DeSanctis and Gallupe (1985). The four models differed in regard to the participant's closeness as well as the duration of the decision-making session. Their taxonomy helped to define GDSS, possible settings and application. The communications needs for different group decisions were evaluated by Bui and Jarke (1986). They also proposed an architecture for the definition and implementation of protocols at the dynamic application level that organize group interaction.

DeSanctis and Gallupe (1987) in produced a GDSS typology based on three stages, with different degrees of involvement. Level 1 GDSS is intended to enable decision-makers' communication. For the support of stakeholders Level 2 GDSS uses decision modeling approaches. Multi-criteria decision maps, multi-attribute utility methodology, decision-making bodies may include such strategies. Level 3 GDSS has integrated knowledge and can provide expert systems with guidance and explanation.

Three environmental contingencies, namely group size, have also been highlighted as crucial to GDSS design. The vicinity of the member and the group's task. A comprehensive framework that links the behavioral percentages of group decision-making to the technical requirements driven by Gr6S was proposed by Jelassi and Beauclair (1987). The GDSS comportemental concerns include responsibility dissemination, deindividualisation, desire to reach consensus group 13 and communication concerns. The GDSS "shells" should take these problems into account. The management of these systems tries to reduce these behavioral problems' detrimental impacts.

The links between task and technology were investigated by experts (1989) in order to help decision-making groups based on studies carried out at the Arizona University. They presented a number of perspectives on group circumstances, including system theory, communication. They argued that a multidisciplinary strategy was necessary to research such environments. This study is based on a literature foundation on the behavior and group psychology of organizations. The scientific investigations of electronic meetings Pinsonneault and Kraemer analyzed the effect of group activities and results (Dalal & Brooks, 2013). The "Negotiable Alternatives Identifier," which might be utilized with preference aggregation approaches, is another proponent of Prsus' search method. A threefold operation: expansion, compression, and intersection characterizes the algorithm. A general strategy for arranging and modeling negotiations was created by another specialist. The focus is on the use of case-based rationale. The methodology The recommended concept was incorporated in a work-management computer application. Another offered an interactive decision-making and negotiations approach for the group. It is founded on the philosophy of aspiration and uses a satisfactory and optimistic approach. The result of the modeling method is a compromise option that can meet fairness and fairness requirements and also an efficient solution. Mainly two concerns linked with the NSS were addressed by Jelassi and Jones (1988): How can technology support talks? In such intricate settings as multi-party negotiations, what appropriate systems can we develop? The analytical mediation method addressed these issues. On the basis of an examination of the prior literature, Jelassi and Foroughi (1989) examined the NSS design problems. They also discussed existing systems to support the bargaining process.

The essay established the ground for the creation of a broad range of tools to enhance individual and group negotiations. The authors suggested five critical considerations for the design of the SSN after the difference between "hard" (NSS) and "soft" (WinWin) discussions. These variables include:

- Separating individuals from the problem;
- Communicating with negotiators;
- Helping negotiators to recognize their true interests;
- Generating reciprocal winning solutions; and
- Using objective standards.

In a following work and proposals to decrease or overcome these, the experts addressed the key hurdles for successful negotiations. They also have recently established a conceptual framework for computer-aided conflict resolution in a recent publication. In the context of mediation, the following barriers were addressed: cognitive distortions of negotiators, socio-emotional issues, and analysis problems. In order to create NSS able to address the foregoing difficulty, a variety of practical design problems and application principles were presented.

The above-mentioned and other theoretical foundation presented in this research is related to various perspectives: management science, operational research, information systems and computer science. Competence in organization, communication, etc. They serve to promote the GDSS and NSS principles by presenting complementing and enlightening views on group decisions and procedure of negotiations. The next phase for researchers is to use these concepts to construct computer-based support systems and assess their usefulness realistically (Cheek & Goebel, 2020).

6.7.2. Examples of GDSS and NSS Implementations

An expanding number of academics are devoting significant time and money in computer-based information systems in order to support collective decision-making and negotiations. Some sixty GDSS and NSS were recognized as the culmination of all these experts. GDSS was the subject of major experiments, particularly at the University of Arizona, where the

PLEXsyS system was established and at the University of Minnesota, the home of the SAMM system, were carried out in North American university laboratories. Two GDSS rooms operate at the University of Arizona. The more broad system offers sixteen personal PCs which have U-shaped screens.

The display on the facilitator's screen can be shown by public screen. The system and information are based on a data host which is also utilized as a desktop for the facilitator. The second, larger system consists of 24 workstations and two amphitheater projection panels. The same technology is in use for this system, which was implemented in 1987. PLEXSYS offers a variety of tools for brainstorming, analysis, votes, identification of stakeholders, assumptions and documenting what transpired at a meeting. The facilitator station gives the group support tools with access and management. In order to communicate with the users the system uses pop-up panels, navigation cursors and computer commands.

The GDSS University uses 4 microcomputing terminals and its software is a public program that manages individual users' what displays on each screen and private applications. All communications from and on the private programs of the participants during the conference are communicated to the public. In the beginning, the private program gives each member with a broad agenda which comprises choices like problem formulation, description or selection of criteria/alternatives, rating, 16 rankings and voting. Notice, instead of incorporated into the table, that personal screens face the public screen. In the NSS sector, the type and degree of support available for existing implementations vary widely differing. NSS consists of a computerized model at one end of the scale that carries out calculations or quantitative analyses employed during the negotiating procedure. These systems act as "backroom processors" and so serve a subordinate role. DECISION TREE and DECISION MAKER are illustrations of these NSS. Interaction solutions that assist a human mediator and/or the negotiating parties are located in the middle of the NSS operational range.

MEDIATOR and GDS1 are two examples of such implementations. Pich use multicriteria decision making methodologies, preference inference approaches, and electronic communication capabilities. MEDIATOR is a database-driven, micro-mainframe NSS that assists negotiators and human mediators in resolving conflict. It is useful at the pre-negotiation phase, when players determine their beginning negotiating leverage. It is also used during the negotiating stage to assist in the selection and evaluation of alternatives.

MEDIATOR examines decision-maker preferences for various solutions using subjective (qualitative) and objective (quantitative) data (agreements). PREFCALC, a single-user multicriteria DSS, is used by each negotiation party to define their particular preferences and challenge description which are subsequently translated to the shared (mainframe) database. The human mediator combines these individual challenge models to generate an initial group joint 17 problem representation exploiting relational inquiry language capabilities (Charness & Sutter, 2012). Consensus is sought through the exchange of knowledge and compromise during negotiations. MEDIATOR is useful for multi-player, multi-criteria, poorly structured, and dynamic situations. Moving along the spectrum, we come across two recently suggested systems: the KAJ NSS and the MEDIANSS. By the use of GDSS characteristics, such as electronic communication and group dynamics design, these NSS offer active help for the full negotiation process as well as use of quantitative analytical approaches and game theory models for conflict resolution. The KAJ paradigm had a significant impact on MEDIANSS. The mediator leads bargaining teams through a planned set of digital stages. Rule setup, reversal of roles, issue and cause identification, issue consolidation, ranking, package construction, proposal presentation, connecting, house trading, and agreement phrasing are among them.

At the opposite end of the range are rules based NSS that play an active part in the negotiating process with expert system methodologies. The NSS such as RUNE is used to evaluate negotiations and simulate negotiation methods by using an artificial intelligence approach to issue representation and solution. Nevertheless, RUNE simply offers pre-negotiation planning for one part of the process. Experts have indicated that regulatory involvement may possibly involve negotiations include:

- conflict contingencies analysis,
- recommendation of relevant formats or analytical frameworks for structuring processes,
- surveillance of electronic communications' semantine content in order to impose interaction rules pre-programmed, mutually agreed,
- proposal of large common benefits settlements,
- (5) and automatic mediation;
- Parliamentary automatic process.

New opportunities to provide effective support for decision-making and negotiating parties are opened up by recent research in the use of artificial intelligence. The knowledge of negotiators is one of the variables that shape and influence the process. These information increases and grows dynamically throughout time, and quantum computing hence may potentially provide 18 adequate representation and handling strategies and methods. The ultimate goal here is to offer a mechanism of defining and evaluating prospective solutions for negotiation parties. This assistance system will therefore empower negotiators to serve as their own mediator, instead of being subjected to an imposed third party, a human or a software. Realizing this target would represent an important step to improve the negotiation process' efficiency and efficiency.

In conclusion, the purpose of this work was to offer certain formal models of group decision-making and negotiations and to discuss how to use recent advancements in information technology to such managers. The computer support approach for such many, complex, dynamic, and unstructured operations was a particular emphasis of the study. In spite of his early years, considerable improvements in the subject have been seen in the section on conceptual frames and practical implementation of group decision-making and negotiating assistance systems (Colombo et al., 2003). However, even though the GDSS and NSS potentials have been acknowledged, limited empirical proof remains that computer-based instruments can help decision-making and negotiators best and under which situations. For instances of GDSS and NSS empirical evaluations. More rigorous research is needed on the function of computers in group choices and disputes and their effects on the results and attitudes of processes. In conjunction with the development of NSS and GDSS technology, additional theoretical research are needed to improve the quality. The real-world "live" testing of these computer-based systems should be an essential subsequent stage in such a research agenda to assess its genuine advantage and weaknesses.

These MCDM strategies are designed to increase the quality of risk-related decisions, multiple criteria and various interests by explicitly, rationally or effectively making choices. This is tried in three different ways:

- Through explaining trade-offs and ambiguities between targets so that negotiating parties are able to comprehend the relative benefits and disadvantages of alternatives;
- By diverting the debate away from alternatives and to fundamental goals. This contributes to negotiations, because it encourages people to reflect on their common interests and prevent defensive

arguments that arise from anchoring themselves on a chosen choice.

- By assisting people to think, articulate and apply judgments of worth consistently, they are producing rational and recorded recommendations that each party prefers alternatives most.

Chapter 7

The Role of Emotions in Negotiation

CONTENTS

7.1. INTRODUCTION

There are different areas of life where negotiation is involved. It could be when one is bargaining for the price of an item in a store or a child negotiating with their parent on the time to get home. This means that there are various reasons for negotiation. However, even though negotiations are a day-to-day activity, there a common misunderstanding that often causes the negotiations to end up in jeopardy. There are different perceptions of negotiation among individuals. There are those who perceive it as a rational decision process. However, what people fail to understand negotiation is a different dimension usually ignored. This dimension is emotion. Emotions have both positive and negative effects on negotiation. Some of the negative emotions include guilt and disappointment while some of the positive emotions are joy and happiness. All the different types of emotions affect negotiations.

The major challenge with negotiation is the fact that very few individuals understand the extent to which emotions affect negotiation. This results in the creation of negotiation strategies that do not take into consideration emotions. If it was understood that emotions could improve emotions negotiations then it could be involved in the negotiation strategies (Caemmerer et al., 2021). This will drastically improve the results of the negotiation process. It is important to note that the various emotions affect negotiation. It is also important to understand that there are certain knowledge and skills needed to ensure emotional intelligence during the negotiation process. For us to understand the importance and the effects of emotion in negotiation, we should get the definition of negotiation, emotions, characteristics and principles of negotiation. There are different types of negotiations and different negotiators possess certain emotions during the negotiation process.

7.2. NEGOTIATION

The major cause of negotiation among individuals is the presence of conflict among the individuals. Without conflict then there is no need for negotiations. This is because all the parties would have the similar interests. For this reason there are different levels and types of conflict. Also there are different styles of negotiation. As negotiations are as a result of conflicts, we define conflict by stating that conflict is the process where individuals interact with disagreement, dissonance or incompatibility being manifested between the social entities. There are different definitions of conflict as a result of certain elements. Some of these elements include different interests being recognized by involved parties, activities by one of the parties causing a thwart in the goal of the other party, different groups having different interests, different parties having different beliefs resulting in one of the parties thwarting and conflict is an interactive process developed as a result of a previous or present interaction. Therefore, conflict can be defined as a continuous process that entails different interests while in some instances there may be negative feelings or perceptions of the opposing individual or group.

One of the ways conflicts can be solved without individuals being physically involved; negotiation is the best method of solving the conflict. One of the definition of negotiation is that it is a two way process if communication done with the goal of reaching a common ground or an agreement with some individuals or groups agreeing with some of if the issue raised while some being opposed. There are different areas where negotiations are done. They can be done in both formal and informal settings. There are six main characteristics of negotiations used in both formal and informal setting. Some the characteristics are as follows:

The negotiation process should involve two or more people, groups or organizations. There should be a conflict between the individuals. The conflict should reflect the desires and needs of the individuals. The process of negotiation should be voluntary in that both sides are willing to come to a common ground. The process should be based on the fundamental principle that it should be a give-and-take process. The process should be done with the main aim of resolving the conflict in the case where there is no familiar way of solving it. The process should entail both intangible and tangible factors (Brodbeck et al., 2002).

7.3. EMOTIONS

With regards to emotions there are different terms, theories and functions with relation to negotiation. However, there is no theory on the nature of emotions recognized globally. This has resulted in numerous theories being developed. Some of the theories are commonly acknowledged. The theory is defining the term emotion. Emotions are experienced, recognized and shown in a daily basis. Even so it is hard for is quite hard for individuals to give an elaborate definition of the term emotion. There are those who argue that emotions can look at as a prototype perspective. However, it is clear that though people experience emotions, very few are able to define it once they are asked what it is. The various theories have presented a challenge of defining emotions. Throughout the 20th century, different theories have been developed. The most commonly acknowledged definition of emotion incorporates different aspects of emotion. This theory is known as the component theory which was developed by Klaus Scherer.

The developer defines emotion as a temporary synchronization between crucial human sub-systems using all major elements of an emotion. Some of the major components of emotions include monitoring, physiological regulation, cognitive appraisal, motor expression and motivation. All these components were established as a result of subjective evaluations in either external or internal stimulus that is relevant to the wants and desires of the person in question (Bolaños et al., 2005). However, the developer failed to create the line between emotions and moods in the definition. Though the terms can be utilized interchangeably they are different in terms of characteristics. Among the differentiating factors between mood and emotion is the fact that emotions can last for a few seconds while moods may be felt for longer durations of time. Also with regards to emotions it is usually directed towards a certain object or individual while moods are not directed towards any Individual nor do they have a certain source. Finally emotions are usually more intense compared to moods.

7.4. FORMS OF NEGOTIATION AND ITS RELATION TO EMOTION

There are two main types of negotiations namely integrative and distribute negotiations:

- *Interrogative negotiations* are said to be cooperative as the arguments are done with the main aim of achieving a win-win for both parties. The main element of this form of negotiation is free information flow allowing identification of interests by involved parties. This means that involved parties can identify, develop and choose an alternative after looking at their differences and similarities. The alternatives should be fair to both parties. In this case there is an increase in the initial 'pie' size due to the exchange in information.
- *Distributive negotiations* are competitive with the case resulting in a win-lose situation in the negotiation. The negotiation is done over limited and fixed resources. Interests presented by both parties should be alike. In most cases the negotiation results in

one side winning while the other loses. This means that a win for one group or individual causes a loss in for the other side. In this case, information is shared with the interest of the other side. The information shared should enable them get their win. This is because the resources are limited. This is why the negotiation is said to be a competition as both side has to present themselves in a manner that ensures winning.

Depending on the situation at hand, the negotiation can either be distributive or interrogative. The manner in which negotiators present themselves and use their emotions will determine their success. There are different types of negotiators. These negotiators may use the three main types of negotiation styles. The classification of negotiators is dependent on the type of negotiation style they use. All the three different type of negotiations make use of different emotions bringing about the difference in the effectiveness of the negotiation. These include:

i. **The hard negotiator**. In most cases there is a stereotype that hard negotiators usually takes the leading role or one who does not change their position in a negotiation. In this case the individual views the negotiation as a form of rivalry in that the other individual who insists on claiming more and is more lenient during the negotiation process holds the most powerful position. As both sides want to win the negotiation they may present the case in a manner that will ensure their win. This causes a competitive behavior in both sides. Each side will try to meet the competitive behavior presented by their counterparts.

Hard bargaining can well be demonstrated by children. Take the case where a mother and child go to a store for groceries. During the shopping process the child may ask the mother to purchase candy, and the mother will the decline. As the shopping draws to an end, the child will insist that the mother purchases some candy. The mother may refuse as there are other candies at home causing no need to purchase more. The mother may try to negotiate rationally with the child who may not want to hear anything as they want candy. The child may begin to cry or misbehave due to the refusal by the mother. In this case, the rational method of negotiation may not be effective as the child will not give in. Moreover, it is not the best type of approach in a hard negotiation as both parties want their way to be chosen. The negotiation will end if one of the parties decides to withdraw their needs. For this reason most of such negotiations results in distributive behavior as the negotiation will be competitive in nature. Both parties will have to use all their resources and in some cases they may not come to a common ground.

ii. **Soft negotiators.** They are the total opposite of the hard bargainers. They are the total opposite in that they do not place much emphasis on their personal position. They tend to avoid personal conflicts with their counterparts. This causes most soft negotiators to make concessions and not insist in their position (Ambrus et al., 2009).

This results in amiable settlements. In the case where hard and soft negotiators are involved in a negotiation, the negotiation may be distributive as on side will lose while the other wins hence the win-lose situation. In most cases, these kinds of negotiations are known to trigger emotions such as disgust, fear and anger towards their opposer. This results in the professional and personal relationship being ruined. The final type of negotiator is the principled negotiator. This last category was established as a result of a project done by Harvard.

This kind of negotiation is also referred to as the interest-based negotiator. This alternative form of negotiation is neither the soft nor hard approach. It makes use of some of the components presented by both. For instance it utilizes merits of hard negotiation while making the negotiation is presented in a soft manner to the people. The negotiation works by trying to separate people from the problem. This form of negotiation is aimed at attaining a superior agreement while solving the interest-based conflicts is removing emotions. This form of negotiation is based on the assumption that negotiations could jeopardize the relationship of parties. Though this form of negotiation may seem to be more rational, it completely ignores the importance of emotions in negotiations. Therefore emotional behavior is not taken into consideration. There are four major steps in this kind of negotiation process. They are as follows: the first step is separating people from the problem. The next step is to place more emphasis on the subject of interest rather than the position. Then parties should proceed to invent various options resulting in mutual gain. While in the negotiation process, the above criteria should be emphasized on.

It is important to note that while the separation step occurs, the involve emotions should not be neglected. In this case, emotions are viewed as a useful intangible factor rather than a threat. This is because emotions affect the negotiation and therefore should be taken into consideration. This alternative of negotiation takes in to consideration the fact that individuals involved negotiations are human beings and not abstract representatives. Therefore emotions should be taken into consideration whether the emotional reaction has either positive or negative effects on the negotiation process. Therefore it is important for both parties to pay attention to the emotions portrayed by their counterparts. They should also know how to handle the different emotions while using certain negotiation skills. Excellent negotiators are able to use such skills to handle different emotions in the negotiation process.

7.5. FUNCTIONS OF EMOTIONS IN THE NEGOTIATION PROCESS

We are able to understand the functions of emotions in negotiation after establishing what it is. Also knowledge on the source of emotions is useful in understanding their functions. With regards to negotiation there are three main functions of emotion. They include decision making, motivation and communication. To better understand the functions, we look at each function looking at how it is related to emotion and negotiation.

7.5.1. Motivation

The main function of emotion in negotiations is motivating Individuals and the resultant behavior. To better understand this function we ask ourselves why some Individuals outshine others in other areas of life. When asked to other Individuals, some answered that those who outshine others may have a lucky streak or possess certain talents. Those known for their expertise in certain fields may say that the harder or the more they practice the better they become. This means that some Individuals perform better than others because of luck or talent but they have motivated themselves to perform well in the activity they are doing. This means that the Individual has a specific goal they want to reach. In this context the emotions they possess will drive and encourage them to achieve their goals. This is because they become a form of guidance by directing Individuals. It also keeps them motivated to be focused while pursuing their goals.

In most cases, if an individual loses a negotiation or a game they experience frustration and anger. By nature, the individual will strive to get better outcomes in future negotiations. For human beings the need for positive emotions is very essential. This is in addition to the fact that it helps them feel much better. Motivation to do a certain task is achieved through emotion. It helps Individuals strive towards improving their personal life situations. The goal is to main rain the life situation and improves it while keeping off every form of negative situations that will hinder the progress made (Wu et al., 2012). Therefore human motivation is achieved through certain emotions. It helps ensure that human beings do not harm themselves and also it keeps them in check. They should continuously seek to improve their life. The main aim of human motivation is to ensure that human beings experience more positive emotion and less negative emotions. The positive emotions will keep them motivated while few negative emotions will enable them learn. Too much negative emotion will result in lack of interest in an individual more so in negotiation. If they tend to lose in every negotiation they may lose interest or have less interest in being involved in negotiations.

7.5.2. Communication

A major part of negotiation is communication. This is because all parties will have to state their grievances through communication. While in a social environmental, emotions enables human beings thrive in such environments. While in such an environments different aspects are used to rely the type of emotion possessed by the Individual. Some of these aspects include the facial expressions, body-language and language. These aspects allow Individuals express what they are feeling and thinking. There are two main roles of emotions in the communication process. The first function is that expressed emotions enable other Individuals perceive how the Individual feels. The second role is once the emotion has been expressed and perceived. Those at the receiving end will exhibit a certain behavior.

This is well demonstrated in a case where an adult expresses fear to children or other adults causing them to be fearful hence a state of panic will be fostered. However, if an individual smiles as an expression of positive emotion then it will result in those perceiving the emotion being calm therefore diffusing the sense of fear or danger. In the negotiation process emotions expressed by Individuals will be useful in determining whether or not the Individuals or groups appreciate their negotiation partners and the subject of discussion. This means that emotions are an important factor in the communication process as it enables those involved understand what their opposer feel and think. With emotions, Individuals need to know how to express and perceive emotions being portrayed. This will help ensure that the process is successful while in the social environment (Weller et al., 2007).

7.5.3. Decision Making

Decisions are made throughout the life if an individual. The decision making process forms part of daily life. For instance in a typical day one decides whether or not they will get up. They will decide whether they will walk to work or drive to work and where they will have lunch or dinner. The decision making process takes the rational approach as the Individual will have to decide on the best option that will enable them achieve their goals. There are different types of decision makers. There are those who make decisions on the basis of a cost-benefit evaluation. Such kind of decision making is no longer used currently though they were referred to as homo-economicus. The term economics is used in showing that they are focused getting economic benefits. Research done showed that a different decision making process is used by humans. In the current research done, it is very evident that emotions will majorly influence the decision making process. In some of the experiments, individuals suffering from brain damage were involved in the study. Researchers were evaluating their ability to make decisions based in their emotions.

When writing books based on the experiment, 12 patients were involved. These patients had prefrontal brain damage which greatly influenced their ability to feel different emotions and also make certain decisions. Different tests were done on the patients who generated results that indicated that emotion mostly influenced their ability to make certain decisions. One of the tests involved rational options being presented to patients. One of the patients said that they would still be unable to make a decision (Van Ginkel & Van Knippenberg, 2009). For such patients, it was determined that brain damage affected their ability to use emotions when making a decision. This is because they were unable to use emotional evaluation when assessing different options as ordinary people would. They were able to use the rational approach in making decisions as they are able to perceive rational differences. Though the rational approach in making decisions is valid, it presents a challenge. These individuals are unable to reach a final decision as they do not know whether the results of the action will benefit of harm them. These possess a threat to their personal goals.

It was later discovered that every person's decisions are affected by their emotions. Emotions enable us make decisions faster and those that benefit us. Emotions enable us weigh the pros and cons of a decision. This means that when making rational decisions emotions will be given their own space in the process for the outcome to be beneficial. Therefore emotions should be included during the decision making process.

7.6. PERCEPTION OF EMOTIONS IN THE NEGOTIATION PROCESS

During the process of effective negotiation, it is important for both sides to be able to perceive the emotion of the other group. This making it crucial for those involved in the argument to be able to perceive emotions. This brings about the concept of emotional intelligence in an effective negotiation process.

7.6.1. The Concept of Emotional Intelligence

This is a new development in the context of intelligence as there are significant deviations from the previous concept of intelligence. Initially the intelligent quotient was used in defining the traditional view of intelligence. There are numerous theories of intelligence used in defining the term emotional intelligence. The major intelligence theory used in negotiation is the concept of multiple intelligence which was developed between the 1979s–1980s. This theory is a major concept and brought a new understanding of the concept of intelligence as it embraces a new perspective to the traditional understanding of intelligence. While developing the theory/concept the developer states that the old understanding of intelligence is way too limited. This means that it cannot fully represent or reflect the full meaning of intelligence. In his new definition of intelligence the developer highlight right types of intelligence namely intrapersonal, naturalist, linguistic, spatial, interpersonal, bodily-kinesthetic and logical-mathematical intelligence.

However, with regards to personal intelligence there are two elements of intelligence forming its foundation. This means that there are two main dimensions of personal intelligence. One of the dimensions of personal intelligence is interpersonal intelligence. It is referred to as the core capacity as it accesses an individual's feelings. It identifies the range of emotions exhibited by an individual. The core capacity is able to affect negative perceptions against some of the feelings. It is used in labeling these emotions (Tang & Liao, 2021). The labeling makes it easy to enmesh emotions in symbolic codes and can therefore be drawn upon. This creates an avenue allowing an individual understand and direct another human being's behavior. Knowledge on interpersonal intelligence is very advanced as it enables an individual to detect and also symbolize differentiated and advanced varieties of emotions.

By definition, the core capacity when dealing with interpersonal intelligence is referred to as the ability of an individual to notice and make distinct variations between individuals. Some if the distinctions can be made based in the individual's motivations, moods, intentions and temperaments. For an individual who has been able to study advanced interpersonal intelligence they may be able to use their skills in reading the desires and intentions of an individual. Though the desires and intentions may be hidden these skills enable an individual perceive then. For those who are able, they may be able to use this knowledge to their advantage. For instance, if they have noted a certain behavior they may advise members of their group to behave in a certain manner for the negotiation to be effective.

On the basis of the multiple intelligence theory while focusing on interpersonal intelligence, emotional intelligence is defined as one's ability to express and perceive emotions. Through thought they are able to assimilate the emotions allowing them to reason and understand the emotions by so doing they are able to regulate emotions in others and in themselves. When dealing with emotional intelligence, there are five main areas identified during the definition. These main areas include self-awareness. This form the foundation for emotional intelligence. This is because an individual has the ability to understand and recognize different emotions once they occur. In a bid to stay in charge and also retain the clear sight if emotional responses and decisions making process one will have to recognize and monitor.

Laying on the foundation of self-awareness is self-regulation which involves the ability of an individual to control their personal emotions allowing them regulating their emotions. These way individuals can increase positive emotions while reducing negative emotions. Emotions can be used to motivate individuals by increasing their creativity and aids in maintaining focus when certain tasks are being performed making the process more productive and efficient (Sorkin et al., 2001). The other area of emotional intelligence is empathy. In this case, one individual understands the emotions of another human being. While defining empathy, one can refer to it as a crucial aspect in interpersonal relationships. During the process of identify and perceiving emotions, one requires social skills. These set of skills enable an individual handle perceived emotions. This enables them create rapport. It is also a useful resource in building personal relationships.

All the five main areas of emotional intelligence make up the list of fundamental skills shared among emotionally intelligent individuals. With perception of emotions, it is very important for individuals to look out for non-verbal ques. As emotions play a major role in helping individuals interact between each other they also help ensure that people are motivated and can make sound decisions. There are different ways in which emotions are expressed. Usually one does not have to say that they are happy or sad. Instead those interacting with them will have to perceive these emotions among them. However, perception of emotions is still a challenge for most individuals as most of them do not give much attention to the different signs of emotion. This makes it difficult for negotiations to be successful. For a negotiation to be successful, one has to possess the ability to identify an emotion in their counterparts and use this knowledge to react to the emotion. By balancing out the emotions the process of negotiation will be more fruitful. When dealing with negotiation, one has to know that there are six types of basic emotions which when perceived would help improve the process of negotiation.

7.6.2. Six Basic Emotions Used in Negotiation

In the study of the recent theory on emotional intelligence, six emotions were found to be the base of other emotions. Among the scholars who studied human emotions is Charles Darwin. From his studies it was established that emotions are innate implying that they cannot be culturally learnt. From the study, he came to the conclusion that there are certain facial expressions 0resent universally among all individuals. One can then state that some of these emotions are inherited therefore they are part of the evolutionary inheritance.

In the 20th century the ideology of evolutionary inheritance of facial expressions and some of them being universally used was embraced by most anthropologists. This resulted in some of them publishing books and among them was Silvan Tomkins who did embrace the ideology presented by Darwin. However, in his book, he was unable to back all his claims as there wasn't any sufficient evidence to prove the claims. Different researchers conducted their own experiments on facial expressions. There were researchers who were against Darwin's ideology of emotions being evolutionary inherited. Among these researchers was Paul Ekman . From his research, the ideology of Darwin stood strong in that there are certain emotions developed among human being through a natural process called evolution. This means that such emotions will be universally present among all humans though different characteristics will be used to express the emotions (Schulz-Hardt et al., 2002).

From the research he was able to discover that the face of a human being is able to express different emotions. These facial expressions were more than ten thousand. Though there are different facial expressions, there are six main basic emotions universally present. They are said to be universally present as they can be identified throughout the world. For the other emotions, there are expressed differently across different cultures. The six basic emotions include surprise, anger, fear, sadness, disgust and happiness. There are other emotions other than these six main emotions. The six are well known as they have been universally identified to be present among people across the globe. The other emotions such as love, trust, satisfaction, shame, excitement, embarrassment, envy and interest are present among individuals globally but exhibit different universal appearance. This may pose a challenge to individuals across different states to interpret these emotions when engaging in negotiations.

As emotions are known to affect the emotions of an individual, a lot of research has been done to evaluate how certain emotions can influence the manner in which individuals negotiate with others. Research revolved around certain emotions namely excitement, anger, regret, sadness, anxiety, envy and disappointment. The research focused on the effects of these emotions being expressed through actions or words while in the negotiation process.

A negotiation involving individuals in a long-term relationship, emotions play a very significant role. This may not be the case for transactional deals. Further research shows that individuals posses the ability to control the manner in which emotions are experienced. There are certain strategies that have been developed to help individuals control expression of emotions. This allows an individual to monitor the manner in which they express their emotions. There are certain ways in which some emotions can be clocked to the advantage of the individual. For instance, expressing anxiety may result in the negotiation process being suboptimal. However, with the developed emotion control strategies those who suffer from anxiety can follow some of the steps to help them limit their anxiety or manage it are such a manner that the other negotiator does not notice. The same case applies for other emotions. There are different coping strategies for various emotions that will help negotiations become more effective (Song, 2009).

7.6.3. Anxiety

Before the negotiation process begins, some of the negotiators may feel anxious. The same may be experienced during the early stages of the negotiation. As the negotiation continues there are those who will experience excitement or anger. The result of the negotiation may result in individual feeling sad, disappointed or attrition. To better understand how anxiety negatively affects the negotiation process it is crucial that we define it. Anxiety is referred to a state of anguish that threatens an individual's stimuli. This is normally experienced among individuals who read novels with unexpected results. Anxiety and anger are quite opposite in that anxiety is said to trigger "flight" which causes individuals to want to end or leave the negotiation process while anger makes individuals want to expound the situation by fighting it. In most negotiations, it is crucial for important for negotiators to exhibit persistence and patience. These two qualities are desired for the process to be effective. It is known to make the process be faster and is very productive. However, for individuals dealing with anxiety the negotiation process may be counterproductive.

Other than making the process counterproductive, anxiety can also negatively affect the negotiation process in other ways. Further research shows negative impact of anxiety in the negotiation process shows that negotiators dealing with anxiety tend to exhibit low expectations and aspirations. This makes them prone to offering timid requests. Such tendencies could result in low negotiation effects. Research done on the effects of anxiety in the negotiation process involved different groups of people negotiating for different items. There were those who negotiated with car dealers, others negotiated with strangers while others negotiated with their bosses for a salary increase. For those who were negotiating for a salary increase or with a stranger they recorded high levels of anxiety. In this case it was the dominant emotion. Those negotiating for a car recorded high levels excitement followed by anxiety. In anxiety is introduced during the negotiation process, some negotiators will exhibit different expressions of anxiety. There are those who will have sweaty palms while others become jumpy.

Generally, anxiety negatively affects the negotiation process. Those exhibiting high-level anxiety may not be able to effectively relay their information. Some may stammer while some may get upset stomach. If such an individual was involved in a competitive negotiation then they may be unable to win the arguments as they may not properly present their ideas. They may also limit themselves by not defending their arguments. Most negotiators used this to their advantage. They ensure that they instill anxiety in their opponents for them to win the negotiation. A good demonstration is the famous TV show Shark Tank. In the show, there are negotiators who want to purchase ideas or invest in entrepreneurial ideas (Schulze & Newell, 2016). All the entrepreneurs will have to put h their ideas to potential investors. In most cases, investors will ask questions that are unnerving and aggressive to create stress in the environment. The pressure mounted on entrepreneurs may result in stress or anxiety among them. The investors are usually equipped with negotiation skills which gives them the ability to through entrepreneurs off guard giving them an opportunity to get the best ideas at a price if their choice. In cases where there several investors who want to be involved in the business; they may give remarks intended to create anxiety in entrepreneurs.

In such a case scenario, entrepreneurs who know how to handle such situations or can use different strategies to manage their anxiety are able to comfortably negotiate with the investors and in the end heat the best offers. There are numerous strategies used in managing anxiety. One of the most common strategies is involving a third party skilled in the art of negotiation. It is crucial for negotiators to ensure that they do not demonstrate any form anxiety. For those who tend to exhibit anxiety they may take various steps to help them work on the situation. Some opt to take training classes; others practice while others conduct several rehearsals before the presentation day. For such individuals, it is in their best interest for them to constantly work on their skills. As anxiety is the body's response to novel stimuli, familiarizing with different negotiation situations will help the individual feel less anxious as they will be comfortable with the situation. For those undertaking treatments to deal with anxiety, most therapists will use exposure therapy. This is when people are exposed to elements or situations that Mae them nervous. Statistics show that there is an increase in the number of individuals enrolled in negotiation classes.

In such classes, there are first taught on different strategies they can use to control their anxiety. Afterwards, they are equipped with different skills useful in the negotiation process. In such classes participants are exposed to different negotiation situations which are a form of simulations. By taking in such exercises negation becomes more natural and in a real life negotiation situation the environment will not induce anxiety. For those who are not able to properly manage their anxiety, it is advisable for them to involve an expert during the negotiation process who will handle all the negotiations. This is crucial for the individual to be an experienced negotiator. They should be able to control their anxiety while using their negotiation skills during the process. In most cases, individuals involve third parties who have taken part in other negotiations as the process will be normal for them and they know how to leverage themselves to ensure that the process is successful. Though involving a third party may be deemed to be a coo-out, it is a common practice in most companies.

This is evident in real estate marketing when families involve brokers to negotiate for better house prices. However, one should take into consideration that they may have to incur more costs due to the hiring of a third party. One will have to weigh the benefits (Sari, 2008). If hiring a third party will help increase the chances of winning numbers, the negotiation then it may be the best way to go. This method is highly advised for individuals who have high levels of anxiety in the sense that it is a challenge for them to regulate these emotions when placed in an uncomfortable environment. This party can also be involved when a negotiation begins to go south.

7.6.4. Anger

Among the negative emotions is anger. When categorized according to its effects in negotiations, it is among the emotions known to negatively affect the negotiation process. Anger and anxiety fall under the same category though they are different in certain ways. Anxiety as an emotion is self-focused different from anger which is directed to another individual. An effective negotiation process requires both negotiators to be able to keep their anger in check though there are those who do not agree with this ideology. There are those who perceive anger as the best emotion for the negotiation process as it could lead to productive results of the process. For these reason some refer to it as a productive emotion as it is useful in helping them acquire the best deals. This is applicable in the case where individuals perceive the negotiation process in a competitive perspective. This ideology if anger as a productive emotion may not hold in other negotiation process that is collaborative in nature.

This form of bias is what research refers to as the fixed-pie bias. In this case, the negotiator, more so those who are not familiar with negotiation processes, have the ideology that the other negotiator's interests are not similar to theirs. This makes the process take the form of a zero-sum game. For such negotiators, they view the negotiation process as competitive. This is not the case for negotiators with much experience. This kind of negotiators uses different means to achieve their win. They try to obtain the best solution rather than seeking for their own interests being used. In most cases, anger is viewed as an empowering emotion as it makes one appear powerful, strong and highly successful. This can be proven in different case scenarios as the individual is able to confidently support their ideas (Saaty & Peniwati, 2013).

Many individuals will report that they have felt anger during or after a negotiation process. Though some view anger to be a productive emotion, it is still a negative emotion and negatively affects the negotiation process. It poses a threat to the negotiation process as it could result several biased perceptions, increased conflicts and numerous impasses being made. The emotion is not beneficial for the process as it minimizes joint gains; increases offer rejection rates, reduces cooperation among members and creates an environment for competitive behavior among individuals. In most cases when negotiators are expressing their ideas while angry may end up giving inaccurate information as they may not be able to remember their own interests. In this state individuals have already developed a perception about the Individual making them less likely to be understanding. For those who are able to use anger in the negotiation process use the emotion with the aim of causing other negotiators to retaliate. This emotion is not good as there are other methods that can be used during the process while producing effective results.

7.6.5. Fear

Fear is among the six basic emotions. It results in negative effects on the negotiation process. It is known to be experienced after one experiences surprise. This emotion is really important for individuals at it enables them handle threats by placing much emphasis on the origin of the threat or harm giving time for one to come up with ways to overcome the threat. It is a crucial emotion as it enables one to gain skills needed to ensure their survival. This means that the individual should use knowledge to allow them keep away from harm or danger. It is the emotion needed in protecting one from harm as they will be able to perceive and deal with the threat. This emotion is usually triggered by harm. The human body is made in a way that it is able to perceive and protect itself from harm. There are two dimensions of fear as a result of the harm threatened. It can either be psychological or physical.

In the case of physical harm, it is triggered by a threatened bodily harm. This triggers fear which may result in the individual wanting to protect themselves from the impending bodily harm. For the case of psychological fear, it is triggered by things that would normally affect humans psychologically. Some if these triggers include loss if a loved one, loss of a job or disappointment. Certain fear triggers can be identified globally (Saka et al., 2008). Some of these fears include the fear if being harmed by an animal, learnt fear triggers or sudden changes in gravity. Fear triggers are different among individuals universally. These fears are brought about by the type of social surrounding and educational environment among others. For instance, western cultures possess a high fear for insects compared to those in eastern cultures.

There are different levels of fear. In all different levels, fear negatively impacts the learning environment. This is because such a negotiator may not be able to properly present their interests. In the case where the negotiation took the competitive approach the negotiator may not be able to win the negotiation. The basic level of fear is anxiety. As the level of stress and pressure increases in the negotiation process then fear levels increase. The highest level of fear is terror. The level of fear is dependent on the type of stimuli introduced making fear intensities be dependent on the subjective cognitive appraisal of the exposed stimuli. If a negotiator threatens the other negotiator then it will introduce fear in the other individual resulting in negative results of the negotiation process. This is because some individuals do not respond well to fear. There are those who will run away from the situation while there are those who may not be able to work well in such an environment. There are three main responses to fear namely freezing, fleeing and fright. These responses are survival tactics of the body to help them cope with the situation at hand.

Fear can also be noted among individuals who are participating in their first negotiation. They are anticipating for the process to be smooth sailing and successful. If things do not go as planned they will experience anxiety which may then lead to fear. If this happens in a group negotiation, it is important for the leader to use identify the emotion and try to manage it. There are several facial expressions that depict fear. One of the common indicators us when eye brows are drawn together in a manner that they are much closer than usual. For others they will have raised eyebrows that are straightened. There are those face will have horizontal wrinkles. In other cases, fear may be noted through word of mouth. Once the emotion has been identified, the leader should try to reassure the individual. This will help them calm down. This will enable the individuals compose himself before they present their interests. For such negotiation environments it may be beneficial if another negotiator involved. This is because if their counterparts perceive fear in the negotiator, they will use it to their advantage ensuring that the individual is not interested in speaking.

While perceiving emotions, it is crucial for one to know the difference between fear and surprise. In most cases facial expressions demonstrating such kind of emotions tend to be similar. Though it might be quite hard to distinguish the two emotions, there are certain differences that can be used in distinguish them. It requires a lot of keenness and attention for one to properly identify certain emotions and properly differentiate between them to avoid any forms of misunderstanding.

7.6.6. Enjoyment and Happiness

These emotions are positive in nature. Among all the six emotions, happiness is the only positive emotion. There is still a sense of contradiction with surprise as it can be classified as either negative or positive. With regards to happiness, there are four main types of such an emotion namely intro-spectional happiness, excitement, pleasure and relief. In the case of pleasure, it is happiness caused by physical sensations while happiness due to psychological sensations is referred to as excitement in that the subject or matter in question is attractive or interests an individual. Relief is a form of happiness caused by the removal of a burden or a form of fear. In the case of intro-spectional happiness, it is happiness as a result of a changed or modified perception of one's self in a positive manner (Risco & Duffy, 2011).

In the negotiation process, positive emotions are known to contribute to effective negotiations. This is because such kinds of emotion influence negotiators in both sides in a positive manner that results in the negotiation process becoming integrative in nature. According to research, if negotiators in either side bear positive emotions towards their counterparts then both parties aim at achieving integrative agreements. In most cases, flexibility will be embraced throughout the process allowing the development of the best solutions. If negotiators bear positive emotions then it becomes quite easy for them to develop a positive attitude towards their counterparts. If the feeling is mutual among both parties then there will be a lot of flexibility throughout the process.

Happiness and enjoyment amongst all negotiators increases chances of the negotiation process being more productive and it reduces the likelihood of a conflict arising among both sides. Such positive emotion makes it easier for both sides to develop trust. Such emotions are known to cultivate persistence among individuals. The emotions create a conducive environment for both sides causing negotiators to be more confident giving them the push they need to raise their concerns and interests and persist on getting certain issues to be addressed. This makes the negotiation process to be more effective. Research also shows that positive emotions influence a negotiation making it more effective as solutions can be achieved faster than usual. Also, positive emotions among negotiators will increase chances of both parties wanting to interact in future.

7.7. MANAGING COUNTERPART'S EMOTION DURING NEGOTIATIONS

Effective negotiation requires one's emotion to be controlled in the sense that it does not disrupt the process. This is very crucial as negotiation processes is interpersonal in nature. The process involves more than two individuals negotiating their interests. In other cases large groups if individuals are involved in the negotiation. There are different ways one can manage their emotions. In some cases, the counterpart may be required to manage the emotions of the negotiator. This is possible if the negotiator can proper manage their emotions. In most cases there are two common strategies used are negotiators. The first strategy requires the negotiator to be observant. By observing their counterparts, the negotiator can perceive the kind of emotions they are experiencing. This is a crucial element in the concept of emotional intelligence. It is an important element in negotiations. While observing, the negotiator will have to take note of the body language of the counterpart, the type of words used to express their interest and the tone of their voice.

In the case where both non-verbal and verbal cues are not aligned, the negotiator may have to inquire about the counterpart's decision whether they agree with the arrangement, why they are uneasy, whether there is something that makes them uncomfortable or whether they are trying to intimidate others. By observing the counterpart, it becomes much easier to as pointed questions. This is because the questions will be structured according the perceived emotions of the counterpart. Based on the emotions and the answer it will become much easier for the negotiator to understand their counterpart's perspective. Answers given by the counterpart are likely to be accurate as pointed questions make it difficult for them to lay or omit certain information.

The second strategy requires the negotiator to be brave in that they can be able to directly influence emotions. Though this strategy may appear to be manipulative it may be advantageous for the negotiating if the influence is positive. Take an instance where in the negotiation, the counterpart expressed anger or anxiety then it may be advisable for the other negotiator to add humor to the situation or a form of emphatic reassurance to alter the interaction tone. In the case where the counterpart exhibits overconfidence or arrogance the other negotiator can induce a healthy dose of fear by using strategized anger (Reynolds et al., 2009). This may be useful in modifying the emotions other than these two strategies there other strategies that have proven effective. For instance, the negotiator can present a certain emotion which will be perceived by the counterpart who will then make an interpretation of the emotion and react according to it. If one employee comes to work crying then others will feel compassionate and want to know the problem. They will then choose words that will full encompass their emotion.

Chapter 8

Role of Justice in Negotiation

CONTENTS

8.1. INTRODUCTION

We live in a world where we always agree to disagree. Human beings are known to be social beings in that; we survive through interactions; and as the saying goes: "*No man is an island*" is prove enough that we need each other for life to have some meaning or have purpose. Through our interactions, there are times that we do agree on the same thing, and other times which we disagree. In most cases, the disagreements turn into conflicts which cause unnecessary enmity and in serious situations, the conflicts might lead to violence.

For the purposes of avoiding violence, a new method of reaching an amicable decision has slowly become part of the human race.

Negotiation is a term used to refer to the process by which, two or more parties reach a win-win agreement after all of them having had different opinions. The win-win agreement ensures that each party is comfortable with the final decision, and that neither of them feels ignored or a bit pressed against the wall (Reinalda & Verbeek, 2004). However, not all individuals have managed to master the art of negotiation, and for this reason; it is important that the subject of negotiation be taught in all learning institutions to help people master the art of negotiation at an early age.

Figure 8.1. An image showing a group of individuals negotiating.

Source: https://www.inc.com/thomas-koulopoulos/the-one-thing-you-should-never-do-when-you-negotiate-hint-put-away-the-gloves.html.

Negotiation ought to be a process whereby, all the parties involved will do their best to increase the chances of them reaching an amicable decision; do their best to avoid occurrence of any conflicts; ensure that, even after the discussion, they will be able to maintain a mutual relationship; and that, they all benefit from the negotiation process. The parties involved in negotiations should also ensure that, they trust each, for without trust, the role of respecting each other's opinion and taking it in a positive way will be low.

The process of negotiation has always been part of the human race for eternity. We negotiate in schools, in churches, in offices, in government; basically, every place where more than one individual interact, there must exists negotiations.

With negotiation, there exist professional negotiators and regular ones. Professional negotiators include the likes of: union negotiators, who represent a union during the process of making deals with other unions; peace negotiators, whom, as the name suggests, their sole responsibility is to ensure that they help in settling conflicts and bringing peace in environments where normal negotiations was impossible, they are more of arbitrators, that is, third parties; hostage negotiators, whom as the name suggests, help in negotiating with kidnappers or other individuals to let go of the hostages, in order to give them something else in return for the purposes of a win-win situation (Rassin et al., 2008). The process of negotiation has also been introduced to computers. With the latest technological advancement, artificial intelligence has been used in invention of computing devices which mimic the normal functioning of human beings in their day to day lives. Since, human beings do require negotiations to live a peaceful life, so do the AI machines. The machine negotiation is referred to as the autonomous negotiation; which is a process whereby different computer components have to agree on how to function strategically for a desired positive output.

8.2. INTRODUCTION TO JUSTICE

Negotiation process needs to be a fair and just process, and for this reason, there is need for justice to be considered during the negotiation process. Justice is the process by which people get to experience what they deserve based on their actions. With justice, the experiences might be based on ethics, equality, religious beliefs, and fairness, among others. Furthermore, justice is believed to be derived from the mutual understanding that, we as human beings have.

Figure 8.2. An image illustrating how justice is determined during negotiation proceedings.

Source: https://hiscreation.co.ke/justice-be-our-shield-and-defender/.

The relation between negotiations and justice comes in when ensuring that, the negotiation process does not lead to chaos; and that, as state severally in the above section, the process will benefit both parties; whereby they will have to reach a mutual understanding. With the presence of justice, the negotiating parties are guaranteed of maintaining a harmonious relationship with each other which does even promote friendship, a move that could benefit both of them.

The process of justice is believed to be more than a mortal thing; rather, it is believed to a divine thing. For individuals who believe in God, or any other supernatural being; they are sure that the divine authority requires them to live together in harmony and peace; and for them to do so, negotiations must exist and that they should be just so as to promote the principle of harmony and peace and for the purposes of obeying their divine authority.

However, the aspect of justice has faced some serious opposition more so among individuals who believe that justice is just a way of the individuals in power oppressing their subjects. Such people believe that, human beings should be free to live life as they want to; and that disagreements are part of life, and in fact, that they are necessary in order for respect to be represent and also for loyalty to last (Pérez et al., 2010).

For justice to serve its purpose during negotiations; the parties involved should first define what is right and what is wrong according to their beliefs.

This is necessary because, not all people believe on same things to be right; sometimes, what seems to be right to one individual is wrong to the other individual; and with such misunderstandings, an amicable decision is next to impossible. Furthermore, parties involved in negotiations should be able to understand that, justice is not all about proving oneself right or to revenge on the other party; rather, that, justice is necessary to avoid revenge or comparisons.

Justice is necessary in negotiations for it helps in equally weighing out the opinions of both parties, and ensuring that; each opinion receives and equal measure and that no one side has been favored. This applies mostly in cases, where an arbitrator or a peace negotiator is required to solve a certain conflict.

8.3. ROLE OF JUSTICE IN NEGOTIATIONS

As stated severally in the previous section, justice does play several roles in negotiation. One, justice plays a role of guiding the parties involved throughout their negotiation process by ensuring that; they present their proposal in a fair manner that ensures that each proposal is heard and respected. Secondly, justice ensures that the discussion process is conducted in a friendly manner, and that each proposal presented at the beginning of the discussion is reviewed thoroughly and that there is limited criticism. Thirdly, justice helps in the formulation of the agreements by ensuring that; all the possible solutions presented by each party are respected and that, the decision on which agreement is the most suitable one is respected.

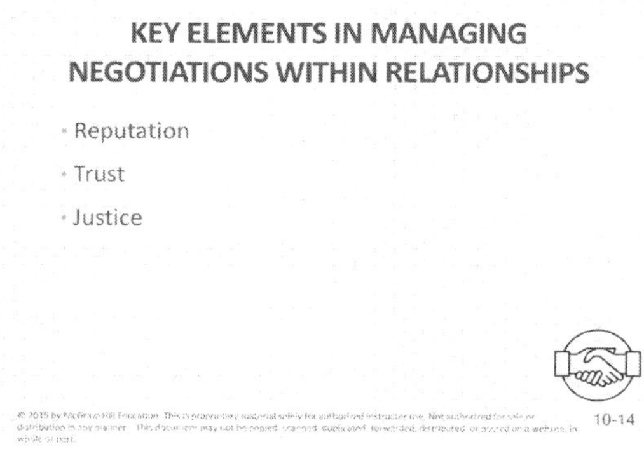

Figure 8.3. An image showing the key roles of justice in negotiations.

Source: https://slideplayer.com/slide/13596955/.

Reciprocity should always be taken in consideration so as to ensure that the process is fair and just. The principle of reciprocity exists in different dimensions. One, there is comparative responsiveness which ensures that, each negotiating party is given enough time to compare their opinion with the other parties opinion; and thoroughly analyze the similarities and difference; and what they would do if they were in the other parties shoes. With comparative responsiveness, before a common decision is reached, both parties are able to at least understand each other's point of view and their difference before an amicable decision is reached.

The second dimension of the reciprocity principle is the diffuse reciprocity. Diffuse reciprocity, as the name suggests, ensures that the involved parties at least get a chance to at least try to understand each other's opinions roughly (Patalano & LeClair, 2011). The difference between diffuse reciprocity and comparative reciprocity is that; with diffuse, the parties do not have to compare their opinions with each other, all they have to do is at least try and understand what could have made the other party suggest such an opinion; unlike in comparative reciprocity where both parties have the role of understanding and also comparing their opinions. The main goal for diffuse reciprocity is to ensure that, before a decision is made, that both parties, at least have a clue of each other's opinions.

Justice ensures that, stalemates and deadlocks are avoided during a negotiation process. Negotiations which require the making of a decision that might affect large populations for instance a country; are mostly faced with deadlocks. As the name suggests, deadlocks prevent parties from reaching an amicable decision. With deadlocks, one party tries to withhold important information which is needed by the other party for a solid decision to be reached. An instance of deadlocks is when, either of the parties present is not willing to share their view of the other party's suggestions; a move that discouraging the discussed party from sharing their opinions too. Stalemates occur when, both parties are unable to reach an agreement because neither of the parties' proposals are suitable enough for either of them (Nutt, 2006). For instance, stalemate could be a situation whereby, both parties are only pushing for the passing of their own opinions; and neither of them is interested in trying to apply the reciprocity principle. Justice avoids the occurrence of stalemate and deadlocks by ensuring that common laws are formulated to guide the entire negotiation process; at least, with the presence of common laws, both parties will be discussing while aiming at remaining within the constraints of the formulated laws, a move which fastens the negotiation process, making it easy for a decision to be reached. The laws being formulated should win the respect of all involved parties so as to ensure that some parties do not feel cornered. If the negotiations are being conducted with the help of a negotiator, the negotiator should ensure they run the negotiations process in a reasonable and balanced manner.

The aspect of justice in negotiations could be divided into two major techniques:

1. *Forward looking justice technique.* As the name suggest, the forward looking technique ensures that, the main role for justice during negotiations is to ensure of a bright and positive future for the parties involved. For instance, in situations where laws have to be formulated to guide in the negotiation process; the laws have to lead to the yielding of positive results for both parties; both in the present and the future, but more so in the future. With forward looking justice technique, the negotiating parties could agree on coming up with a decision that benefits them in the future, allowing them to let go of their current conflicts and instead focus on working hard for the future. However, with the forward looking technique, both parties ought to understand their cause of conflicts and amicably agree on letting go of their conflicting opinions; a move which ensures that, the union which they form for their future will be solid and there will be no grudges between them.
2. *Backward looking justice technique.* As the name suggests, the backward looking technique is a justice technique which aims reaching an amicable decision by referring to past events that affected the negotiating parties either in a positive or negative way (LeClair, 2010). The backward looking technique aims at settling both present and past scores of the involved parties. With this technique, the negotiating process focuses on knowing the main root cause of the issue, and helping both parties open their eyes to the root case by; digging deep into the cause of the problems they are trying to solve. In most cases, negotiations which are solved using the backward looking technique might take some time before an amicable decision is reached. This is because, the parties will have solved the problem, but they will not have addressed the way forward.

Currently, the involvement of justice into negotiation process has reached the level of digitization. With digitization of negotiation process, applications which are able to draw hypothesis of different justice techniques and the possible outcomes have been invented. At least this way, the negotiator is able to predict what the possible results could be during the negotiation process if a certain justice method justice has been used.

8.4. TYPES OF JUSTICE USED IN NEGOTIATIONS

Justice system is divided into several types which could all be applied during negotiations to help the conflicting parties to reach an amicable agreement. However, there exist two main types of negotiations. The first type is the distributive justice which ensures that there is fairness during the negotiation process. The second most common type of justice is the retributive justice.

8.4.1. Distributive Justice in Negotiations

Distributive justice, as the name suggests, is a certain type of justice which majorly focuses on ensuring that the negotiation process is conducted in a manner that is fair to all parties involved. Distributive justice is determined by use of emotional evaluations whereby, the all the involved parties are asked of their emotional expectations during the negotiation process. If either of the parties feels that they have been oppressed, then the justice system used during the negotiation process is considered to be non-distributive justice.

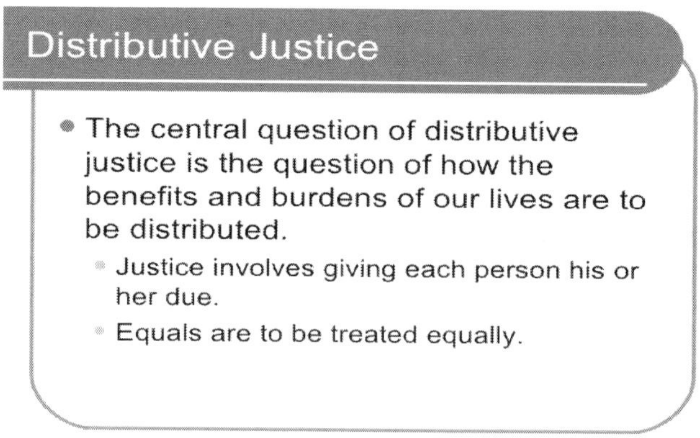

Figure 8.4. An image showing the description of distributive justice which is used during negotiations.

Source: https://www.slideshare.net/stevenjkashdan/types-of-justice.

Distributive justice operates under the six factors which guide how it is executed. The first factor is that equality. The method of justice should ensure that there is equality during the entire process of negotiation. For instance, as stated severally in the above section, each and every proposal for all the negotiating parties ought to be respected. The equality factor supports both the justice categories in that; the forward looking negotiation technique requires that all opinions of the involved parties be heard and respected, before they agree on a common goal which they all aim to achieve in future; the backward looking justice technique does also require equality in that, all negotiating parties ought to be heard for the purposes of understanding the common cause of the problem at hand.

The second factor is proportionality. Proportionality plays a big role in negotiations more so during conclusion of the entire process. The principle of proportionality ensures that, each concluding suggestion is given a specific percentage depending on its weight in terms of how relevant it is. Proportionally applies in both categories for it ensures that each and every opinion of the involved parties is weighed according to its relevance to the negotiation process (Leclercq, 2018).

The third factors are compensation. Compensation ensures that, the category of justice being selected serves the purpose of ensuring that the unfairly treated negotiating parties are compensated in a just way. For instance, during the forward looking justice technique, some of the opinions from maybe the minority negotiating parties might be ignored, and the parties with more influence manage to push for their suggestion. In such an instance, the compensation principle ensures that, the final agreement does also consider the "*previously oppressed party*" and ensures that it is a win-win agreement.

The fourth factor is need. The need principle applies in all justice negotiation skills in that; the forward looking justice technique requires all the needs of the involved parties be considered and respected. The backward looking justice technique does also require that all the needs of the negotiating parties to be heard and respected.

Power is the fifth factor which influences the execution of the distributive form of justice. During negotiation process, individuals who are much influential or in authority should accept the rule that they have to receive less attention; and allow more attention to be given to individuals who are in less influential. However, this does not mean that, opinions from influential individuals should be ignored; rather it means that, their opinions should not be favored based on the fact that they are influential. The power factor is mostly considered if the forward looking justice technique is being used. This is because most influential individuals push for agendas that will benefit most in the future, not minding about the future of the less influential individuals within their midst.

Last but not least, is the sixth factor which influences distributive factor, responsibility. Responsibility plays a role in negotiation by ensuring that all involved parties understand the fact they have to play their part in ensuring that the negotiation process is a success.

The above mentioned factors do also influence the final decision to be made in the negotiation process. For instance, the need factors might play a much bigger role in influencing the final decision to be made such that, the other factors do influence the process of reaching an amicable agreement that much.

Not all negotiation processes which turn out to be successes. This means that, some negotiation agreements might only last for a short period immediately after the negotiation process has been completed. For this reason, it is necessary that the rules set before the negotiation process was initiated, be set in a manner that ensures that they are to be strictly adhered to during and also after the negotiation process; in order to ensure that the agreement still holds even after the negotiation process is complete (Mustakallio et al., 2002).

8.4.2. Theories of Distributive Justice in Negotiation

The application of distributive justice in negotiations has led to the existence of several theories of how the justice type helps in negotiation process. One of the theories is that, application of distributive justice in negotiation should always promote fairness. With this theory, it is believed that no negotiation should be conducted under distributive justice and there be cases of inequality, or oppression of people rights such as the likes of right to express oneself, or even cases of disrespect. The fairness theory has been shared among people to the extent that it seems to be true because, it has helped in so many cases, by fastening the negotiation process.

The second theory that is associated with application of distributive justice in negotiation process is the theory that believes in determination of the original cause of the conflict and the original procedure to be followed during the negotiation process. This theory helps in ensuring that, both parties are able to understand the root cause of the conflict they are addressing. The original position theory ensures that, during the entire process, the negotiation follows a certain procedure that is fair and just.

The other theory is the veil of ignorance. As the name suggests, the veil of ignorance encourages the negotiators to hide their titles or rank in certain places. This gives them the advantage of being able to negotiate peacefully without any favors during the negotiating process. The veil of ignorance supports the power factors of distributive justice.

The fourth theory is the principle of just distribution. As the name suggests, the basic principle of just distribution pushes for equal recognition of all individuals during the negotiation process. With basic principle of just distribution, each present member is given an opportunity to air their opinions; and each aired opinion is given same weight. The theory of principle of just distribution is further divided into two more categories. The first category is the liberty principle (Mukherjee et al., 2016). As the name suggests, the liberty principle gives negotiators a chance to understand their right throughout the negotiation process and what it is expected of them. The rights should be equal among all members present during the negotiation process. The second category associated with the principle of just distribution is the difference principle. As the name suggests, the difference principle pushes for the recognition of all members present during the negotiation process despite their differences. In a negotiating platform, there are different categories of negotiators present. Some of them are more influential whereas others are not that influential. The difference principle encourages that, if there are any nominations being done for the board responsible for controlling the negotiation process, members who are less influential should be given more seats compared to members who are more influential; at least this way, each and every individual will be represented and the chances of favors will be minimal.

The fifth theory associated with the distributive form of justice used in negotiations is the utilitarianism. The utilitarianism supports fairness during the negotiation process by pushing for the belief that, anything that supports the well-being of the entire society from the negotiation process is good, and anything that attempts to degrade the goodness in the society during the negotiation process is bad. Basically, the application of this theory as a form of justice during the negotiation process pushes for the greater good of not only the negotiators present during the negotiation process, but also for the entire society at large which will be affected either directly or indirectly (Martinsons & Davison, 2007). The theory of utilitarianism is further divided into one justice categories. The category referred to as the conceptualizing welfare. The conceptualizing welfare, as the name suggests, pushes for the application of certain concepts which will lead to positive results which benefit the welfare of not only negotiators but also the individuals to be affected by the final agreement indirectly. With conceptualization welfare sub-theory of utilitarianism, the negotiation process has to evaluate the satisfaction of the involved parties and their level of happiness with the proceedings. This way, the negotiation process will yield to a positive agreement which will leave all negotiators happy and satisfied.

The sixth theory associated with the distributive form of justice is referred to as the egalitarianism. Egalitarianism is a theory which evaluates how the negotiation process is being conducted and ensures that all roles are distributed in a fair manner and justifies how the entire negotiation process proceeds from the first step of addressing the root cause of the conflict, to the presentation of proposal, to the evaluation and understanding of all the proposals, and finally to the conclusion of the negotiation process whereby the final decision is made. The egalitarianism theory promotes the equality factor of distributive justice whereby all parties are given the opportunity to relate with each other form an equality perspective.

8.4.3. Reasons for Use of Distributive Justice in Negotiation

Distributive justice is used during negotiation processes for various reasons. The first reason is that, it promotes efficiency of the negotiation process and makes it more productive for it pushes for equality and fairness during the entire negotiation process. With distributive justice, the negotiating parties are given the opportunity to appreciate the beauty of justice, for it is a friendly form of justice where each party is treated in fair manner without employment of harshness for the purposes of affirming the negotiation process. Distributive justice encourages individuals to go for negotiations as a way of solving their differences; for they are at least assured that the process will definitely lead to positive results.

The second reason as to why the distributive type of justice is used because it promotes the principle of proportionality. With distributive justice, individuals who are less privileged or less influential are not discouraged from engaging in negotiation process since they are sure they will not be disadvantaged. With proportionality, each and every individual, despite their rank is treated in a proportional manner depending on the weight of their proposal.

Negotiations which involve making decisions which affects not only the negotiating parties prefer the use of distributive type of justice. This is because; distributive justice promotes fairness not only for the negotiators but for the other parties to be affected indirectly by the final agreement; by use of the utilitarianism theory which pushes for them making of decisions for the good of the entire society.

The other main reason as to why the distributive form of justice is used during negotiation processes is because it promotes the policy of helping one another. With distributive justice, the forward looking technique of justice works well during negotiation since it will push for understanding of each party's point of view before a final decision is made.

8.4.4. Retributive Justice in Negotiation

Retributive justice is the other type of justice that is mostly used in negotiation process. Retributive justice is mostly used in instances where, the negotiation process involves the solving of a conflict which could lead to violence and damage of property. As the name suggests, retributive justice involves the use of harshness and punishment before an agreement is reached (Kugler et al., 2012). It supports the belief that, there must always exists permanent laws which will always guide the negotiation process and the consequences to the breaking of such laws should be clearly outlined from the word go. If no laws have been implemented before the negotiation process, retributive type of justice pushes for a negotiation process whereby the negotiating party will focus more on finding a form of punishment that suits the offender; and the punishment ought to be proportional with the offense committed.

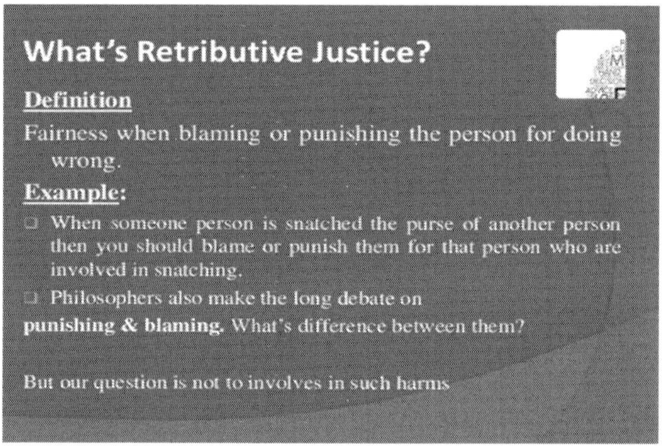

Figure 8.5. An image defining retributive justice and stating an example of how it is applied in negotiations.

Source: https://www.slideshare.net/muhammadshehrozafzal/ethics-retributive-justice-objections-to-ethics-of-care.

The use of retributive justice during negotiations does not mean that the negotiation process is all about seeking a perfect punishment for the offenders; rather, it promotes the reaching of an agreement of a suitable punishment for the offenders and the way forward, ensuring that the agreement will be amicable among all the involved parties; and that no parties will feel oppressed; and still that justice will be served. An instance of use of retributive justice is during post-election violence in different countries whereby, peace negotiators have to come together; understand the root cause of the violence; listen to the suspect's side of their story; agree on the suitable punishment for the law breakers; and agree on the way forward that will lead to peace instead of conflicts. Application of retributive justice in negotiation mostly involves the use of peace negotiators for the purposes of reaching an amicable agreement which is fair and just too all parties involved in the entire negotiation process.

Retributive justice promotes fairness and justice and eliminates the theme of revenge during negotiations. It mostly discourages the carrying out of negotiation processes with the aim of revenging for a wrongdoing committed. Retributive justice is not about the suffering of the law offenders; but it is about the affirming of the laws of a certain country or region, and discouraging other individuals from committing the same mistake; this might seem as an act of using the offenders to serve as an example to the want-to-be offenders; however, it is not, rather its main aim is to promote the theme of justice. Most people confuse the use of retributive justice in negotiations for the purposes of rehabilitation of the offenders; however, retributive justice focuses on making the offender understand the weight of the offense they committed. This does not mean it focuses on the suffering of the offender, rather, on making them know what they did is wrong, and there is no excuse whatsoever for the offense they committed (Kulcsár et al., 2020).

8.4.5. Reasons for Use of Retributive Justice in Negotiations

Retributive justice is mostly used in negotiations for many reasons. Retributive justice is used in negotiations mainly because; it discourages any form of favors during the negotiation process or the defense of the offender by one party. It sticks with, the need for execution of justice and that no individual should be favored because they are known or because they are special in any way. The other reason as to why retributive justice is used during negotiation processes is because it promotes discipline during negotiation process. With retributive justice, the use of negotiation to form major conflicts is respected for the final outcome ensures that justice is served; and that negotiation process will never be viewed as just a normal process which solves issues which addressing the root cause of the conflict and pushing for the rightful punishment for an offense committed.

Most individuals in the society have eroded their principle in the sense that, anyone who does not break the law is considered to not be man enough or to be a coward. The use of retributive justice during negotiations affirms not only to the negotiators but also to the individuals to be affected by the decision made indirectly that; all laws are important, and that, the adherence to the laws and regulations of a certain region is not a cowardice move, rather it is a bold move.

8.4.6. Principles Governing the Use of Retributive Justice in Negotiation

During negotiation process, there is need for use of various principles which guide the application of retributive justice to avoid occurrence of more conflicts during the negotiation process (Hwang & Lin, 2012). One of the main principle which govern the use of retributive justice during negotiations is the belief that, all law offenders should be willing to pay for the crimes they commit in manner proportional to the harm they caused. With this principle, during the entire negotiation process, all negotiating parties will be focusing on which is the most appropriate punishment and not on how to relieve the offender of the crimes they commit. The principle of proportionality could be likened to the mosaic forms of punishment in the bible where the negotiations focused on an eye to an eye form of punishment.

The second principle which guide the use of retributive justice is that, during the negotiation process, the reaching of a final agreement should not be influenced by the fact the offender might have committed the crime with the right intentions in mind. Basically, this principle focuses on the fact that, the negotiation process should not be compromised in any way, rather, it should focus on ensuring that justice and fairness are served in the most appropriate way.

The principle of fairness helps in guiding the negotiation process. With fairness, the negotiating parties should be able to understand the main cause of the problem. They should also be able to proof the guiltiness of the suspects. This principle of fairness ensures that, the rightful offender is punished and avoids the punishment of innocent individuals. This principle of fairness also ensures that the final decision made is fair to all parties.

8.4.7. Divisions of the Retributive Type of Justice

Retributive justice is further divided into different categories which could either be used during the negotiation process. The first category is referred to as the one that beliefs that, the negotiation process should focus on applying a proportional amount of punishments to the individuals who cause the conflict.

The second category of retributive justice believes that, during negotiations, the negotiators have the authority to change the punishment to impose on the wrong doer based on their reasons for committing a certain offense. For instance, some might have been on the influence of drugs the time they committed a certain offense, meaning that the negotiators have the obligation of judging the offense from a drug influence point of view; and at least try to reduce the amount of punishments. However, this category of retributive justice does not let wrong doers go scot free; they have to face some form of punishment for the to understand that what they did was wrong and is not acceptable at all.

The use of retributive justice in the negotiation process has faced a lot of criticism. Most individuals believe that it is an outdated way of guiding the negotiation process; and that, in most cases it leads to harsh decisions which are considered to be too much in our current generation. Furthermore, the retributive justice is opposed because, instead of focusing on the reformation of the wrong doer, it focuses on making sure the offender experience the same amount of pain they caused to others; not as a form of revenge, but as a way of forcing them understand what they did was wrong and that the same amount of pain they are currently experiencing, is the same amount of pain they caused to others.

Traditionally, several forms of punishments which were decided in negotiations guided by the retributive justice included the likes of sending the wrong doers into exile or shunning them completely from the society. This was a fair form of justice since most of them could survive away from their loved ones and find livelihood in other communities or in the forests. However, in our current society, sending an individual into exile is impossible, since our societies have advanced technologically such that, by the time an individual moves to the nearby society, their wrong doings will have been known by the whole world and it will be a challenge for them to find a society which will accept them and live with them (Herrera et al., 2005). The current forms of punishments imposed by negotiating committees guided by retributive justice include the likes of transformative justice whereby the offender is send to a rehabilitation center whereby they will be punished severely and given a chance to change their behaviors; the second one is restorative justice, whereby the offenders is send to prison and exposed to almost the same amount of pain they caused to others, giving them a chance to restore themselves and vow to never cause any form of harm to any other individual; and the last most common form of punishment under retributive justice in negotiations is the psychiatric imprisonment, which as the name suggests, is given to individuals who are considered to not be mentally unstable, and they have to undergo some form of treatment where they will go back to being normal and never attempt to cause any harm to anyone for they are now able to differentiate what is right and what is wrong.

8.5. BENEFITS OF USE OF JUSTICE DURING NEGOTIATIONS

The use of justice during negotiations benefits the negotiation process in so many ways. One, it ensures that the negotiators willingly agree to the negotiation process and that they are not forced by anyone or in any way to engage in the negotiation process. Furthermore, with presence of justice, the negotiators are free to accept or reject the final agreement if they feel that it does not suit them or they are not comfortable with how things turn out. Justice promotes the principle of representation in that; if an individual does not feel comfortable participating in negotiation proceedings which are to affect them directly, they are free to choose either a close friend, or a colleague, or a professional lawyer, to represent them in the negotiation proceedings.

Justice ensures that, the number of negotiating parties is not limited in number. This means that, the negotiation proceeding could be between two individuals, or even three, or even a dozen; whichever number, the negotiating individuals agree on. Basically, justice promotes fair representation of all negotiating parties in numbers which the negotiators feel comfortable with.

The use of different justice techniques during the negotiation process promotes the principle of equality in that, no third parties will be involved in the negotiating process; and that the final decision agreed upon by the negotiators will not in any way be altered by an external force; unless the negotiators feel that the final agreement is not fair, and they convene again to make the necessary changes to the agreement. However, if any changes are to be made to the previous final agreement, they should be done without the influence of any third parties (Haghani et al., 2019). The application of justice during negotiation proceedings ensure that the negotiation process is not tied to the adherence to certain rules. With justice, the negotiating parties are free to choose whichever form of justice technique they are to use; they are also free to set their rules which will govern their negotiation process; the duration for the negotiation is not specified; the number of meetings to be conducted during the entire negotiating period is not specified; among other freedoms that negotiation processes enjoy so long as the process remains to be just. Basically, negotiation processes could be said to be informal.

The use of justice techniques during negotiations gives negotiators the freedom to choose whether their negotiating proceedings will be made public or private. If they are to be made public, the justice system in place ensures that the negotiators do not face any form of criticism or they are not influenced by third parties in making certain decisions; and if they are to be private negotiations, the justice system ensures that the negotiators are not under any form of pressure to finalize their negotiations and present the agreed upon solution to the public.

Justice promotes flexibility during the negotiation proceedings. This means that, the negotiating parties have the freedom of choosing the most appropriate method for them during the negotiation process. If the method chosen does not suit them after few days into the negotiation proceedings; the parties are free to choose different methods that suit them. For instance, at the beginning of the negotiations they might have decided to choose the forward looking technique of justice to guide their discussions, but after few days, they realize that technique will challenge them while deciding on an amicable solution; hence, they are free to go for the backward looking justice technique which will help them understand the conflict better and fasten the process of agreeing on a common solution which benefits all of them.

The use of different justice techniques during negotiations promote the principle of maintaining good relations even days or weeks or even years after the negotiation process was completed. This is because, with justice, the negotiation process will be fair, and all parties involved will be given equal opportunity to present their opinions, and by the time the parties will have agreed on a common solution; they will have understood each other's point of view, and they will uniformly agree to a common solution without having been forced to. This way, they will still remain in good terms even after the negotiation process because, they were never forced to say yes to the final agreement they all signed at the end of the negotiation process. Negotiations are known to be one of the cheapest forms of solving disputes. Furthermore, the presence of justice ensures that the negotiations process will be smooth and that no additional costs will be incurred during the negotiation process either due to violence causes by disagreements among other things (Gillet, 2009).

Justice increases the chances of attaining the desired outcome from a negotiation process. With justice, the entire negotiation process will be conducted in such a manner that, no individuals will feel like they have been left out, and all the proposals presented will be equally reviewed, and an amicable decision will be made benefiting all the parties. Justice does also ensure that the final agreement is documented so as to avoid occurrence of any conflicts in the future based on the current negotiation. Most documentation processes of the final agreements are done under the supervision of courts which affirm that, the agreement is legal and it is to be adhered to, and that, failure to adhere to the agreement, there are certain consequences which will follow.

As stated earlier, the negotiation process conducted under the governance of a certain justice technique, allows for representation of the directly affected individuals. The justice system ensures that, the individual representing a certain client operates under direct instructions by their clients; and that they are not biased to make any decisions for the client during the negotiation proceedings before they consult the client first; a move which promotes fairness. The client must also be updates frequently, even if it means that, the individual representing the client has to consult them in between the negotiation proceeding. This principle of justice ensures that, everybody is equally represented and that their opinions, whether passed directly or indirectly are heard and respected.

The use of justice during negotiation proceedings promotes the principle of appreciation of differences during the negotiation process. Most negotiation are affected by not only the opinion differences; but also tribunal differences; race differences among other types of difference. Justice is required to ensure that, not only the opinion of each negotiator, but also their race, their tribe, their level of exposure to the outside world, their gender, and their language is respected. Without respect, reaching an amicable solution seems impossible.

Use of different justice techniques during the negotiation proceedings promotes the principle of discipline. Not all negotiating parties are willing to maintain a high level of discipline during the negotiation process. In some cases, negotiating parties which are way too egocentric, might end up using intimidation as a way of negotiation; whereby they intimidate their fellow negotiators in order to push them to agree to their opinions. Some negotiating parties might even get to the point of causing chaos all in attempt of disrupting the negotiation proceeding and pushing for the support of their opinion (Gati et al., 2011). In other cases, bribing might be present whereby certain parties pay their opposing parties to drop their stand of reaching an amicable solution and instead go for the bribing party's opinion. The use of justice ensures that such indiscipline is dealt with either by suspending the negotiating party or giving them less priority. However, the use of justice during negotiations ensures that, even before the negotiation proceedings are commenced, the parties lay out rules which will guide the negotiation process and that no indiscipline will be tolerated.

Justice promotes the principle of planning even before the negotiation process has been commenced. For instance, once it has been agreed upon that a certain dispute will be solved through negotiations; the negotiating parties have to agree on which justice technique they will use. After selecting the justice techniques, the parties go ahead and choose the type of negotiation they are to use during the negotiation proceedings. The credibility of the negotiating parties is determined with the help of justice system in place to ensure that, they are individuals who only have the interest of coming up with a common solution, and not individuals who will attempt causing chaos. With justice, the voluntary level of the negotiating parties is determined to ensure that, the negotiators have not been forced to participate in the negotiation process. The relationship between all the negotiating parties is determined. This step is important for it helps in the formulation of the laws which will guide the negotiation process in that; some negotiating parties might have a bad past together which if not checked up on frequently, they might cause chaos. Justice does also ensure that, before the negotiation process has commenced, all parties agree on negotiation as their preferred way of solving the dispute.

After all the negotiating parties have been formulated, justice helps in linking all of them and ensuring that they both have a mutual understanding of each other, and know what is expected of them during the entire negotiation process. With the help of justice, all the negotiating parties are able to lay down their agendas, and similar agendas from different parties are combined and the complete list of all the agendas is shared with every individual from all the negotiating parties. After the formulation and the combination of the agendas; the negotiating parties are able to agree on the timetable, which is, the specific dates on which they will be meeting based on the availability of every individual from all parties. The timetable does not have to be fixed, for as stated earlier, one of the benefits of using justice during negotiation process is that, it allows the negotiations to be flexible in terms of changing the dates of meeting and also changing the agendas which were specified in the first negotiation meetings (Forbes & Milliken, 2008). The second step which is done smoothly due to the presence of justice is the selection of the meeting point. The meeting point ought to be neutral to all members and easily accessible to all them depending on their means of transport; it would not make any sense if the meeting point was only accessible by means of walking, yet there are members who own vehicles. The last step is the determination of the type of negotiation which should be done before the official commencement of the negotiation, and whether it will be confidential or made public from the first day of the negotiation process.

Depending on the justice system put in place, each negotiating party has certain responsibilities which they have to fulfill. One, each member has the responsibility of understanding the dispute even before the negotiation proceedings commence; and also try to understand the reasoning of the other negotiating parties. This way, all parties are able to engage in the discussions in a peaceful way and there will be no confusions or anything of that sort. After every discussion, if any conflicting interests arise, they should be addressed in a peaceful way and ensure that during the next negotiation session, all the burning issues will have been tackled to avoid stalemate. Each individual has the responsibility of challenging their creativity level. A move which helps in coming up with better solutions to the different problems at hand. Negotiation proceedings which involve the presence of a peace negotiator should ensure that, all the members of the negotiating committee are presented with a detailed profile of the peace negotiator in advance before the negotiation proceedings officially commence. This way, the members will at least have a clue of how to interact with their leader, for in most negotiations which require a peace negotiator, the peace negotiator is the leader.

With the help of justice system, all the negotiation procedures are strictly adhered to from the word go. In the first meeting, the negotiating parties should only focus on the interests of each other, instead of the different positions they hold in the government or even in the negotiation committee. Secondly, with the help justice, members of the negotiating committee are encouraged to focus on the problem at hand, not on the individuals who present the possible solution; a move which eliminates the taking of ideas personally which could lead to conflicts and holding of grudges between the negotiating parties. All the members of the negotiating committee are challenged to pay keen attention to the negotiation proceedings and not take any idea lightly. The most important step which turns out to be a success if the justice system in place is adhered to be that, the negotiation proceedings turn out to be a complete success by ensuring that the final agreement is a win-win solution. For a win-win solution to be arrived at, the negotiating parties should be willing to make the negotiation process to not only be bounded to the rules set to guide the negotiation proceedings; but also make it to be free process whereby all members are able to think outside the box for an amicable solution to be found. All members of the negotiating committee should be able to understand the main objectives of the negotiation process; and if possible, in each meeting, the member's awareness of the objectives should be refreshed whereby the objectives will be read out loud to all of them before each session begins (Escobar & Moreno-Jimenéz, 2007). If the negotiation proceedings feel a bit toxic, justice system allows the parties to make a decision of taking a break from the negotiations; and once all the members are ready to continue with the proceedings, they communicate with each other and resume to the negotiation sessions. Most negotiation proceedings end up with so many conflicting ideas, meaning that, the members should remain within the constraints of the justice system in place by ensuring that they differ in a respectful way and they do not turn their conflicting discussions into chaos. If the conflicting discussions take time before they are solved, it is advisable that the negotiation session be terminated; the parties be given time to recover from the discussion and clear their head and know the way forward.

The benefits which are enjoyed from the involvement of justice in negotiation proceedings are numerous.

In conclusion, negotiations have always been part of the human race, and they will continue to be part of the human race. There is needed to make negotiations be more appreciated in the society for they are part of our daily lives. If possible, negotiation skills should be taught in learning institutions from an early age; and most important, the role of justice in negotiation proceedings; be it official negotiation proceedings or even informal negotiation proceedings; justice should be present.

Chapter 9

Advantages and Disadvantages of Group Decision Making

CONTENTS

9.1. INTRODUCTION

Figure 9.1. Group members brainstorming on ideas.

Source: http://www.free-management-ebooks.com/news/effective-group-decision-making/.

Group decision-making is the concept of providing a discussion topic to the target group, in which individuals mutually decide their opinions. After making a collective decision, no team member or anybody outside the team can change it. Group discussions frequently include two or more individuals. Decision making is critical in any organization, and it is crucial to conduct proper research and choose the right method before making any workplace decision.

Group decision-making often leads to improved decisions, since strong ideas come from proper brainstorming. All employees in the organization are important in the process. Consent of everyone involved in the group decision-making process will produce effective decisions. For smaller issues, decisions can be made individually, but when deciding on larger matters, the collective decision-making process is necessary.

9.2. GROUP DECISION MAKING ADVANTAGES

9.2.1. Helpful and Understanding Contributors

Figure 9.2. A group of people can achieve more than one individual.

Source: https://courses.lumenlearning.com/boundless-management/chapter/defining-teams-and-teamwork/.

Typically, contributors within the organization need to have an understanding of the topic and accept the final choice irrespective of what the risk can be because the choice impacts on the entire organization. Popularity of the idea and opinions convey appreciation among individuals within the institution, accordingly generating a first-rate consideration. Different studies show that when accepted as truth, the idea tends to encourage participation from most members which helps it to be successful. So preparing the employees for group participation and fulfillment will result to better results (Eden & Ackermann, 2001).

Leaders set the tone for a lifestyle this is effective and impart into everybody's strengths and motivations. A great leader is likewise a model of stability and addressing as much challenges as possible. Research shows personnel perform better when managers care about them. Leaders who are in touch with employees allow them to contribute more in the decision-making process resulting in better delight and commitment. Leaders who don't connect properly with their staff have a tendency to overlook people, work relations and consciousness on duties or knowledge. Connectivity is a mind element that requires leaders to absolutely embrace their feelings in a way that others can see them, and they can also examine the emotions of others.

Making associations within the group helps with interfacing and quick decision making. The support for one another and the information they trade can help in putting forth a valiant effort. What's more, having exclusive requirements doesn't simply mean setting high expectations. It implies thinking the best of individuals in your group and anticipating that they should succeed. Various studies show that when you accept somebody will succeed, you will in general give them absolutely the consolation and backing that helps them succeed. So setting up the workers for progress will improve results. Making positive associations with colleagues should be possible through routinely planned one-on-one gatherings, successive, significant grateful and useful input, and through giving freedoms to development and adaptability. Checking on objectives is a useful method to invest energy as a manager.

Leaders should inquire as to whether ventures or groups have room for everybody to participate. They should work with representatives to determine issues when working on different tasks, considering local needs and duties in group and undertaking policy assessment (Dyer et al., 2008). Essentially, effective managers must build a culture that promotes work-life balance since they realize that doing so pays off. How adaptable would you say you are in balancing work-life needs? Are workers able to get some much needed space to address personal issues?

9.2.2. Team Building and Collective Contribution of Ideas

The organization must be facilitated in getting rid of the barrier of monopoly in the decision-making process. When a decision occurs by way of a single person its way unreliable. As a result, with collective ideation unreliability can be removed in the decision-making process. When considering group decision making, games must be put aside in preference to seeing the real advantages of the activity. Right from the inception, group activities must be interactive and allow leaders and teams to collectively suggest new ideas and duties. This will allow every member of the group to function as a frontrunner, and not just a team member. So how does group work help organizations? A properly constituted group develops a stronger team, strengthens relationships in the team and improves the capacity on your group to reap real-time results.

Figure 9.3. Games provide an opportunity for colleagues to bond and networking.

Source: https://www.teambonding.com/6-reasons-for-team-building/.

A well-designed team ensures that every member gets an opportunity to share their ideas. The group can accomplish much larger projects than any one person can, because they work collectively to fulfill their purpose, cooperate and collaborate. The common goal gets placed before individual feelings, so the team becomes more potent by completing their responsibilities collectively and achieving more. This includes collaborative tasks within the office, where employees work collectively on targets to fulfill the company's goals (Di Fabio et al., 2015).

Operating collectively allows team members to get to test new techniques to fixing pressing issues, and being attentive to other group members. Everyone gets to recognize their team mates better, and to accept as truth the team's collective ideas. Team members who agree with one another and care about each other are extra effective contributors to the team. When they care about their fellow group members, employees are more likely to be engaged, stay along with the employer, become more targeted on results and demonstrate dedication to fulfill group desires and objectives. Team building develops interpersonal skills and requires crew members to cooperate in order to complete their duties. Group work is becoming increasingly important at the workplace, and its how a success project manifests.

Figure 9.4. Technology makes team collaboration much easier.

Source: https://www.entrepreneur.com/article/302126.

Most importantly, team work increases employee morale and builds enthusiasm. It's now not most effective due to the fact tea building events frequently imply a day trip out of the workplace, for bonding among the employees. Group work allows team mates to enhance individual talents and become more assured of their team's strengths. It builds self-esteem and encourages others to offer compliments and reward. The team that works collectively – achieves together.

Teamwork facilitates businesses grow in many aspects that are not typically apparent to participants. It makes groups stronger and can increase their ability to collectively fulfill their desires. Reaping these benefits doesn't require giant steps, or extraneous team building events or special equipment. Internal training programs can help develop capacity around effective teamwork, and alignment of critical internal priorities within the business. Professional development can be achieved at the workplace through teamwork and cooperation.

Dynamic participation from everyone within the group helps in building the capacity of the group, and constructs a solid and coordinative relationship between individuals within the group and to foster specific interests. As this happens, the team members foster certain abilities of the dynamic interaction which benefits the individuals and group in general. Group building is the way toward transforming group dynamics, and factors contributing to stability within the group (Bazerman & Moore, 2012). Team building makes more grounded bonds between individuals in the group. The individuals regard one another and their differences as shared objectives and assumptions. Team building involves both the everyday association that team members participate in when cooperating to complete the group goals. This form of team building is common and can be facilitated when the team gathers to find solutions and group standards. These standards help individuals realize how to fittingly connect within the group and the entire company.

Figure 9.5. Putting heads together ensures the best decisions are reached.

Source: https://sightsinplus.com/insight/emotion/strategies-to-resolve-work-place-conflict/.

Team building can likewise include organized exercises and activities drawn by colleagues. Or on the other hand, with the legitimate spending plan and objectives, leaders can contract out certain roles to for external assistance. Outsourcing can be accomplished where other individuals can give your group a helping hand. Group building will empower employees to achieve the work and objectives of the company more successfully. An emphasis in team building ensures achievement within the group.

Regularly, the manager will work with other group representatives to become more acquainted with one another and foster strong working relations. In the bigger picture, greater efficiency will be achieved. HR officials should additionally be contented with fostering team building meetings. What's more, with a little practice, groups can work towards achieving certain common goals. Be that as it may, team building doesn't generally have to follow a particular script. You can strengthen teams by organizing exercises and fun occasions that colleagues can do together.

9.2.3. Team-Building Ideas

Figure 9.6. Writing down ideas during a group discussion ensures that they are not forgotten.

For instance, you could begin with an office outing, or a few hours during the workday visit a close by park. Barbecue some food and propose that workers carry a dish to pass. The objective is that you assemble to share some quality talking time over the dinner. In the event that workers take their snacks to their individual workplaces to eat alone, it overcomes the objective of group building. You can likewise support exercises where representatives get together for no particular reason (Davenport, 2009). Bowling, painting pictures at an artistic creation shop, waterway travels on a traveler boat, satire club trips, and ball games all fit the bill. Truly, any occasion that your group can do or go to as a gathering will help bond them. Occasions that are truly difficult, for example, rock climbing and ropes courses, can cause fear and dread for truly idle or tested representatives. Thus, for group building, avoid the sort of occasion that a few workers would be not able to partake in serenely and without anxiety. The best group building exercises are cheap, fun, and successful—also neighborhood and simple to do.

9.2.4. Utilizing External Assistance

When utilizing an external facilitator for team building, groups can participate in organized exercises that are structured to assist the staff with blending a powerful group. By and large, the facilitator operates alongside other representatives to configure team building exercises or meetings. You can gain from these team building exercises when they are tweaked to meet the requirements of your group. Nonexclusive team building can also have a positive effect; however, it is not even close as significant as a personalized event. These meetings may incorporate icebreakers, conversation points, games, agreeable tasks, and group conceptualization. The objective of the outside facilitator in these occasions is to help you arrive at your objectives.

9.3. DEMOCRATIC DECISION-MAKING PROCESS

Figure 9.7. Decision making is a rigorous process with multiple steps.

Source: https://senseiuke.com/2015/03/decisions-decisions-decisions/.

The democratic choice making process involves the greater aggregate support so it is; thus, vote based in contrast with the individual decision-making process which is more dictatorial. When the choice is vote based, it is all the more effectively discernible and worthy and in line with those it represents. Hence it is consistently best that the decision involves more than the two people (Beynon, 2005).

While the group votes and the dominant voice carries the day, no one individual is answerable for the choices made and the group may not feel obligated if the entirety of the individuals didn't cast a ballot. There might be no obligation taken for the choice. Vote based dynamic actions work best when your group is very much educated about the topic, and when your employees accept majority share rule. Democratic dynamism is the point at which a leader surrenders authority over a choice and presents a progression of choices to the full gathering to decide on. The alternative acknowledged by most of the group is then enacted. The popularity based framework, or "rule of the greater part," is generally based on antiquity Greece. In spite of the fact that it's likely that individuals have been casting a ballot in some form all through mankind existence.

Benefits include a genuinely quick choice, and a higher measure of group interest. The inconvenience of this process is that the individual isn't answerable for the result. Even the group feels no genuine obligation since certain individuals will say, "I didn't vote in favor of that." Absence of group and moral duty thus appears to preclude this style of decision making; but in any case, the popularity based style has its followers in business.

Vote based initiative, otherwise called participative administration or shared authority, is a kind of administration style in which individuals from the group play a more participative role in the dynamic process. This sort of administration can apply to any organization, from private establishments to schools and government. Everybody is offered the chance to take part, thoughts are traded uninhibitedly, and conversation is encouraged (Beekun & Westerman, 2012). While the majority rule measure will in general zero in on group correspondence and the free will of thoughts, the head of the group is still there to offer direction and control. The majority rule system involves collective participation, who is in the group and who will add to the choices that are made. Analysts have determined that the majority rule style is quite possibly the best and prompts higher efficiency, increased commitments, and expanded team spirit.

Figure 9.8. Board stickers provide a map for group based activities.

Source: https://integrispa.com/blog/team-decisions/.

Some of the essential qualities of vote based initiative include: (a) Group individuals are urged to impart opinions and insights, despite the fact that the leader holds the last say over choices; (b) Members of the group feel more occupied with the process; (c) Creativity is energized and rewarded. Researchers propose that great majority rule process has explicit characteristics that include genuineness, insight, boldness, innovativeness, ability, and decency. Majority rule requires trust and consideration among followers.

Democratic leaders are true and settle on choices dependent on their ethics and qualities. Staff will in general feel motivated to make a move and add to the group. These leaders additionally will general look for different conclusions and won't attempt to quiet contradicting voices, or those that offer a less meaningful perspective. The term 'democracy' comes from Greek roots, and signifies "rule by individuals." In fair systems, individuals have a say in the principles and laws that will at last govern them. Winston Churchill once said about democracy: "No one imagines that popular government is awesome or all-wise. For sure, it has been said that vote based system is a weak type of leadership, with the exception of each one of those different structures that have been attempted from time to time."

Here, he suggests that while imperfect, majority rule is still more successful than other alternatives. When discussing popularity based governance in the work environment, this statement isn't excessively farfetched. Involving subordinates in the democratic cycle may not be great, since their decisions may not be well-informed. Be that as it may, the advantages it can convey are priceless and numerous. Democratic authority encourages participation. By its actual definition, this administration style welcomes participation and association from those within the organization who may not in any case be (or feel) represented (Bolaños et al., 2005). By encouraging feelings of contribution and incorporation, colleagues are caused to feel more significant. By having their interests heard, they feel more esteemed and incorporated into the organization. Democracy also brings more perspectives to the table. Drawing on a more extensive pool of participation and assessment carries more weight to the decision making process. This free progression of ideas, fortified by varying perspectives mirroring group variety may prompt choices being made that have been held to better expectations than they could have been otherwise. And albeit only a few of every suggested decision can be made, viable execution of vote based management includes clarifying that commitments are followed through in any case.

Figure 9.9. Group members should be prepared to face the consequences of their decisions.

Source: https://www.linkedin.com/pulse/choices-have-consequencesfor-elections-leaders-dave-ulrich.

Organizational democracy also allows for extra efficient problem solving. With extra minds running on a project, the range of potential solutions will increase. Even as choices may be reached much less quickly than in other management styles – such as autocratic management -it's likely that the eventual solution could be arrived at through a more rigorous manner. The ability to remark – and criticism – from participants of the group is a good way to become aware of weaknesses and downsides earlier before implementation, as opposed to cleansing up the mess in a go (Dalal & Brooks, 2013). When you deliver an idea to the table and its well heard, discussed, and properly applied within the movement, it's easier to sense extra involvement for the group. As group democracy becomes more established, groups emerge as a tight-knit unit, and team members are likely to get better commitment and involvement. When used correctly, democratic management can foster a wholesome organizational culture. Besides, with the help of an administrative center in which people speak, ideas float, and discussions are heard, the seeds are sown for stronger team relationships. In democratic leadership, discussion turns into the norm. More communication among colleagues – especially around topics which have direct effect on company processes- can form the basis for more effective professional (and personal) relationships.

Increase in morale among employees is also feasible. Group decision making creates a business environment in which project satisfaction and morale are probable, much better than they would be in any other case. In a business where all members feel valued, and in which their contributions are reputable and now and again taken on board, group members will possibly feel more delightful. Anyone who has the experience of being subordinate to a leader who has no interest in what they are saying or suppose, and who sees workers as only an extra pair of hands can attest to the value of democratic management. Honesty is prioritized in democracy. If the route decided upon by the leader is at odds with guidelines in the group (which, except unanimous, will continually be a case to point), then they must provide a powerful explanation to the ones whose opinions are longer taken on board. In this situation, honesty is the ultimate goal. It permits for the protection of goodwill, and guarantees that contributions will be coming more often.

Figure 9.10. A decision is a doorway that leads to a particular route.

Source: https://www.forbes.com/sites/allbusiness/2019/10/16/business-decision-making-tips/.

A strong and clear imagination is fundamental, and a democratic leader must outline and articulate an imaginative and prescient process for the group members. A strong organizational approach is fundamental. Within the context of an articulated imaginative and prescient process, it is easier to articulate an idea and adjustments can be made even amidst disagreements. Instead of rejecting an idea, shooting it down, or criticizing, team members are much more likely to scrutinize and offer positive comments. Multiethnic organization is also possible in the workplace. Whereas a few leadership patterns perform well in a narrow range of settings (bureaucratic leadership, for example), democratic management is able to thrive in lots of work places and not just a few.

9.4. ABUNDANT INFORMATION FOR IMPROVED DECISION MAKING

When a group is sharing their ideas and critiques, they normally pass a lot of records and some ideas to evaluate for decision making and final passing. So, institutional decision-making is more of a bonus and useful in making a clear and accurate choice, in order to have a long-lasting impact on the end result of the plan.

Brainstorming is quite common in group decision making, it's a method for swiftly producing ideas with the aid of asking contributors to put in their ideas and exchanging thoughts in place of randomly shouting out ideas. It is closely related to brain writing, which is much less widely known than conventional organization brainstorming. There is proof that brain writing often produces better thoughts than group brainstorming (Brodbeck et al., 2002). Because people are writing down their thoughts equally, the method is parallel to brainstorming where one idea may be suggested at a time. If there are four persons in a 20-mins brainstorming consultation, you're brainstorming for 20 mins, however, in case the four persons spend 20 minutes writing down solutions (as rapidly as possible) in a brain writing session, the whole process can be completed in 8-mins.

9.4.1. Brain Writing

Figure 9.11. A brain writing session where group members jot down their ideas and share it with others.

Source: https://manualthinking.com/methods/brainwriting/.

Brain writing is not yet a commonplace approach for generating ideas; however, it has some blessings over institutionalized brainstorming wherein people present their ideas in a collection. One advantage is that the blockading effects determined in face-to-face brainstorming are reduced as group members write their ideas privately as opposed to shouting them out. Brain writing is also simpler than brainstorming as it does not require an experienced facilitator—nearly each person can conduct a brain writing session with self-belief that the outcomes will be useful. The most popular forms of brain writing are "nominal" and interactive.

For the duration of brain writing, individuals are given a question or subject matter and list down their thoughts privately for a distinctive time period without dialogue. You may keep in mind the set of lists, where you ask a set to listing as many thoughts as feasible to a question, as type of brain writing. All the thoughts are collected, once more without dialogue, and any duplicates are eliminated (Caemmerer et al., 2021).For interactive (group) brain writing, members are requested to be as participatory as possible. After an interactive brain writing consultation, all the ideas may be accumulated for evaluation or published for assessment at once. Participants can then "vote" on the exceptional ideas or use another method to determine what thoughts to put into practice. Broadly speaking an interactive brain writing session entails a small group of individuals, who presents some synergy of thoughts due to the fact that every person reads the thoughts of others before listing new ideas.

9.4.2. Brainstorming

On the contrary, a brainstorming consultation is a meeting where leadership can get together and come up with ideas on a certain subject matter or issue. It's all about getting creative thoughts flowing without shooting down anyone's thoughts.

Brainstorms allow for others to freely advocate their thoughts. It may be difficult to provide new ideas being the person closest to the solution. However, inviting others into the verbal exchange to parent out new methods of doing matters lets in people familiar on the problem to talk overtly about ideas they're considering. Not every idea is going to be excellent, but that's where the subsequent factor comes in.

Every idea that is introduced should not stand on its own. It's vital to discuss thoughts despite the fact that they aren't the perfect solution, because it may assist to make something click on for somebody else. The concept of brainstorming is sharing ideas, which triggers new thoughts, which creates a sequence of recent thoughts. The most effective concept building strategy can thrive in a brainstorming session if ideas are presented without any delay. This may discourage people from sharing and in turn will restrict any achievement of the session.

A brainstorming session over a task can also be beneficial because it could reveal improvements you didn't even recognize you needed. Every consultation should have at least one person writing ideas down, so no concept is misplaced. One of the excellent parts of a brainstorming consultation is the list of thoughts you could take with you and construct off of within the path. Not the entirety can be relevant straight away, but a list of thoughts permits you to assume some creative ideas after the actual brainstorming session (Colombo et al., 2003).

Brainstorming sessions create a team atmosphere. Brainstorms don't happen without people. Inviting co-workers right into a brainstorming session allows team solidification, that you are in the same group and further opens up the choice to seek for assist from others. If you are stuck on an idea or just need clear thoughts, a brainstorming session can be beneficial. At the very least it's going to get you questioning more creatively about the subject you are discussing. If it's possible, set a schedule of brainstorming classes and rotate who's managing it. This way absolutely everyone has a chance to have each person think creatively for the appropriate answers.

The advantages no longer have any effect on the individual the session is surrounding, but anyone who's taking part in the group and thinking outdoor the box is welcome in brainstorming. Sometimes, brainstorming may feel like a total waste of time. If you agree then it is important to get your team's focus on a subject, and the consultation should not simply become some people bickering, and the contributors achieving nothing at all. Although it may turn into an amazing session with stable ideas, the group notes (if there are any) will most likely be lost in a communication chain abyss and by no means to be determined again.

However, there are a few classic examples of brainstorming gone wrong.

When venturing into the world of brainstorming, preserve a few vital matters in mind. First, the top precedence of brainstorming is quantity over quality. Yes, you read that right: Amount, not first-class ideas. Brainstorming is the first step in exploration of a brand new idea, so it is critical to be open to all thoughts and opportunities. Troubles rise up when team participants separate potentially the best thoughts from the not-so-good ones out of a fear of rejection or judgment. Another possible problem with brainstorming is that some people think it could be finished in one session: an open dialogue in a meeting room with each person concerned. This approach is not necessarily wrong, but results in large part are unrecognized social drawbacks that may contribute to a nonproductive session (Charness & Sutter, 2012). For instance, whilst the initial few ideas are shared throughout a session, there may be an inclination to only pay attention to those thoughts all through the brainstorming session. The greatest risk with brainstorming is only a few people may do the talking as others are ignored. This bias, often called "anchoring," can often prevent different new thoughts from coming to light.

9.5. NEW FORMS OF BRAINSTORMING

9.5.1. Figure Storming

Figure 9.12. Figure storming involves picturing what a historical figure like Winston Churchill would do when faced with a similar situation.

Source: https://www.dailymail.co.uk/news/article-9503495/How-war-hero-Winston-Churchill-LOST-1945-election-despite-leading-Britain-WWII-victory.html.

Ever taken into account how somebody else would possibly deal with a situation? Or what they may say about a selected topic? With figure storming, you intend to simply do that. The idea is to reflect on how someone like your boss, a famous celebrity, or even the might cope with a similar scenario. Setting yourself in someone else's shoes can provide the team a distinctive angle, supporting them see the opportunities from fresh ideas. This approach works satisfactory for groups who find themselves coming across identical thoughts in repetitive projects. One easy question can be: What would Winston Churchill Lincoln do? While you brainstorm questions that revolve around the possible actions, you unlock thoughts that are not limited on yourself. It's one of those group activities that provide everyone with a distinctive perspective.

9.5.2. Online Brainstorming (Brain-Netting)

Digital teams have become increasingly commonplace throughout all industries. The evolution of e-mail and collaboration networks makes working remotely the norm in many groups. However, what takes place when the group desires to come collectively to brainstorm? Sure, thoughts can be tossed to and fro via e-mail, but then it becomes difficult to archive these thoughts for future reference. Developing a relevant system wherein group members can collaborate is essential for these digital groups—taking into account cloud-based record storage or online collaboration tool (Cheek & Goebel, 2020). There are also a ton of tremendous brainstorming tools that make on-line brainstorming more of a visual and collaborative experience. One brainstorming tool for companies involves the use of an online mind-mapping device to answer very specific questions or generate ideas tangential to the primary problem. What different ideas surround this concept? These examples can be mapped out, visually.

9.5.3. Rapid Ideation

Every so often, time limitations can help generate thoughts speedily, due to the fact you don't have time to filter or overthink each one. With this method, the team leader offers context ahead with information or questions about the topic, finances, cut-off date, and so on. Then, a time restriction is set for individuals to put in writing down as many thoughts across the subject matter as possible, and the usage of any communication mediums.

The great thing about this style of brainstorming is that it's completely customizable to fulfill the desires of the team and task. Several unique mediums can be used, consisting of pen and paper, white forums, submission forms.. whatever to get the creative ideas flowing. The time restriction for speedy ideation sessions can be anywhere from 5 to 45minutes, depending on the complexity of your subject matter. This method is good for groups with a tendency to get sidetracked, teams who hate conferences, or for placing a time limit on brainstorming periods that regularly take longer than predicted. At the same time as brainstorming is the fundamental technique for growing ideas, and getting people to assume new principles and answers, there may be a very real threat to overthink things. It is easy to get bogged down with the aid of each new concept and its information. This is exactly the hassle that rapid ideation seeks to remedy (Wu et al., 2012).

9.5.4. Round Robin Brainstorming

Groups develop a circle to kick off this approach. As soon as the subject is shared, it moves around the circle of group members where everyone provides a concept till each person has had a go. Concurrently, a facilitator records all thoughts so they can be discussed once the session is over. It's crucial to not compare any thoughts until everybody has contributed. This method is great when some of the team members have a propensity to remain quiet all through the meeting.

The round robin technique of brainstorming lets in anybody to pitch in and make contributions. Just ensure to treat each concept with same weight. And try and discourage members from saying "X already cited my concept." If this does occur, say you will revisit it at the end in order that they have time to think about something new. Well, as a group has a number of participants and them as individuals come from unique backgrounds, so in the long run they have got distinct thoughts and reviews regarding the matter on the hand. All the thoughts may be distinct in comparison for a better decision making process. With a variety of thoughts, it's possible to create a wide variety of options and ultimately come to a successful end. With dedication and interest, group decision making promotes progressive ideas and plans which make decisions more promising. When involved, people present their ideas to the institution more actively which makes the participation more involving and powerful. Some individuals may additionally or won't be the professionals in that particular subject matter, however, their opinion still matters because of the proven concept of participation and dedication.

9.6. GROUP-DECISION MAKING DISADVANTAGES

9.6.1. Ambiguity in the Risk-Bearing Factor

When decisions are made on behalf of the organization, the component of risk-bearing will constantly show up. So in some instances, the organization may choose proceeding rather than taking much less risk, or taking greater hazard for the company as a whole. When a company opts for taking more risk, it can result in getting a greater and extra reward after the goal has been met. However, to achieve more within the company, some types of risks must be undertaken by the organization. Dialogue can be used to give updates about any variations on risk bearing, and uncertainty within the firm. The two phrases 'risk' and 'uncertainty' are frequently used interchangeably to mean a situation of capacity loss of the firm's resources, as a consequence of the truth that it's far operating in an indefinite business environment. Risk bearing means having to or sharing obligations, for accepting the losses in case the project doesn't go as expected (Weller et al., 2007).

Figure 9.13. Groups decision making has its own benefits and risks that the teams must beware of.

Source: https://www.dreamstime.com/photos-images/group-decision-making.html.

Many financial activities are capable of causing losses under some situations, however, accurate the predicted effects may be. Any business has to endure the risk of meeting any losses. In a private company, the primary risk-bearer for any challenge is the entrepreneur, or the shareholders. If the losses are sufficiently massive, different people linked with a firm also are at risk, which includes creditors, the tax regime, customers who've paid deposits on goods to be added later, and employees left unpaid whilst a business collapses. Certain risks are insurable (as an example, the risks of fire or theft of the firm's inventory), however, not the company's ability to survive and prosper. The firm itself must anticipate the risks of the market place. If it can't sell its products it's going to cross into bankruptcy; but if it's successful it's going to make income. Besides, risk-taking is to be considered as an integral part of the technique of supplying products and offerings and in developing new products.

On account those managers do not recognize for sure what the future holds, they're pressured to bet what the maximum possibly outcome of any choice could be, effectively assigning a statistical profitability to the likelihood of future happenings. All such estimates of the risk of future happenings must, by way of their very nature, be subjective, even though a few estimates are possibly to be higher than others depending upon the quantity of information available. Where large amounts of information are to be considered, in order that accurate statistical probabilities can be formulated, we might also talk of risk in place of uncertainty. As an instance, an insurance company handling health coverage regulations and claims for fire outbreak and the amount of damage achieved, might use these statistics to predict the chance of a commercial enterprise experiencing these risks.

These statistics allow for the health coverage organization to charge manufacturers top rate for covering them in case of losses, and helps them to continue making income in the process. By way of assessment, a manufacturer may find it difficult to predict the likelihood of his premises being broken into, experiencing fire or any other form of damage, for the reason that such an event may be a completely unique experience for him.

Faced with a possibility of fire, the producer can both choose to bear the risk of losses resulting from an extreme fire or can avoid it altogether by paying a coverage company to prevent the hazard. Uncertainty, not like risk, arises from changes which might be tough, and resulting from cases whose risk cannot be correctly estimated (Ambrus et al., 2009). Uncertainty refers to lack of expertise or records about present information or destiny possibilities; uncertainty arises especially due to unpredictability of future events. There may be a distinction between risk and uncertainty.

Risk covers involve cases wherein when events are not regarded, people can consider recognizing the frequency with which an occasion occurs (or is probable to arise). But uncertainty exists wherein such beliefs are absent. Events of the type blanketed by risk, consisting of individual deaths, fires, or motor accidents, are potentially insurable, even as activities of the types included by using uncertainty are not. Regrettably, maximum management decisions are taken in uncertain situations, considering they're not often repetitive in nature and there's little past data available to act as a guide to the future. Such marketplace uncertainty as to the probability and amount of losses, which would possibly get up in launching a brand new product can best be assessed by managers through combining the limited statistics available with their individual judgment. Managers can improve upon their subjective estimates about the future by way of gathering statistics from forecasts, marketplace research, feasibility studies, and so forth. However, they need to balance the value of collecting such records towards its value in improving choices. Wherein such statistics expenses are prohibitive, managers may additionally turn to various regulations of thumb like complete-cost pricing which provide fairly exact (though not most advantageous) choices.

The traditional principle of the firm envisages a firm armed with best knowledge about its destiny expenses and sales, pricing and output selections on the premise of a marginal weighting of costs and sales. This cognitive assumption of ideal information is open to criticism for diverse motives. The entrepreneur has to take risks but must weigh the risk and capital in anticipation of a successful outcome—they cannot guarantee fulfillment, neither can they ensure protection due to the risk of failure. Earnings are typically described as a reward for bearing the weight of uncertainty, or as a return to the habit of risk-bearing (Bazerman & Moore, 2012).

The dangers incurred in operating a commercial enterprise are of many sorts. a number of these, including the risk of loss due to flooding, fire, or theft, and injuries to personnel, which are insurable, because the legal guidelines of possibility may be implemented to such occasions and coverage companies can calculate the level of danger concerned. However, no statistician can calculate the numerical risk that a firm, or organization of companies, will make in terms of earnings or losses in the future. Economic conditions are frequently changing, and the achievement or failure of a particular employer is not in any case comparable to any future achievement or failure.

9.6.2. Procrastination

Procrastination occurs when the decision-making process within the group is such that a few decisions are slow in precedence, and some choices are of low consideration in the eyes of the members of the institution. Sometimes certain high precedence responsibilities are changed for low priority responsibilities. This method of doing things is referred to as procrastination, the participants of the organization keep away from such tasks which might be excessive in precedence as they no longer observe them or find trade solutions to replace them. They may also not discuss them as an alternative to replace them with obligations of much less significance.

Figure 9.14. Procrastination delays group projects.

Source: https://ct.counseling.org/2019/10/procrastination-an-emotional-struggle/.

Most people procrastinate from time to time. Statistics vary broadly, however, a number of them mention that 95% of folks are occasional offenders, with routine procrastination probably affecting approximately 20% of the populace. To clarify the issue, there's needed to start with the definition of procrastination. Eliminating matters wanted now in favor of doing something that seems easier or fun. Procrastination is characterized as pointless delaying which results in negative results, because of the pointless putting off of projects. Procrastination can costly because the decision to delay without any clear expectations can be detrimental. This irrational choice can delay progress in addition to negatively impacting a decision before and after it is made (Van Ginkel & Van Knippenberg, 2009).

Standard reasons of procrastination consist of; tasks being boring, feeling overwhelmed, feeling stressed, fear of failure, fear of the unknown, and anxiety among other factors. What does this inform us? The various causes of procrastination point to possible missing or unresolved decisions, and feelings influencing decision making. Emotions of fear, doubt and uncertainty are evident within the possible reasons. Lack of motivation, an expression of unmet needs, is also closely related to procrastination.

9.6.3. Avoiding Procrastination

Stopping procrastination is possible with proper planning. Making choices and following them through is the remedy for procrastination, and it's a good idea to be cognizant of possible prevention efforts. Perseverance, recognition and decision-making can aid in keeping off procrastination by ensuring projects are set in motion. It's important to set aside some time to reflect and examine your lifestyles choices. The self-understanding that comes from these choices can reduce worry, uncertainty, and doubt that may motive procrastination. (i) Take note of feelings that negatively impact on decisions. They may be signaling the need for a decision that might save you later inaction. (ii) Develop your decision-making efforts in an effort to figure out, make out and implement the necessary choices. (iii) Recognize your values and remain balanced as unmet needs can result in procrastination. (iv) Find ways to measure development and offer rewards. (v) Encourage a sense of duty. We can greatly benefit in getting things accomplished. Overcoming procrastination is choosing to make a better decision.

9.6.4. Social Pressures

When a person within the organization remains silent during the time of decision-making, one of the reasons can be due to social pressures in that unique environment. Hence, this results in the failure of being an active member. The social pressure of the group can affect a person's mindset and other traits and features of the individual, in turn, changing their conduct absolutely which affects the decision.

How common has the word "do it and you'll be cool" been said to get someone to do something they in any other case wouldn't? It's somewhat of a universal law that humans revel in when handling the pressure to suit in. But does social pressure actually affect an individual's selection making? Humans are social creatures by nature, and as such will do things that they may now not believe so one can be familiar and fit into a group. Right from the early days, man used this principle to ensure the survival of the species.

If someone feels that the continuation of a valued friendship hinges on a particular movement or opinion, it is very probably that they may relook what they are intending to do. A psychological study conducted in December 2014 examined the effects and impacts of social and peer pressure on adults and youngsters when making decisions. A part of what this study and experiment observed was that both adults and adolescents are willing to make unstable decisions, or trade in their ideas based on advice and comments from their friends (Tang & Liao, 2021).

Humans are much more likely to exhibit brash decision-making when with friends rather than around strangers or new buddies. Even in the family, parents ask their children after they make a bad decision with the common decision being. "All my friends are already doing it?" The reality is that the child will feel neglected and fearful when they don't participate in what their peers suggesting. As it turns out, life is simply peer-focused and absolutely everyone wants to feel like they match in, and in a few instances this means changing or not admitting what their mind tells them. It's this fear about not being accepted or kicked out of the organization that makes people crave things like repute, followers and admiration. If a person within the group says something is cool to do or think, then the chances are that others will go together with it. Social pressures certainly affect a person character and decision making.

Chapter 10

Factors That Affect Negotiations and Group Participation

CONTENTS

10.1. INTRODUCTION

Making decisions is one of the most crucial actions that everyone in any type of business performs on a daily basis. Either the decision is simple and can be made alone, or it is difficult and requires a group effort and a lot of information. According to Botero, Hollingshead, and Wittenbaum, organizations who use GSS have a greater possibility of sharing more information and producing more innovative ideas, particularly when such systems foster anonymity to reduce personal conflict and communication issues. A situation in which a group of individuals is involved in assessing, evaluating, and selecting the most appropriate option is referred to as group decision making.

The decision-making of a group can happen in three levels: advisory decision-making, which is used to consult the members of the group before the decision is taken. The second is consensus decision making, which works together both group leaders and group members to develop, evaluate and make the ultimate decision (Beynon, 2005). The second is consensus decision making. The third issue is democratic decision-making, which empowers group members to start making decisions. According to different research, two categories of qualities affect group performance: usually transparent traits that can be easily recognized in person (e.g., gender, age, etc.) and underlying traits that are difficult to identify (e.g., knowledge level, personality characteristics, etc.).

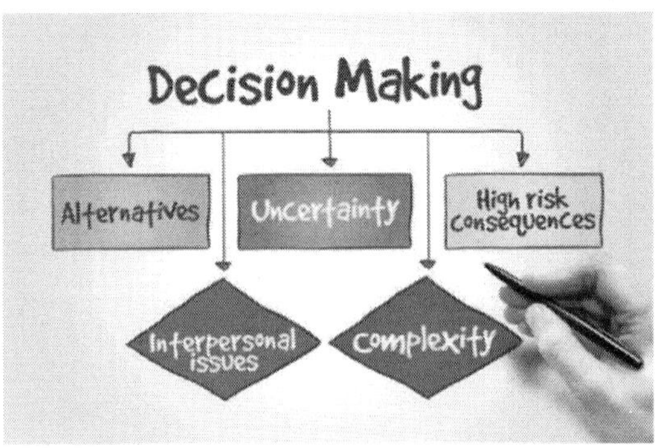

Figure 10.1. In the Japanese organizational system, for example, a decision-maker makes a choice after consulting with others.

Source: https://www.managementstudyhq.com/factors-affecting-decision-making.html.

We come into a variety of bargaining situations in our daily lives. A potential employee can bargain with his employer about his wage, a customer can bargain with the salesman about the price of a product, and management can bargain with the workers union about work-related concerns. Parties determine what each of them gets and gives in their partnership through negotiation (Sorkin et al., 2001).

It's crucial to understand conflict before diving into the many parts of negotiation. Negotiation and conflict are inextricably linked. Conflict is defined as "a state of mind whereby one finds it hard to make a decision or a choice" or "severe dispute or conflict about anything essential." Conflicts are an unavoidable element of running a business. The following are the essential ingredients of conflict, according to K.K. Sinha:

- incompatible personality;
- poor or inadequate communication;
- difficulty in making a decision;
- clash of perceptions, interests, and goals;
- argument;
- disagreement.

Conflict resolution is crucial, and there are several approaches to it. Negotiation, on the other hand, is the greatest way to resolve a disagreement. As a result, negotiation can be defined as "the interaction of two parties to resolve a conflict." Negotiation is a process through which two or more individuals or organizations with both common and conflicting interests' state and discuss suggestions for the particular terms of a possible agreement. Negotiation, according to J.L. Graham, is "a face-to-face decision-making procedure among parties about a particular product." Negotiation is thus an immersive process of communication that can happen whenever something else or somebody else wants from us.

10.2. FACTORS THAT INFLUENCE GROUP DECISION

Decision-making is affected by a number of crucial elements. Past experiences, various cognitive biases, an escalation of commitment and sunken results, individual characteristics, such as age and socioeconomic position, and a sense in personal relevance are all significant contributors. All of these factors have an impact on the decision-making process and the decisions that are made.

Figure 10.2. The decision-approach maker's is influenced significantly by social and group norms. A social norm, according to Ebert and Mitchell, is an assessing scale that designates acceptable and objectionable latitude for conduct, events, beliefs, or any other object of interest to members of a social unit. To put it another way, the social norm is the acceptable style of making decisions.' Similarly, an individual's decision-making style is influenced by his or her cultural upbringing and many cultural characteristics. In the Japanese organizational system, for example, a decision-maker makes a choice after consulting with others.

Source: https://www.managementstudyhq.com/factors-influencing-negotiations.html.

Decisions made in the past can influence decisions made in the future. Past decisions, according to Garling, Karlsson, and Juliusson (2005), have an impact on future decisions. It comes to reason that when a decision yields a positive result, people are more likely to make the same option in comparable circumstances. People, on the other hand, try to avoid making the same mistakes they have made in the past (Friedland and Sagi, 2007). This is essential because future decisions based on previous experiences are not always the optimal judgments. Highly successful people in financial decision-making do not make investment selections based on prior sunk outcomes, but rather by assessing options without respect for past experiences; this approach differs from what one may expect (Juliusson et al., 2005).

There are many cognitive preconditions in addition to past perceptions that influence decision-making. Cognitive impairment is thinking patterns which can lead to memory errors, imprecise judgments and faulty logic based on observations and generalizations. Cognitive preconditions include but are not limited to: bias of faith, over-reliance on pre-knowledge when reaching decisions, back-sight bias, the facts tend to be inevitable once an event has taken place; bias of omission generally leads people to omit information perceived to be risky. Cognitive biases affect people's decision-making by enabling them to over-rely on or give greater credibility to expected observations and prior knowledge, while discarding information or views that are viewed as unclear, without taking the whole picture into account. While this impact can occasionally lead to poor conclusions, cognitive biases sometimes allow people to make effective decisions with the help of heuristics (Shah & Oppenheimer, 2008).

In addition to previous perceptions and cognitive distinctions, decision-making can be driven by an increase in engagement and sunk results, which are unrepairable costs. Juliusson, Karlsson and Garling (2005) finalized that the individuals take decisions based on an irrational scale-up of commitment, i.e., invest more time, money, and effort to make decisions to be committed to; and, when they feel that they have responsibility for the sunk costs, time, money and effort spent on projects, they tend to continue making risky decisions. Consequently, decisions may sometimes be influenced by "how far in a hole" the person feels (Juliusson et al., 2005).

Individual variations may also have an impact on decision-making. According to research, decision-making is influenced by age, socioeconomic level (SES), and cognitive capacities. Finucane et al., discovered a substantial difference in decision-making performance as people get older; that is, when cognitive capabilities degrade, decision-making performance may deteriorate as well. Furthermore, elderly adults may be overconfident in their decision-making abilities, which limit their capacity to implement solutions (de Bruin et al., 2007). Finally, there is evidence to support the idea that elderly people prefer fewer options than younger people (Reed, Mikels, & Simon, 2008).

Individual differences in age are merely one factor that affects decision-making. People in lower SES groups, as per de Bruin et al. (2007), may have less educational opportunities and resources, making them more vulnerable to unfavorable life events, many of which are out of their control; as a consequence, low SES persons may make poorer decisions based on previous choices.

Figure 10.3. Leaders are always negotiating, both within and outside of their businesses.

Source: https://www.imd.org/research-knowledge/articles/negotiation-and-dispute-resolution/.

Aside from prior experiences, cognitive biases, and physical characteristics, the belief in personal importance has an impact on decision-making. People are more inclined to make a decision if they believe what they decide matters. Krueger and Acevedo looked into people's voting behaviors and found that people are more likely to vote when they believe their views are representative of the overall public's views, as well as when they believe they have a stake in the outcome. When people believe their vote matters, they vote. The irony of this voting occurrence, according to Krueger and Acevedo, is that when more people vote, individual ballots weigh less in electoral calculations.

Heuristics are mental shortcuts that decrease the cognitive load associated with decision-making. They are general decision-making methods that individual's use that are premised on little data but are frequently correct; heuristics are mental short cuts that decrease the cognitive load associated with decision-making. Heuristics, according to Shah and Oppenheimer, minimize work in decision-making in various ways (Schulz-Hardt et al., 2002). Heuristics allow the user to examine a limited number of signals and/or alternative options before making a decision. Furthermore, heuristics reduce the effort required to get and store information in memory, speeding the decision-making process by lowering the quantity of integrated data required to make a decision or pass judgment.

Cognitive psychologists have identified a variety of decision-making heuristics as a result of study and theorizing. Heuristics can be broad or narrow, and they can be used for a variety of purposes. The price heuristic, in which people assess more-priced items to be of higher quality than lower-priced products, is exclusive to consumer behavior; however, the outrage heuristic, in which people weigh how despicable a crime is while deciding on punishment, is not (Shah and Oppenheimer, 2008). The representation, accessibility, and grounding and modification heuristics are three important heuristics according to Shah and Oppenheimer.

People use a variety of heuristics to make decisions for the sake of ease and quickness. The representative heuristic (RH), which is a very cost-effective heuristic, is one of the most essential heuristics (Hertwig and Pachur, 2006). When one of two items is identifiable, people will tend to choose the identifiable thing, putting the least amount of effort or knowledge into making a decision. It is difficult to research and answer definitively whether someone is utilizing the RH alone or if they are using additional information in forming a conclusion, according to Pohl and Hilbig.

As a result, the RH research is contradictory (Gigerenzer and Goldstein, 2002; see also Pohl and Hilbig, 2006). RH research was pioneered by Gigerenzer and Goldstein. They claimed that recognition memory is more intuitive, trustworthy, and precise than randomness alone; they also claimed that less recognition results in more correct decisions. People, on the other hand, often use extra information while using the RH, according to Pohl and Hilbig; that is, they do not rely exclusively on recognition when making decisions. Furthermore, Pohl and Hilbig found that people employ other information in addition to the RH even after sound recognition is achieved.

The availability heuristic is another well-studied heuristic. People are more likely to use the information that is most readily available when making a decision, according to this heuristic (Redelmeier, 2005). This is an intriguing heuristic because it serves as the foundation for many of our decisions and judgments (Redelmeier, 2005; McKelvie, 2000). When people are asked to read a list and then identify names from it, for example, the names that are frequently identified are those of renowned people with whom the participants are familiar (McKelvie, 2000).

In the medical field, Redelmeier claimed that heuristics are to blame for many missed medical diagnoses, with the availability heuristic being one of them. Heuristics, according to Redelmeier, are advantageous because they are cognitively efficient, but doctors and practitioners must identify when heuristics must be overridden in favor of more thorough decision-making processes. In circumstances where some assessment of value is required, the adjustment and anchoring heuristic is the core decision making heuristic

(Epley and Gilovich, 2006). Individuals that utilize this heuristic first employ an anchor, or a ballpark estimate, that surfaces first, and then tweak their estimations until they achieve a satisfying response. The anchoring and adjustment heurist might be used, for example, to answer the question, "In what year did John F. Kennedy assume office?"

Figure 10.4. Past encounters, various cognitive biases, an escalation of commitment and sunken results, individual characteristics, such as age and economic status, and a sense in self efficacy are all significant contributors. All of these factors have an impact on the decision-making process and the decisions that are made.

Source: https://www.managementstudyhq.com/features-and-components-of-group-decision-support-system.html.

Starting with a given date, like the day he was shot, November 22, 1963, the person can next create an estimate based on the available information (Epley and Gilovich, 2006). In negotiations, people use the anchoring and adjustment heuristic to make counter offers based on the anchor that is given to them. People commonly generate estimations that trend towards the anchor side, where actual values are farther away from the anchor initially placed, according to Epley and Gilovich. Furthermore, anchoring necessitates effort; this effort is critical in preventing anchor bias.

People have a range of reactions after making a decision. Furthermore, current decisions have an impact on future decisions. Regret or contentment is two possible results of a decision, both of which might affect future decisions. One possible effect of decision making is regret, disappointment, or unhappiness with a choice made. Regrettably, regret has been shown to influence decision-making. Anticipated regrets as per Sheeran and Abraham

(2003), is the notion that a decision will be regretted because of inaction. Anticipated regret may motivate activity; that is, when a person says they will do something, such as exercise, they are more likely to follow through on their promise to prevent regret. Once a decision is taken, the consequences of that decision, if remorse is felt, will have an impact on future decisions. People are prone to obsessing over the other possibilities that are available to them. The path not pursued.

People may feel regret depending on how a decision was made, according to Friedland and Sagi (2007); regret may be reliant on the amount of options accessible throughout the decision-making procedure; and how diverse the options were may affect how regret is perceived after the decision was taken. Friedland and Sagi found after a series of experiments that people feel guilt because they believe they might have made a better decision if they had looked at additional information, previously ignored, and carefully weighed the pros and drawbacks of each option. Surprisingly, people who are unhappy with their choices feel forced to accept it in order to alleviate their anxiety about the decision's quality. When a job candidate isn't hired, for instance, he may reorganize his experiences and come up with a variety of reasons why he didn't want to work for the organization.

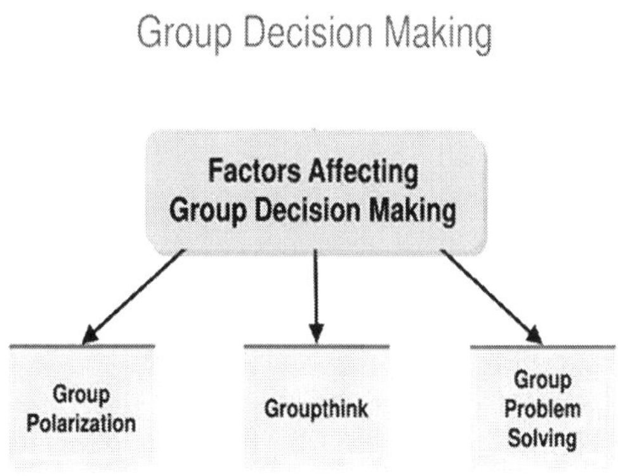

Figure 10.5. Cognitive biases affect individual decision by leading them to over-rely on or give greater credibility to expected views and prior knowledge, while discarding facts or perceptions that are viewed as unclear, without taking the whole picture into account. While this impact can occasionally lead to poor conclusions, cognitive biases sometimes allow people to make effective decisions with the help of heuristics.

Source: https://slideplayer.com/amp/13475979/.

In addition to remorse, individuals can also be satisfied with their choices. Satisfaction of the decision-maker with the result of the decision is called satisfaction. Numerous factors influence satisfaction levels. People like to make their own decisions and think that, according to Botti and Iyengar (2004), they are better satisfied with their choices, but decision-makers are less satisfied than those with their choices.

As previously stated, future decisions are influenced by past choices as well as emotions of satisfaction or regret. Even if there is evidence to support this theory, decisions may be made based on the reversibility factor in many circumstances, especially when the decision can be reversed. People are willing to pay a premium for the chance to change their opinions at a later point, which is important to their pleasure. Catalogue shoppers, for example, make a two-step purchasing decision: first, they decide to buy the products, and then, once the products arrive, they determine whether or not to keep them. Gilbert and Ebert investigated whether people prefer to make reversible judgments.

In cognitive psychology, decision-making is an important topic of study. It's crucial to understand how people make decisions in order to comprehend the decisions they make. Decision-making is influenced by a number of things. Past experiences, cognitive biases, age and personality differences, conviction in personal relevance, and an increase in commitment are among these influences. Heuristics are mental shortcuts that relieve decision-makers of some of their cognitive load. Although there are many other types of heuristics, three of the most essential and often employed are availability, representational, and adjustment and anchoring.

There are various different consequences once a person takes a decision, including regret and contentment. Reversible decisions are more desirable, and people are prepared to pay a premium for the ability to change their minds, even if reversibility does not always result in positive or satisfactory outcomes (Beekun & Westerman, 2012). Cognitive psychologists have suggested many decision-making models to explain how people make intelligent decisions. The foundation of a unique model is objectives and planning. There are still many more decisions to be researched that will make it possible for psychologists and educators to impact well on the lives of many people.

10.3. FACTORS IN WHICH NEGOTIATIONS ARE INFLUENCED

One would not anticipate vague dreams and aspirations to cut much ice when negotiating the terms of a lease, where devotion entails a multi-year contract and a considerable number of money. The mere mention of a desire to create a "Kid's corner" playground in a retail arcade, on the other hand, appears to be enough to bring stalled negotiations back into the conversation. This research looks for an answer in the concept of cognitive closure, and claims that its benefits are greatly underestimated.

Negotiation occurs when two or more mutually dependent people wish to share money, goods, services, or other valuable assets. There's no point in negotiation if a powerful party a can dictate to a weaker party B, or if there's no underlying conflict of interest. If there is a conflict of interest, however, it is prudent to learn what the other person experiences the most in order to arrive at a mutually acceptable prioritization.

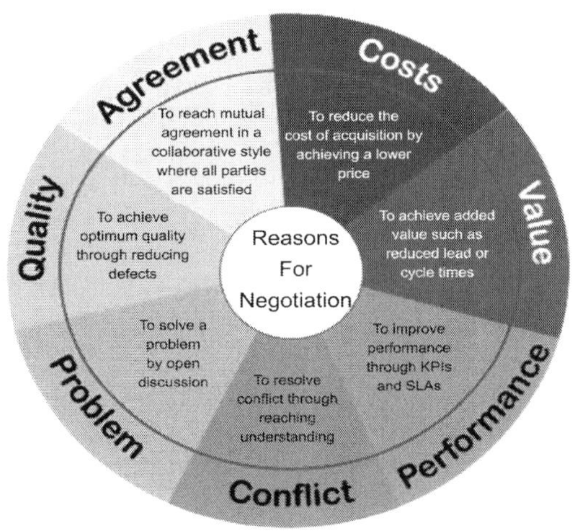

Figure 10.6. Negotiation between another procurement expert and supply chain parties can occur for a variety of reasons.

Source: https://www.cips.org/knowledge/procurement-topics-and-skills/strategy-policy/negotiation/.

This method is taught to negotiators during their training. In training, substantially life-like negotiations are carried out in the absence of a pay-off sheet and under conditions of great uncertainty. As a result, when negotiators seek information about their counterpart's preferences, they consider all information as justifications for a stance that may be conflicting with their own.

As in the renowned tradition of Petty and Cacioppo, much research on persuasion begins with the assumption that there is a persuader and a target that may or may not completely understand the arguments (1986). However, in a negotiation, both parties are attempting to persuade one another using reasons that are not only incompatible but also incommensurable, such as money and justice.

The dual interacting role of persuader and target is a convoluted communicative starting point for agreement – so convoluted, in fact, that the presence of argumentation may be a predictor of standstill. As a result, Roloff et al., (1989) show that compelling argumentation is adversely connected to integrative solutions, while Bülow-Mller (2005) speculates that excessive argumentation is a signal of a negotiator with a weak case. However, the processing processes of contentious negotiators provide a more convincing explanation: the more one person argues, the less time he or she spends hearing. Parties that do not listen are unlikely to address the primary problems of their partners, and hence their self-directed argumentation is ineffective.

There is also confusion about the objectives of the partner, which van Kleef et al., call "situational bogusness," for those who negotiate (2010). Since dealers fear to be used, they are likely to concentrate on facts that support their skepticism, i.e., on hypothesis-consisting information selectively. The concept of cognitive closure provides a great explaining force for the unnecessary deadlock, and it was the subject of research on many dimensions, fast judgments and resistance of the closed mind.

The collection of research that underpins early closure prediction has introduced the model given in Kruglanski and Webster (1996) and Webster and Kruglanski (1996, 1997). Again, the key concepts are epistemic incentive, selective analysis, and the cognitive environment, like time constraint or cognitive activity, for the purposes of this paper. People epistemic drive impacts whether they analyze knowledge in a shallow (heuristic) or deep (systematic) manner. Increased information search is a benefit for negotiators when epistemic motive is high. As a result, it's been proven time and time again that persistent information gathering leads to greater joint outcomes.

However, the more a person feels the need to have a definite answer, to clarify, or to see a structure, the more likely they are to use shortcuts.

Importantly, this applies not only once, but often in a complex choice process like a negotiation: with many minor judgments to make, such as whether to believe or not trust a certain move made by the partner, heuristics make the process easier. If a conflict of interests is the place to start, selective processing of data in line with group biases and affirmation of convictions can be expected. There is a lot of information that needs to be tracked on the relative complexity of the multi-issue negotiations; faithful evidence is found to be easier to keep in mind when there is ambiguous evidence that might have delayed the closure.

Figure 10.7. It is critical to take the view that a project leader must be an expert negotiator and that all about a project can be negotiated.

Source: https://www.coursera.org/learn/art-of-negotiation.

Historically, laboratory activities like the retention of a nine-digit number have been used to manipulate cognitive workload. While negotiators in realistic simulations are not under this kind of pressure, they do try to mix a lot of various data and considerations in order to create a type of proactive, chess-like strategy, and can thus be considered to be working under great cognitive load, which comes at a high price. It has been shown that under time constraint, negotiators tend to keep to pre-formed views, such as a fixed-pie situation or a stereotype of the out-group; and it has been shown that under situations of cognitive busyness, originality suffers.

Therefore, negotiations with complex options and ambiguity could be presumed as leading participants to seek a conclusion by heuristics and search for closure along the original lines of Kruglanski and Webster, that of information shifting by early anchors and stereotypes, a reduction in decision-making and a reduction in perspectives in order to understand the partners. As a result, people can focus on important and easy to process topics, reducing the probability of integrative solutions (Song, 2009).

Because this pessimistic forecast does not hold true for good negotiators, there must be other factors at play. It is suggested that if negotiation experiments are conducted with elevated verisimilitude, i.e., with enough background detail, partly communal, partly personal to one party, and if the incident involved the option of some selective logrolling of aspirations rather than negotiating or attempting to reach a logically correct decision, therefore the process of joint knowledge construction can be observed in action.

As portions of private information are presented, acknowledged, and included into the common ground that every negotiation strives to create, the closure of the mind, which has had such a poor rap in negotiation research, can be demonstrated to have a good consequence. The influence of specific examples, in particular, is intriguing, as they reflect a classical rhetorical prescription to engage the audience by requiring it to contribute representations. The most important instances are really simple to comprehend. Though actual instances can be presented to make a negotiator jump on a piece of information supplied by the opponent, even if it is plainly in the opponent's own best interests, then skepticism and confirmation bias must have been dissolved. In other words, I believe that not enough attention has been devoted to the actual phrase, i.e., the framing and subsequent detail selection that "sells" a piece of information to a negotiating partner to the point where it becomes common knowledge.

While the use of instances is neither required nor enough for immediate settlement, their existence is favorably correlated with it, according to the findings of this study. Their purpose appears to be to contribute to overall clarity, i.e., the rejection of skepticism, so that discussion can continue on a trust-based foundation. Negotiators who stick to the abstract level, such as "we must be flexible enough to change with the times," on the other hand, fail to soothe anxieties. Thus, in terms of negotiation theory, the instances appear to relocate the conflict's locus into manageable grounds.

While the use of instances is neither essential nor sufficient for immediate settlement, the findings of this study show that their presence is positively connected with it (Schulze & Newell, 2016). Their goal appears to be to contribute to total clarity, i.e., the rejection of skepticism, so that dialogue can continue on a foundation of confidence. On the other hand, negotiators who stay to the abstract level, such as "we must be flexible enough to evolve with the times," fail to calm nerves. As a result, the instances appear to shift the conflict's locus into more manageable grounds, according to negotiation theory.

It is important to emphasize that we are working with just one issue among many, and that such "little closes" do not determine the outcome of a negotiation. However, I believe that this particular component has not been investigated and that it helps to our understanding of decision-making cognitive processes. Clearly, there are concerns concerning pupils' mental abilities, given that they have been provided with facts concerning a fictional universe. A whole effort should seek evidence outside of the classroom laboratory for development.

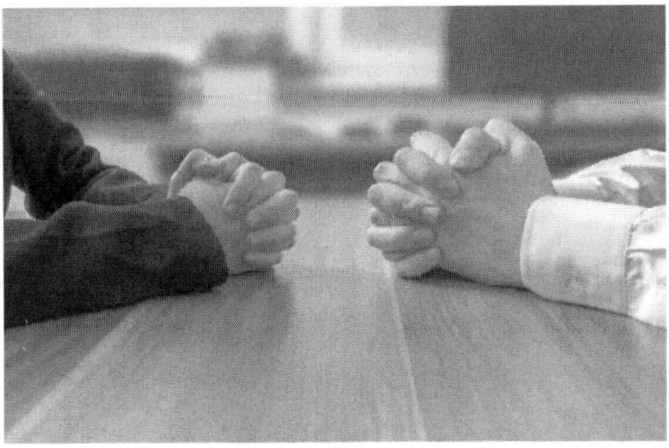

Figure 10.8. Power has determined how tribes, countries, businesses, and people operate since the beginning of time.

Source: https://lerablog.org/business/marketing-business/communication/factors-that-influence-business-negotiation/.

10.3.1. Pre-Negotiations

The majority of academics think that training and scheduling are essential for good negotiating. Furthermore, commercial negotiators and negotiation practitioners from both Europe and the United States agree that preparing is the most critical attribute to have in any successful negotiation. Even so, much of the research has thus far concentrated on what happens at the negotiating table. However, at-the-table discussions are merely a part of a larger conflict-resolution process (Saunders, 1985), and little is known about what is really planned during negotiations (Jordan and Roloff, 1997). As a result, scholars in the field of negotiation are calling for additional in-depth research to better comprehend how inter-organizational pre-negotiation works (Peterson and Shepherd, 2010). From a methodological standpoint, the goal of this study is to correct the equilibrium.

A key gap in the research, in my opinion, is our lack of comprehension of how real-life inter-organizational pre-negotiations are handled. This study explores the alternatives available to scholars who want to collect rich, rigorous data from practitioners while also proactively mitigating threats to validity and reliability throughout the study process rather than after the fact. Quantitative research often outstrips quantitative research in terms of contextual realism in comparison with quantitative research. A description of a computer supported qualitative research method that combines data from an open end survey, a thirteen-month longitudinal case study of a complex negotiation and participant observation from a 24-month "live" in the organization with a constructivist thematic analysis is presented to raise some key research questions. The doctoral thesis is based on the method, so examples of continuous research that applies the method proposed are mentioned. The hope is that this essay will inspire further negotiators to undertake qualitative research to further promote our negotiating knowledge.

The pre-negotiation phase was not extensively researched by academics (Roloff and Jordan, 1991), while the planning and preparing of negotiations are crucial components (Thompson, 2009; Ghauri, 1986); the main chapters on this subject include checklists and description advice, for example, in Thompson (2009). Fisher and Etrel (based on the seminal book Getting to Yes, in 1995, also devoted a whole book into the pre-negotiation phase (Fisher et al., 1991).

The pre-negotiation review by Lucas and Peterson (2001) proposed to conceptualize the four-part pre-negotiation phase. The first component of the information collection framework is the collection of information, including the BATNA, issues and underlying interests of the other party. BATNA evaluation, reserve price development, target definition, the preparation of a Plan for achieving defined objectives are two and three of the components, Strategy and Formulation Development. The BATNA evaluation. In addition to logistical concerns, the fourth component, Preparation is dedicated to development and testing of the customer presentation. Other pre-negotiation research exists, for example in the fields of international business negotiation and diplomacy, but none of them resolve the activities that take place during the pre-negotiation phase, and thus the knowledge of how negotiators and negotiating teams plan and start preparing for their negotiation process.

Given the economic significance of the result for both the negotiators and the organization, customer negotiations are a touchy subject. The transactions are frequently in the millions of Euros, and the sales manager in charge will probably only complete a few each year. As a result, this is a closed context (Bell, 1969) in which the negotiators are in a high-stress position, rendering entry to the negotiations difficult for the researcher.

In order to mitigate the problem, the researcher applied an insider strategy which, thanks to its support from the business college and the company, transferred the head office to the Sales Manager to a Sales unit. The status of the insider position allows participants to quickly and fully assimilate information, thus increasing the data depth. Coming from the Head Quarter and replying to the Sales Manager has been beneficial for transparency and door maintenance but there has also been a problem of loyalty.

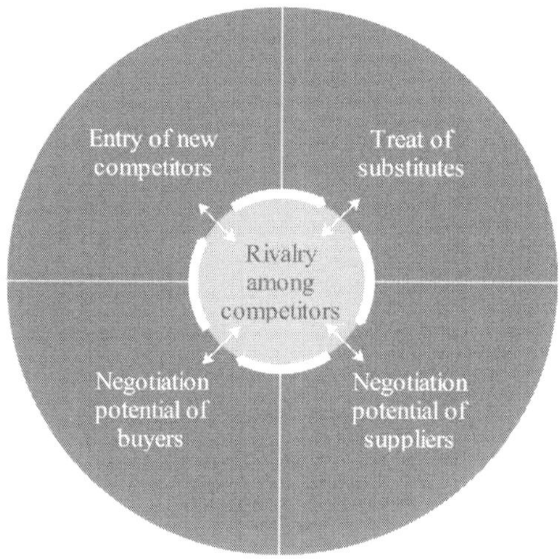

Figure 10.9. Negotiation can result in massive development for a company or its rapid collapse; therefore it should never be taken lightly.

Source: https://www.researchgate.net/figure/Factors-influencing-shipbuilding-competitiveness-and-attractiveness-Porter-1980_fig2_281234068.

Few negotiating parties would welcome the presence of a management spy in their discussions. This problem was solved by a distinct and public agreement with leadership, which stated that the research group goal was to contribute to science and that interactions between the observers and the participants would be considered anonymous. Still, it isn't enough for the Head of Sales to issue an order allowing the observer to participate; negotiators must perceive the advantages of having the observer there. As per interviews conducted, the negotiators' hesitation may arise from the fact that the Company's agreements involve very substantial quantities of money, and the negotiator's compensation, image, and job security are all on the line (Sari, 2008). The researcher selected a humble approach, spending all of his time in the office assisting where he could while also producing a customized high level negotiation skill training tailored to the needs of the negotiators. The goal of these acts was to build confidence and respect so that entry to the negotiations could be gained.

According to casual talks with negotiation course participants, the foregoing measures recently identified the researcher as a helpful and knowledgeable negotiation advisor, and he was immediately invited to multiple negotiations both as an observer and as an advisor. Another significant factor for his acceptance, according to the negotiators, was his own experience as a negotiator over a long period of time, which made him feel like one of them.

Being a member of the inner circle has both benefits and cons. whereas being an insider has the advantage of continuing access to restricted settings and higher data depth, being such a participant-as-observer (Gold, 1957) has the disadvantage of losing one's sense of being a researcher and being engrossed in the world of the negotiators. As a result, where possible, the act of reciprocating was isolated from observing through teaching and coaching.

The negotiation teams agreed that if they wanted the advice, it would be given only at the end of the pre-negotiating discussions, allowing the field to be as unaffected as possible. The benefits and drawbacks of becoming an insider must certainly be considered; however, in the case of the described study, the decision was pretty straightforward because not being an insider would have made data collecting difficult, if not impossible.

10.3.2. Other Basic Influences

Several elements influence the negotiation process due to its complexity. We can divide them into six categories: communication skills, emotional control, time, information, credibility, and authority. These are discussed below:

- *Authority:* The first important consideration in any negotiation is power. Negotiation may begin with contemplation, but it must conclude with a conclusion or settlement in order to be effective. Both sides must have the power or authority to close the contract in order for this to happen. If one party believes the other lacks the power to make commitments or at the very least mediate and push the process ahead, he or she may be reluctant to come to the table.

If the participants' authority comes from a higher power, they should be aware of how far they can go. Exercising their authority beyond its limits may result in the negotiation being canceled. In real-life circumstances, we've seen cases where one side makes concessions or provides services that the higher authority does not approve or honor because of a misunderstanding. Negotiation efficacy is harmed by a lack of authority or ability to stand by the agreements reached.

- *Credibility:* In any negotiation process, reciprocal faith and loyalty are crucial. When it comes to negotiating, people who are known to be honest, truthful, steady, and reliable have an advantage. When another individual talks, the group asks itself, "Can we trust this individual's thoughts and statements?" The answer to this question should be affirmative in order for discussions to move well. The person's experience, skill, track record, and connections all contribute to their credibility. It is critical that both parties have members on their teams who are regarded as trustworthy. The legitimacy of those sitting across the negotiation table must be complemented by the power or authority to embark into a negotiation (Saaty & Peniwati, 2013).

Figure 10.10. Most people under time constraints, on the other hand, use the 'heuristic approach,' which focuses on justifications to reject some alternatives rather than ideal decisions.

Source: https://www.negotiations.com/articles/collective-bargaining/.

- *Information:* Facts, numbers, historical data, future trends and forecasts, studies, empirical data, and computations are frequently used in negotiations. To use a cliché, knowledge is power. The success of a negotiating exercise depends on having enough and credible knowledge about the numerous problems involved. The party with more information has the upper hand. In the lack of the necessary facts, it is impossible to make logical and persuasive arguments. Prior to sitting down to negotiate, each side should make a concerted effort to obtain as much data as feasible on all of the subjects that will be discussed. Hard bargaining is a common part of successful negotiation, and well-informed teams have more negotiating strength. One of the negotiating sides is likely to have more access to information than the other. Information pertinent to talks should be communicated with the opposite party in order to ensure a smooth flow of negotiations. How to share it, when to share it and how to communicate it is all decisions that must be made based on the circumstances (Saka et al., 2008).
- *Time:* Another major component affecting the negotiating process is the time range within which it must be accomplished. One of the parties may feel a sense of urgency, and as a result, they may be in a rush to wrap up the negotiations. Negotiations cannot carry on indefinitely due to time limits, and both sides must agree on a time range within which the process must be finished. At the same time, the negotiation process is designed in such a way that the other party cannot be rushed. Both sides must have sufficient patience. Putting the other party under extreme stress is never a good idea. Negotiations with a broad influence on all parties must adhere to a well-defined process, which takes time. However, as the process develops, the discussions should gain traction, and the deal should be sealed or the settlement reached at the end of the negotiations. Each party must be careful not to overextend themselves, ending in a deadlock.
- *Emotional control:* Humans are not only rational, but also emotional beings. Every individual has attributes of the mind and heart. True, in commercial settings, people make decisions based on logic and reasoning, as well as a thorough examination of the options available to them. However, if we scrape underneath the surface, we may see emotions at work. Emotions have a role in

negotiation, and good negotiators are aware of this. Aside from gauging the emotional condition of the other party's members, the negotiator should exhibit the proper emotional condition himself. Coming on strong with aggressive points is sometimes appropriate. A delicate touch and a whisper would suffice at other times. The concept is that no matter what your perspective is, you should endeavor to match the opposing party's emotional fervor and create an environment that is conducive. While emotional awareness is undoubtedly important, there is no tolerance for excessive emotional display during the bargaining process.

Figure 10.11. Despite the fact that negotiations are a part of everyday life, few people are taught to be effective negotiators.

Source: https://www.donnarossdisputeresolution.com/services/negotiation/.

- *Communication skills:* Negotiation, as previously said, is a time-consuming process requiring the exchange of messages. These communications aren't always information in bits and pieces. A complicated combination of ideas, attitudes, and even emotions would need to be conveyed with others during the negotiation process. Depending on the scenario, the negotiator must state, articulate, explain, reason out, appeal, concede, persuade, persevere, and even keep silent. Silence is an effective tool for good negotiators. They are aware of when it is appropriate to remain silent. Not only does effective negotiating include saying the correct thing at the appropriate moment, but it also necessitates leaving unsaid what does not need to be stated. A competent negotiator must have a strong knowledge of the English language (Risco & Duffy, 2011). The bargaining process is not often taken seriously. There may be times during intercultural group negotiations when jokes, humor, and light-hearted statements are unsuitable since they are likely to be misconstrued. In other cases, where the negotiating teams' relationship is less formal, appropriate humor and lighter moments may aid in creating rapport and reducing stress. Effective negotiators enhance their arguments with anecdotes, metaphors, and analogies in addition to utilizing the appropriate words and tone. Considering the significance of effective communication in the bargaining process, parties select members of negotiating teams who have strong interpersonal skills. Arrogance, nasty statements, sarcastic remarks, temper tantrums, and overly pleasant methods are all detrimental to the negotiation process's smooth flow. Construction organizations use a wide range of group decision-making methods. The groups must create a hierarchy based on prior performance, persuasiveness, and the capacity to assess the relative power or knowledge of the individuals involved. In most circumstances, multinational contractors would form a temporary bidding group for a single project, which will typically consist of a group leader and several technical and business experts from various departments.

The term "group decision and negotiation" encompasses the entire process or flow of activities related to group decision and negotiation, not just the final choice, such as monitoring, interaction, and sharing of information, problem identification (representation), and evolvement, substitute generation, and social-emotional interaction. The perspectives of descriptive normative and design are of interest. As a result, Group Decision and Negotiation is concerned with the relationship and coordination of group processes in general.

Bibliography

1. Ambrus, A., Greiner, B., & Pathak, P. (2009). Group versus individual decision-making: Is there a shift. Institute for Advanced Study, School of Social Science Economics Working Paper, 91.
2. Bazerman, M. H., & Moore, D. A. (2012). Judgment in Managerial Decision Making. John Wiley & Sons. 19(5),
3. Beynon, M. J. (2005). A method of aggregation in DS/AHP for group decision-making with the non-equivalent importance of individuals in the group. Computers & Operations Research, 32(7), 1881–1896.
4. Beekun, R. I., & Westerman, J. W. (2012). Spirituality and national culture as antecedents to ethical decision-making: a comparison between the United States and Norway. Journal of Business Ethics, 110(1), 33–44.
5. Bolaños, R., Fontela, E., Nenclares, A., & Pastor, P. (2005). Using interpretive structural modelling in strategic decision-making groups. Management Decision. 21(4),
6. Brodbeck, F. C., Kerschreiter, R., Mojzisch, A., Frey, D., & Schulz-Hardt, S. (2002). The dissemination of critical, unshared information in decision-making groups: The effects of pre-discussion dissent. European Journal of Social Psychology, 32(1), 35–56.
7. Caemmerer, B., Goerne, J., & Mulki, J. P. (2021). Consequences of managerial indecisiveness. International Journal of Bank Marketing.15(3).
8. Colombo, A., Bendelow, G., Fulford, B., & Williams, S. (2003). Evaluating the influence of implicit models of mental disorder on

processes of shared decision making within community-based multi-disciplinary teams. *Social Science & Medicine*, *56*(7), 1557–1570.

9. Charness, G., & Sutter, M. (2012). Groups make better self-interested decisions. *Journal of Economic Perspectives*, *26*(3), 157–176.
10. Cheek, N. N., & Goebel, J. (2020). What does it mean to maximize? "Decision difficulty," indecisiveness, and the jingle-jangle fallacies in the measurement of maximizing. *Judgment and Decision Making*, *15*(1), 7.
11. Dalal, R. S., & Brooks, M. E. (2013). Individual differences in decision-making skill and style. *Judgment and Decision Making at Work*, 80–101.
12. Davenport, T. H. (2009). Make better decisions. *Harvard Business Review*, *87*(11), 117–123.
13. Di Fabio, A., Palazzeschi, L., Levin, N., & Gati, I. (2015). The role of personality in the career decision-making difficulties of Italian young adults. *Journal of Career Assessment*, *23*(2), 281–293.
14. Dyer, J. R., Ioannou, C. C., Morrell, L. J., Croft, D. P., Couzin, I. D., Waters, D. A., & Krause, J. (2008). Consensus decision making in human crowds. *Animal Behavior*, *75*(2), 461–470.
15. Eden, C., & Ackermann, F. (2001). Group decision and negotiation in strategy making. *Group Decision and Negotiation*, *10*(2), 119–140.
16. Escobar, M. T., & Moreno-Jimenéz, J. M. (2007). Aggregation of individual preference structures in AHP-group decision making. *Group Decision and Negotiation*, *16*(4), 287–301.
17. Forbes, D. P., & Milliken, F. J. (2008). Cognition and corporate governance: Understanding boards of directors as strategic decision making groups. *The Value Creating Board*, 208–236.
18. Gati, I., Gadassi, R., Saka, N., Hadadi, Y., Ansenberg, N., Friedmann, R., & Asulin-Peretz, L. (2011). Emotional and personality-related aspects of career decision-making difficulties: Facets of career indecisiveness. *Journal of Career Assessment*, *19*(1), 3–20.
19. Gillet, J., Schram, A., & Sonnemans, J. (2009). The tragedy of the commons revisited: The importance of group decision-making. *Journal of Public Economics*, *93*(5–6), 785–797.
20. Haghani, M., Sarvi, M., Shahhoseini, Z., & Boltes, M. (2019). Dynamics of social groups' decision-making in evacuations. *Transportation Research Part C: Emerging Technologies*, *104*, 135–157.

21. Herrera, F., Martínez, L., & Sánchez, P. J. (2005). Managing non-homogeneous information in group decision making. *European Journal of Operational Research*, *166*(1), 115–132.

22. Hwang, C. L., & Lin, M. J. (2012). *Group Decision Making Under Multiple Criteria: Methods and Applications (Vol. 281)*. Springer Science & Business Media.

23. Kulcsár, V., Dobrean, A., & Gati, I. (2020). Challenges and difficulties in career decision making: Their causes, and their effects on the process and the decision. *Journal of Vocational Behavior*, *116*, 103346.

24. Kugler, T., Kausel, E. E., & Kocher, M. G. (2012). Are groups more rational than individuals? A review of interactive decision making in groups. *Wiley Interdisciplinary Reviews: Cognitive Science*, *3*(4), 471–482.

25. Martinsons, M. G., & Davison, R. M. (2007). Strategic decision making and support systems: Comparing American, Japanese and Chinese management. *Decision support systems*, *43*(1), 284–300.

26. Mukherjee, N., Dicks, L. V., Shackelford, G. E., Vira, B., & Sutherland, W. J. (2016). Comparing groups versus individuals in decision making: a systematic review protocol. *Environmental Evidence*, *5*(1), 1–9.

27. Mustakallio, M., Autio, E., & Zahra, S. A. (2002). Relational and contractual governance in family firms: Effects on strategic decision making. *Family Business Review*, *15*(3), 205–222.

28. Leclercq, N. (2018). Intermittently indecisive leaders: Understanding leaders, who are otherwise effective, as they abrogate or transfer their decision making responsibilities for urgent and significant decisions, *19*(7).

29. LeClair, Z. A. (2010). The impact of group decision making on indecisiveness-related decisional confidence, *3*(2).

30. Nutt, P. C. (2006). Comparing public and private sector decision-making practices. *Journal of Public Administration Research and Theory*, *16*(2), 289–318.

31. Patalano, A. L., & LeClair, Z. (2011). The influence of group decision making on indecisiveness-related decisional confidence. *Judgment and Decision making*, *6*(2), 163.

32. Pérez, I. J., Cabrerizo, F. J., & Herrera-Viedma, E. (2010). A mobile decision support system for dynamic group decision-making problems.

IEEE Transactions on Systems, Man, and Cybernetics-Part A: Systems and Humans, *40*(6), 1244–1256.

33. Rassin, E., Muris, P., Booster, E., & Kolsloot, I. (2008). Indecisiveness and informational tunnel vision. *Personality and Individual Differences*, *45*(1), 96–102.
34. Reinalda, B., & Verbeek, B. (Eds.). (2004). *Decision Making within International Organizations* (Vol. 31). Routledge.
35. Reynolds, D. B., Joseph, J., & Sherwood, R. (2009). Risky shift versus cautious shift: determining differences in risk taking between private and public management decision-making. *Journal of Business & Economics Research (JBER)*, *7*(1).
36. Risco, C. M., & Duffy, R. D. (2011). A career decision-making profile of Latina/o incoming college students. *Journal of Career Development*, *38*(3), 237–255.
37. Saka, N., Gati, I., & Kelly, K. R. (2008). Emotional and personality-related aspects of career-decision-making difficulties. *Journal of Career Assessment*, *16*(4), 403–424.
38. Saaty, T. L., & Peniwati, K. (2013). *Group Decision Making: Drawing Out and Reconciling Differences*. RWS Publications.
39. Sari, E. (2008). The Relations between Decision Making in Social Relationships and Decision Making Styles. *Online Submission*, *3*(3), 369–381.
40. Schulze, C., & Newell, B. R. (2016). More heads choose better than one: Group decision making can eliminate probability matching. *Psychonomic Bulletin & Review*, *23*(3), 907–914.
41. Song, F. (2009). Intergroup trust and reciprocity in strategic interactions: Effects of group decision-making mechanisms. *Organizational Behavior and Human Decision Processes*, *108*(1), 164–173.
42. Schulz-Hardt, S., Jochims, M., & Frey, D. (2002). Productive conflict in group decision making: Genuine and contrived dissent as strategies to counteract biased information seeking. *Organizational Behavior and Human Decision Processes*, *88*(2), 563–586.
43. Sorkin, R. D., Hays, C. J., & West, R. (2001). Signal-detection analysis of group decision making. *Psychological Review*, *108*(1), 183.

44. Tang, M., & Liao, H. (2021). From conventional group decision making to large-scale group decision making: What are the challenges and how to meet them in big data era? A state-of-the-art survey. *Omega*, *100*, 102141.

45. Van Ginkel, W. P., & Van Knippenberg, D. (2009). Knowledge about the distribution of information and group decision making: when and why does it work? *Organizational Behavior and Human Decision Processes*, *108*(2), 218–229.

46. Weller, J. A., Levin, I. P., Shiv, B., & Bechara, A. (2007). Neural correlates of adaptive decision making for risky gains and losses. *Psychological Science*, *18*(11), 958–964.

47. Wu, W., Kou, G., Peng, Y., & Ergu, D. (2012). Improved AHP-group decision making for investment strategy selection. *Technological and Economic Development of Economy*, *18*(2), 299–316.

INDEX

D

E

F

G

H

I

J

L

M

N